Sylvia Rideoutt Bishop (Oct. 5, 1920-Dec. 27, 2004) was one of seventeen children born to a West Virginia family whose ancestors were enslaved. Sent to live with a nearby childless couple as a toddler, she was indulged with fancy dresses and one mesmerizing pony ride that changed her life. Her love of horses took her to the Charles Town racetrack at age fourteen to work as a groom, hot walker and then trainer, all the time fighting sexism and racial bigotry against a backdrop of the swirling Civil Rights movement.

She prevailed to break barriers, shatter stereotypes and celebrate countless transforming victories in the winner's circle with many wealthy clients. As a single mother after two failed marriages, financial reality forced her to take on extra work in the shipping department at a nearby Doubleday publishing factory. Never wavering in her passion, she returned to the track to train horses at age eighty. And finally, with little fanfare, she was honored for her pioneering accomplishments as the first black woman licensed to train racehorses in the United States.

This never-before-told story will bring to life Sylvia's love of horses and demonstrate her resolve and grit in confronting a litany of obstacles. They included the limited opportunity for an education and the precarious odds of getting her fractious Thoroughbred racehorses to the starting gate when factoring in their health and soundness.

Sylvia Rideoutt Bishop made her mark in the alluring sport of kings long before the tennis-playing Williams sisters or Olympic track star Jackie Joyner ever made the evening news. She traveled Maryland's half-mile track racing and fairground circuit in Cumberland, Timonium and Hagerstown. Well past nightfall, she checked on her charges, often mixing poultices for their aching legs and constantly demonstrating her wonderful way with horses.

ALSO BY VICKY MOON

THE OFFICIAL
MIDDLEBURG LIFE
COOKBOOK

THE MIDDLEBURG MYSTIQUE

BEST DRESSED SOUTHERN SALADS

A SUNDAY HORSE

THE PRIVATE PASSION OF
JACKIE KENNEDY ONASSIS

EQUESTRIAN STYLE

GOLF STYLE

THE STYLISH LIFE EQUESTRIAN

EQUAL PARTS

Sylvia Rideoutt Bishop

HAD A WAY WITH HORSES

**A PIONEERING
AFRICAN AMERICAN
WOMAN'S CAREER
TRAINING RACE HORSES**

VICKY MOON

This September, 1962 ad in the Spirit of Jefferson newspaper is from The Bank of Charles Town. Now 150 years old, the bank has served many members of Sylvia's family to this day.

Sylvia Rideoutt Bishop

HAD A WAY WITH HORSES

**A PIONEERING
AFRICAN AMERICAN
WOMAN'S CAREER
TRAINING RACE HORSES**

VICKY MOON

COUNTRY ZEST

This is a work of creative/narrative non-fiction.

www.vickymoon.com

First Edition, Country ZEST, December 2020

WGA # : 2075301

Moon, Vicky

Sylvia Rideoutt Bishop Had A Way With Horses/Vicky Moon- 1st ed.

ISBN 978-0-9617683-7-9

Cataloging-in-publication data: Biography & Autobiography / Women; Sports & Recreation / Horse Racing; Biography & Autobiography/Cultural, Ethnic & Regional/African America & Black; Biography & Autobiography/Sports; History / Women

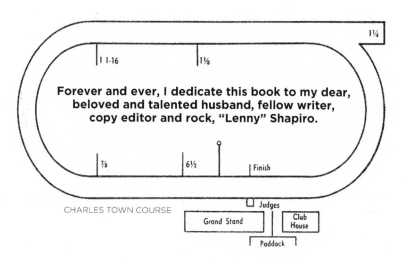

Forever and ever, I dedicate this book to my dear, beloved and talented husband, fellow writer, copy editor and rock, "Lenny" Shapiro.

CHARLES TOWN COURSE

In loving memory to my
magnificent treasured friend
Sharon Ann Maloney,
a brilliant horsewoman
and devoted animal lover.

THE RIDEOUTT FAMILY

James Howard Rideoutt   —— Married 1916 ——   Bertha Athell Snowden
1892-1958   1898-1975

Flora Elaine Rideoutt 1916-1961

Emma Gene Rideoutt- 1933-1935

Mercedes Rideoutt 1917-1977

Clara Howard Rideoutt 1918-1993

Sylvia Augustua Rideoutt 1920-2004

Edgar Rideoutt 1921-1922

James Rideoutt 1921-1923

Robert Lee Rideoutt 1922-1990

Lucille Rideoutt 1923- 2012

Irma Moselle Rideoutt 1925-1988

Leonard Rideoutt 1926-1927

Donald Morris Rideoutt 1931-1967

Veda Marie Rideoutt 1932- 2012

Govenear Paige Rideoutt 1933- 2004

Shirley Rideoutt 1935-

Betty Louise Rideoutt 1936-1961

Madge Virginia Rideoutt 1937- 1993

Magruder Leslie Rideoutt 1939-1961

CONTENTS

CHAPTER 1

I GOT THE HORSE RIGHT HERE

Rita Haywood stalked the pace three wide, moved to the front near the five-sixteenths pole, surged clear in the two path around the far turn and held well clear under a drive in the lane.
- Equibase Company, 2012

Fierce sheets of rain make it impossible to see more than two feet of the road beyond the front of the charter bus. A late summer storm is raking wicked winds across the Blue Ridge Mountains into the Shenandoah Valley of West Virginia.

The bus driver squirms in his seat and leans closer to the windshield, trying to get a clearer view. The immense windshield wipers beat rhythmically and provide no reprieve. The air is thick and stale. The driver grabs a rag and rubs the windshield vapor. This delivers a trifling relief.

The forty-odd passengers murmur. Despite no smoking, the odor of musty cigarette smoke is eternally entwined into the clothing fibers and hair of those addicted to the repugnant habit. The unpleasant, robust odor wafts down the aisle. A twenty-something male passenger is listening to his iPod. Carly Rae Jepsen's folk-style pop best-selling single "Call Me Maybe" peals out from his earbuds three rows in front and behind the

1

music buff as he rocks.

The tempest outside does not deter the optimistic fans as the bus inches along the two lanes of Rt. 340 leading to the Hollywood Casino at the Charles Town Races complex. These gamblers have hope in their hearts. The red and yellow lights of the gambling and horse racing facility twinkle through the downpour as they approach.

The enterprise is owned by Penn National Gaming, based in Wyomissing, Pennsylvania. The company operates or has outright ownership or "interests" in twenty-seven gaming and racing facilities in seventeen jurisdictions, including California, Florida, Illinois, Indiana, Kansas, Maine, Massachusetts, Mississippi, Missouri, Nevada, New Jersey, New Mexico, Ohio, Pennsylvania, Texas, West Virginia and Ontario, Canada. They have 35,000 gaming machines, 800 table games and 4,600 hotel rooms.

The bus halts under a large overhang and a colossal swoosh sounds as the bus door opens. They've been lured to this historic town, initially developed by the brother of George Washington, by anticipation of a whopping jackpot.

Hours and hours later, the same bunch on the bus will depart. Most will sulk after getting soaked at the slots or taking a bath at the pari-mutuel windows, never mind the rain. A fortunate few will have pockets bulging from success.

Back in the stable area, trainers and grooms scramble to stop the rush of water into the stalls. Every available person grabs a shovel or spade in order to dig a trench to divert the unrelenting deluge away from the barn. Visitors must side-step a strategically placed red plastic bucket in the middle of the walkway, intended to catch drips.

Debra Ketterman stands in front of Rita Haywood's stall. "Good girl," she coos, stroking her sleek neck.

A gray and white cat stretches out on top of three bales of hay stacked in the feed room. A bay horse not scheduled to run is pacing around in circles in his stall and fretting. He's a stall-walker. This could easily be called EOCD—Equine Obsessive Compulsive Disorder.

A groom holds two steaming cups of coffee from the hot plate in the tack room. He teeters along so as not to spill and presents one to a co-worker, a hot walker circling the barn, cooling out a bay colt. If a horse defecates, a groom is there within minutes to shovel it up.

To uneducated eyes, a stable might appear to be dirty and messy. The reality is that the horses, their tack and their stalls are immaculate.

No matter what…this was going to be a long, chilly night.

Jeff Runco, a leading trainer, has two horses in the feature race: Navy Chapel and Notayankeefan. Runco began his horse career as a jockey, and in the past thirty-plus years, his stable has grown from a half-dozen horses to around forty. He's always been content at Charles Town, and since the slots came in and created generous purses, he's extremely happy. With 20,356 starts and 4,326 wins, his lifetime earnings have exceeded $59 million. He's a viable competitor and has no intention of letting up.

Over near the track in the cavernous casino, there are 4,000 slot machines inside the faux Vegas wagering multiplex that's open twenty-one hours a day. Long past the last race at 11 p.m., in the wee hours before dawn, most of the 15,000-plus visitors will either catch buses back home or trudge to their cars in the six-level parking garage. As with the bus bunch, they will also leave with heavy hearts and lighter wallets.

An automated button has replaced your grandmother's one-armed bandit slot machine. A numbing, omnipresent computerized droning has supplanted the bygone clamorous resonance of winning bells for triple cherries. Flashing neon is the lighting of the moment. A high-fat food court beckons the gluttonous; pizza is $2.50 a slice. Smokers and non-smokers are segregated, yet visitors suffer burning eyes no matter where they wander.

Compulsive gamblers metastasized to stools at the slots are oblivious to the race about to go off. There's a Western Union desk for cash advances. Credit card machines spit out more bills, big and small. The town's median income is $32,538, and the population is 5,945.

It's almost ten o'clock this August night. Six horses line up in the starting gate, shifting and stomping. A seventh horse, Nicknmina, has been scratched by the veterinarian. Outside, announcer Jeff Cernik beckons the seven horses for a race around the half-mile track, the $50,000 Sylvia Bishop Memorial Race. The familiar bugle horn refrain announcing "Call to Post" is a now a recording. Back when the track opened in 1933, a live professional bugler did the honors.

Hall of Fame jockey Bill Hartack started his career here and went on to win the Kentucky Derby five times. Joe Servis moved to Charles Town in 1948. He began his horse career as a jockey in the 1950s, then toiled as a trainer and later a steward. Two of his sons, both born and raised in Charles Town, took up the sport.

Jason Servis' horses have won more than $52 million in 5,281 starts with 1,306 victories. He won the Kentucky Derby in 2019 with Mary and Gary West's then-undefeated Maximum Security, only to watch as the bay colt was disqualified for interference. His brother, John Servis, won the Kentucky Derby and the Preakness with Smarty Jones in the spring of 2004. He has more than $61 million in lifetime earnings in 10,497 starts, with 1,840 wins.

A pair of hardcore racing punters linger inside the track clubhouse in front of a bank of television monitors. Imagine them as modern-day characters Nathan Detroit and Sky Masterson from Guys and Dolls, the iconic 1955 Broadway musical. They're drinking beer from paper cups. One clutches a hot dog slathered in bright yellow mustard with a sauerkraut garnish. Tucked in the frayed pocket of his lucky blue plaid shirt, he has a ticket for a 7-1 exacta, a daring twenty dollar investment.

The outriders, trainers, jockeys and grooms outside are drenched from the rain. The racing surface is a sloppy soup of mud.

"And…they're off in the $50,000 Sylvia Bishop Stakes," the track public address announcer bellows.

In less than ninety seconds, a chestnut filly named Rita Haywood wins by 4½ lengths. Trained by a woman named Debra Ketterman, the filly wins $30,600 for her effort (a far cry from the $2,275 Sylvia Bishop won in her biggest victory). Horses trained by Debra have gathered $3,314,634 in earnings.

One of the Guys and Dolls characters sets his beer down on a table, pulls a betting ticket out of his plaid shirt, and slaps his friend on the back. "I got the horse right here," he says, without adding "his name is Paul Revere" from the musical. The winner's circle in the now misty evening is crowded with grandchildren, nieces, nephews and friends of the late Sylvia Bishop. The twenty dollar exacta bet pays $318.

At least one customer on this night did not get soaked.

The man devouring the hot dog turns to his pal, his right cheek coated with mustard. He wonders out loud, "Who was this Sylvia Bishop anyway?"

FIVE BLOCKS FROM THE RACETRACK...TODAY

Five blocks from the racetrack, the visitors pass the Turf Motel, opened by the Marcus family on March 1, 1952, and billed as the "first modern amenity-equipped motel in Jefferson County." A succession of fast food drive-through (or "thru," as they're known in these parts) windows follow ad nauseam, where folks are asking: "Where's the beef?" "Specialsaucelettucecheesepicklesonions?" or "finger lickin' good?" usually paired with a New York City Mayor Michael Bloomberg giant-sized Diet Coke.

Just past the artery-clogging food outlets, the road narrows and visitors ease into another time warp on Washington Street. Continuing a few blocks, there's the Jumpin' Java coffee shop, La Mezzaluna Café, a second-hand shop with a lunch counter, a tobacco shop, and the Wooden Shoe antique shop, which specializes in light fixtures. An online phone book lists thirteen pawnshops around town.

CHAPTER 2

HONEY BAKED HAM

The old saying "they don't make 'em like they used to..."
doesn't apply here. We do make 'em like we used to,
because it's still the best way.

– The Honey Baked Ham Co., established in 1957
by Harry J. Hoenselaar

ylvia Rideoutt Bishop sits in a dark Naugahyde vinyl lounge chair in the corner of apartment 5-P of the Charles Towers, just three-tenths of a mile from 122 South West Street, where she lived for most of her eighty-four years. A game show blares out from a large television set on the other side of the room. It is early fall and the weather is still summertime warm. The presidential election of 2004 is in the final stages, with incumbent President George W. Bush, a Republican, running against

Democrat John Kerry, a senator from Massachusetts. Barrack Obama is an obscure community organizer and state legislator in Illinois.

Pine-scented disinfectant wafts through the living area from the hallway along with a hint of boiled cabbage from the kitchen. The window next to the lounge chair faces east, overlooking the back parking lot and is wide open, creating a glare on the TV screen.

The five-story, sandy-colored cinder block building on Augustine Avenue is named after the son of George Washington's brother, Charles, and his wife, Mildred. Their son was George Augustine Washington. The building is wedged between a Citgo station and Bobby's Used Car Lot. It provides low-income housing for senior citizens. A Save-A-Lot grocery store is across the street.

There's a tap, tap, tap, as the brass knocker hits the steel door.

"Door's open," Sylvia warbles sweetly. "Come on in."

She can't locate the remote control to mute the sound and is frantic to find her black plastic cigarette lighter. She's not quite sure which she wants to locate first.

On this warm, humid day, a copy of the Daily Racing Form is laid open on the dining room table. The weekly full-color Food Lion insert from the local newspaper is lying in a chair. Specials include Stouffer's frozen lasagna, Pillsbury biscuits and Wisk liquid detergent. A partially deflated helium birthday balloon is still tied to a chair.

On the wall above the couch there are dozens of photos from the racetrack, all with Sylvia in the winner's circle. In the framed pictures, joyous horse owners, jockeys, family members and smiling friends surround her. As she looks at each photo of the many horses she trained—Classical Herb, Forever Noble, Key Punch, Prince Devil and many others—she reminiscences in detail to her visitor.

"This one liked to come from behind," she begins. "This one had to be led to the paddock by two people, and this little filly had a heart of gold." There is plenty of heartbreak, too, as she continues, "Lost by a nose, she broke her ankle coming out of the gate and had to be put down; the owners decided to move with another trainer."

Her training career was laced with a strangling concoction of sexual discrimination and racial bigotry long before the phrases "sexual harassment," "Me Too" or "Black Lives Matter" entered the lexicon. And it all took place in what appeared to be a mannerly southern town.

A trim woman with her partially gray hair pulled back in a neat knot, Sylvia's hazel eyes sparkle. Her jaw is lean and angular. Her skin is milky caramel, and many have remarked on her near-whiteness. They even go so far as to attribute her success with influential white owners to this.

A flowing, pinkish duster and blue bedroom slippers make up her wardrobe of choice this day. She finds the lighter, fires up one of many

Winston cigarettes, and drums her fingers as she pulls up the past.

She loves to pour through old scrapbooks and photos, reliving days of glorious triumph. She still understands which horses favor oats and which prefer mash. (She even swears a few of them improve form after swallowing a bottle of beer, but that's a story for later.) She mastered their strategy: breeze, gallop, sprint or seven furlongs. When one of her charges hung his head, she was able to pinpoint his aches. She nursed them with potent potions and homemade fixes.

Up before the sun for sixty years, Sylvia trained hundreds of horses and won thousands in purse money. She broke countless racial barriers and shattered sexual/female stereotypes. She also confesses to spoiling all of her charges with plenty of peppermint candy.

Quite simply…Sylvia Bishop had a way with horses.

She speaks of leading a big bay horse named Odd Lot to the paddock one long ago afternoon, recalling a spectator shouting, "Let's just see what you can do today, nigger lady!" She never flinched then, and it doesn't matter much to her now.

Over the next few months, the visitor returns weekly and a golden autumn turns into short, chilly days. She is planning for Christmas. On a later visit, the dining room table is filled with gifts for grandchildren, nieces and nephews. The packages all have small, hand-written name tags.

A horse-loving teenage boy comes by for a holiday visit bearing a gift of a fourteen-pound spiral cut honey-baked ham. "I just love ham," she says, and nods toward the kitchenette for him to place the gift on the crowded counter top.

She shows the young boy her wall of honor with all those framed win pictures, and then points to the one photo that means the most.

The phone rings. "Hello, yeah Brady, busy right this minute."

Boom.

Click.

"The guy lives in the building," she says with a sly smile, "and all he tells me about is all his wives."

She continues, recalling the trail she blazed as a racehorse trainer: "I was the first black woman in the United (pronounced in three strong syllables—you-night-ed) States, not just West Virginia. Just think. I'm still here."

The Jefferson County Courthouse, first built in 1803 on land given by Charles Washington, stands at the intersection of Washington and George Streets in Charles Town. The imposing building has an intriguing history. Now, just feeling the weight of the front door and walking across the creaky floors conjures famous trials, loquacious lawyers, and stern judges. The structure was destroyed by a fire and rebuilt in 1836. Abolitionist John Brown and his co-conspirators were tried for treason in a second floor courtroom in 1859. While the Civil War raged, the building was damaged and precious papers were moved south to Lexington, Virginia and eventually returned unharmed. Just after the war, the county seat was relocated to nearby Shepherdstown, but the West Virginia Court of Appeals transferred it back to Charles Town in 1871. The courthouse was once again rebuilt by December 17, 1872, at a cost of $21,179.18. In 1910, it was expanded, and a jail was added in 1919.

Image Courtesy of the Jefferson County Museum, Charles Town.

CHAPTER 3

JOHN, GEORGE, SAMUEL, LAWRENCE AND MILDRED ... WASHINGTON

*Charles Town is a quiet, small city filled with home loving people of
high culture. For the most part they are not concerned
about attaining great wealth or developing a large city.
What they do want is to live in a happy contented fashion
without too much interference from outside.*

**- Phil M. Conley for West Virginia Publicity Commission,
Farmers Advocate, February 2, 1923**

Sylvia Rideoutt Bishop, the namesake for the August night-time feature race, spent her life at the track in Charles Town and had a never-ending infatuation for horses. As their bus turned east, the Guys and Dolls gamblers settled in for their return trip to Washington. They and most everyone on board had no idea they were heading away from one of the most historic towns in the nation.

Initially developed by Col. Charles Washington, the youngest brother of George Washington, Sylvia Bishop's quaint hometown was established in 1786 by an act of the General Assembly of what was then Virginia. Charles Washington lived on the edge of town at Happy Retreat. He practiced law and is buried here beside his wife, Mildred Thornton.

Charles Washington designed the town of eighty acres and donated the four corner lots at the main intersection of (what else?) Charles and Washington Streets. In addition to naming the streets honoring his wife and his brothers George, Samuel and Lawrence, Charles also named the roads adjacent to the appropriately named main thoroughfare of Washington Street, Liberty and Congress.

First identified as "Charlestown" and located in Berkeley County, Charles Washington left several requests when he died on September 16, 1799. He noted that if ever the county was divided and Charlestown specified as a new county seat, several of his real estate holdings were to be used for public buildings on the town square. Jefferson County was born in 1801, and Charles Washington's posthumous aspirations for the town square on land he bequeathed were established.

At one point in its pre–Civil War history, as many as 4,000 slaves were put to work in surrounding farms in Jefferson County, with a large population of freed slaves also residing in and around town. More than 220 years after Charles Washington died, the town that bears his name continues to have two distinct populations—rich and poor, black and white. Time passes slowly in these ever-so-southern parts of the Shenandoah Valley.

"Colored had their own churches, restaurants, toilets, schools, and everyone seemed content with the arrangement," Buddy Morgan wrote

ROOM IN WHICH DOLLY MADISON WAS MARRIED
HAREWOOD, NEAR CHARLES' TOWN, W.VA.

Located on the outskirts of Charles Town, Harewood was the home of Samuel Washington, George Washington's brother. It was constructed in 1770 using native gray limestone and most likely was designed by British-born architect John Ariss (c.1725–99) around 1751. Samuel was the first Washington in the area. He died in 1781 and is buried on the property in the family graveyard located southwest of the mansion. Harewood was left to Samuel's son, Ferdinand, who died in 1788, and then to his second son, George Steptoe Washington. Both were sons of Anne Steptoe, Samuel's fourth wife. In 1793, George Steptoe Washington married Lucy Payne. In 1794, Dolley Payne Todd, the widowed sister of Lucy Payne Washington, married James Madison in the famed drawing room. The drawing room walls have the original paint and the marble mantelpiece that was a gift to George Washington from the Marquis de Lafayette. Harewood is listed on the National Register of Historic Places and is the only Washington home in Jefferson County that has remained in the Washington family. Of the original 3,000 acres Samuel Washington owned, only 268 are still part of Harewood.

in his memoir, Charles Town 1912-1924: A Boy's Eye-View of Charles Town and Its People, published in 1987. "I liked the colored because they [were] always joking, laughing, telling stories, and seemed to be more happy than the whites. Dad, who was a great favorite of the blacks, and also an admirer of them, once told me that they were truly a remarkable race. More than others they could stand any kind of adversity—pain, suffering, heat, cold, poverty, and come back smiling. But he said one thing they can't stand is prosperity."

Folks now scurry from what was once the jailhouse of abolitionist John Brown's mid-1800s era to the post office of today. Built on the same southwest corner, it was completed in 1923 with Martinsburg wirecut brick. On Saturday, December 1, 1923, the Farmers Advocate newspaper reported an update on the post office: "Charles Town's new post office building on the site of the old county jail at the southwest corner of Washington and George Streets has been completed. By the end of another week, according to the present plans of Postmaster Young, the entire post office force will be transferred to their new quarters."

Architectural details of the post office building included an entrance

Charles Washington, the founder of Charles Town, constructed Happy Retreat out of salmon-colored brick in 1780 on land his brother, Lawrence, left him when he died. Charles brought his family from Fredericksburg, Virginia and constructed the estate as two buildings separated by a breezeway. After Charles died, his son sold the house. The graves of Charles and his wife, Mildred, are located on the far side of Evitts Run, a stream that flows along the back boundary of the property. Both graves are unmarked. Two other historical buildings on the property that predate the house are a stone kitchen and smokehouse and an octagonal wooden powder house (similar to one at Mount Vernon) that was possibly used as a school, but more likely an office. In 1873, Judge Isaac Douglass purchased the property and built the center portion of the house, renaming it Mordington after his ancestral home in Scotland. In 1945, R.J. Funkhouser became the next owner and restored the Happy Retreat name. Happy Retreat is currently a private home, but the non-profit organization, Friends of Happy Retreat, is working to purchase the property.

Images courtesy of the Jefferson County Museum, Charles Town.

vestibule and lobby floors finished in terrazzo with a strip of black Virginia marble and a base of pink Tennessee marble. There was a heart pine floor and fireproof vault in the Postmaster's office. And, oh yes, "The mezzanine floor contains one large room for postal employees and carriers and a men's toilet." Obviously, there was nothing said about women or African American employees and if they were able to use the same toilet?

Doubtful.

These days, post office patrons are often mingling about and discussing recent news: a sexual assault trial about to begin; water bills on the rise; or the Jefferson County High School's girls' basketball team's recent three-point victory over nearby Musselman High.

In October 1859, John Brown had only a short walk catty-corner from the jail to the brick Roman Revival style courthouse with four massive white columns for his treason, conspiracy and murder trial over three and a half days. Brown's wife, Mary, arrived by horse-drawn carriage. The courtroom was packed for "Virginia v. John Brown." He and six of his cohorts, captured in the historic raid at Harpers Ferry, were convicted and sentenced to hang on November 2, 1859, for the death of fourteen people and wounding of nine others.

On December 2, 1859, more than 1,500 soldiers (including a future assassin named John Wilkes Booth) surrounded Brown as he rode on top of his own coffin in the back of a horse-drawn wagon to George Street, a grand residential street. A historical marker recounts the execution, and the current owners of this house are said to welcome all questions.

George Street was named after the nation's first president when Charles designed the town. Other members of the family are honored on streets named Samuel, Lawrence and Mildred. Exquisite, often commanding brick homes with intricate architectural details and broad porches line the street. A lovely brick, four-bedroom, two-and-a-half bath 1897 Victorian beauty is listed for $798,000.

Meanwhile, out on the edge of town, there's the Huntfield subdivision, where a faux historical marker attempts (unsuccessfully) to give it some importance. On a circle at the entrance is a tacky copy of the Washington Monument, located in the nation's capital, sixty-four miles and light years away. In this neighborhood, a four-bedroom, two-and-a-half bath home with synthetic siding sells for $389,500. No boxwood included.

Growing up in an era of continued Jim Crow bigotry, Sylvia had to go to the back door of the town ice cream parlor for a cone. She also watched as history unfolded. In December 1923, when she was only three years old, the Ku Klux Klan set fire to a cross planted in the public square. Back then, there was a local horse show, but it was restricted and called the Charles Town Colored Horse Show. Sylvia, the budding horse lover, was not welcome to the bigger and more prestigious all-white competitions.

Prohibition in West Virginia was repealed by a sixty percent margin on June 27, 1933, and ratified on July 25. It didn't matter to then-teenage Sylvia, but alcohol later would certainly play a role in her life. And then, an epic landmark day for women took place in Charles Town when Carrie Lee Strider became the first woman appointed sheriff of Jefferson County on January 5, 1948.

"If you were black, you lived in a complex society," said James Taylor, one of Sylvia's long-time friends and a leader of a local preservation group.

Said another friend, "Most black women worked in the hospital. You didn't even try for a job as a telephone operator. It was an era when you were presented with two opportunities: cook for a white family or scrub floors for some white woman."

Instead, Sylvia found her opportunities right up the street from the courthouse and the jail at the racetrack. She preferred to clean the stables.

CHAPTER 4

POTATO HILL

I can't sleep at night, I can't eat a bite,
'Cause the man I love, He don't treat me right.

- "Crazy Blues," lyrics by Perry Bradford,
sung by Mamie Smith, the first
African-American to record blues, 1920

Sylvia's mother, Bertha
Athell Snowden Rideoutt

Sylvia's grandfather, Charles Snowden, had to sign a letter of consent for his seventeen-year-old daughter Bertha to marry twenty-three-year-old James Howard Rideoutt.

Rev. Robert J. Johnson performed the ceremony on May 3, 1915, at St. Philip's Episcopal Church on South Lawrence Street in Charles Town.

As World War I consumed Europe on multiple fronts, it was on this day that Lieutenant Colonel John McCrae wrote one of the most memorable war poems from the Second Battle of Ypres, Belgium. It was written in honor of his former student, Alexis Helmer, killed the previous day by a German shell. *"In Flanders fields the poppies blow, Between the crosses, row on row..."*

A tidy nine months after the Rideoutts were married, they welcomed their first daughter,

Flora Elaine, on February 15, 1916. The weather on that day was fair and the temperature was in the low thirties.

Church records reveal Bertha apparently had never been baptized, so she went through that formality on April 2, 1916, with Rev. Robert J. Johnson, the same minister who had married the Rideoutts. Two weeks later, Johnson baptized Flora Elaine.

Their second daughter, Mercedes, followed almost a year after the first, on February 6, 1917. The war shifted into a higher gear as the United States joined in the great conflict. James Rideoutt was drafted into the Army on October 27, 1917, and served as a food service cook in France in Company B, 505th Engineers. Their third daughter, Clara, was born on May 5, 1918.

A family diary notes that in October 1918, the "epidemic of influenza broke out in the U.S." and "about 75-80 white and colored died in Charles Town which had three hospitals." Virtually everyone in town was affected. Entire families were forced to remain indoors. With other outbreaks of measles, scarlet fever or chicken pox, families were quarantined and a large sign was placed on the front door until the chance of contagions passed. Visitors were warned off and no one was allowed to visit except Dr. William "Billy" Neill, a white physician who attended the Rideoutt family. Even the congregational communion cup, used in churches throughout West Virginia, was ruled unlawful by the state's board of health.

As a result, Charles Town's Edge Hill cemetery handled eighty-eight burials, a third of them children, through the end of the year.

By November 1918, the Rideoutt family diary contains bold pencil handwriting: "THE WAR WITH GERMANY ENDED."

James Rideoutt returned home from France by June. He worked briefly as a cook, a trade he mastered while in the service. He later joined the crew at the Miller Chemical plant in nearby Ranson. He eventually became a foreman at the plant, which produced fertilizer.

When the thick, warm liquid mis-labeled as "water" oozed down the stout Bertha's bowed legs on October 5, 1920, she was well-aware of the impending birth. Sylvia was their fourth daughter, all under four years old. As a "baby catcher" (otherwise known as a mid-wife), Bertha, now a seasoned mother herself, was familiar with the three stages to follow: dilation, birth and afterbirth.

"Babies were born at home, usually with the help of a very efficient black mid-wife or relatives," Buddy Morgan recalled in his 1912-1924 memoir about Charles Town. The hospital was segregated. "My mother said she never even thought of going to the hospital and all three of us were born at home. The hospital was directly across the street."

A peculiar onion-like odor unique to women in labor drifted in the second floor room with each wrenching spasm as Bertha struggled while

Dr. William Neill (front row, left) tended to Sylvia's birth and the pages from the county ledger reveal a baby named Cora, born on October 5, 1920, and later known as Sylvia Augustua Rideoutt.

Images courtesy of the Jefferson County Museum, Charles Town and Vicky Moon.

Dr. Neill attended to her. Downstairs, the windows on the back of the house were fogged from the damp steam off the big pots of water boiling on the stove.

That water had to be transported from the hand pump out back. There was no indoor plumbing, and James most likely took a day off from his work as a laborer at a seed mill to help in any way possible. Just like that, a healthy baby girl was born. Over a hundred years later, a look at the Jefferson County courthouse binders reveals the baby girl was first named Cora and later became Sylvia Augustua Rideoutt.

The population of Charles Town was estimated at 2,527. Woodrow Wilson, the twenty-eighth president, was in office. Wheat futures were reported down ten to twelve cents per bushel to $1.95.

Advertisements in the *Farmers Advocate* paper of 1920 featured Scott's Emulsion for weakness with nourishment that protects, to be used after meals for children and adults. Or perhaps one might try Vinol, the "Greatest of All Tonics" with cod liver and beef peptones for run-down nervous and anemic conditions. Hill's Bromide Cascara Quinine promised to break up a cold in twenty-four hours. Male impotency drugs had yet to be created.

For women, Lydia E. Pinkham's Vegetable Compound offered all kinds of benefits, though for what maladies we are not sure. Tutt's Pills offered a cure for malaria. White Caps for headache in a trial size were ten cents. And fifty Bull Durham tobacco cigarettes went for a dime.

Black patrons were not welcome in most restaurants on Washington

Street. "You didn't even try to go in the courthouse or post office," one resident recalled. Ten cents would get everyone a seat for the matinee presentation of Charles (Buck) Jones in *Western Speed* at the Opera House Theatre. But black patrons had to sit in the balcony.

A meal at a restaurant? Black patrons were served at the back door, if at all. They also delivered food orders from the grocery stores. Sugar was the only item any member of the Rideoutt family ever bought. A ten-pound bag sold for fifteen cents at the Great Atlantic & Pacific Tea Company, which many remember simply as the A&P. Two tall cans of Del Monte peaches were twenty-five cents, and three bottles of Yukon Club Ginger Ale sold for twenty-five cents, plus deposit.

The Rideoutts, like most of their neighbors, grew many fruits and vegetables in the back yard. They also raised hogs and chickens.

During the 1920s, the biggest controversy facing local citizens was a debate to change the name of the town. Some argued the designation was too similar to the state's capital city of Charleston. Several freight shipments, including one of wire hoops for apple barrels, were sent by mistake to Charleston. Charles City, Charlesboro, Sir Charles and Jefferson City were suggested. After much debate and an 850-129 vote, Charles Town stayed Charles Town. It was the first time many women had the opportunity to cast a vote.

The *Farmers Advocate* newspaper, published by R.C. Rissler, noted their mission statement on the front page: "Equal Rights to All" and "Special Privileges to None." A one-year subscription was $1.50 "in advance." Front-page news reported the good: "Miss Julia Lane Moore, daughter of Mrs. N.M. Moore and a popular teacher in the Charles Town Graded School, was married Monday evening to Mr. Randolph Barnes of Middleway, a young businessman, salesman for Gilbert Brothers, wholesale druggist of Baltimore." And then there was the grim news under the headline "Death's Harvest": "The death of Mrs. Helen Hurt Byington at her home two miles north of Charles Town Tuesday afternoon brought an end to a long illness."

More news: "Becoming bloated from eating beans and bean vines, three milk cows owned by Thomas Painter died Saturday afternoon." Or "Mr. Dennis Link is suffering from an attack of rheumatism," and "Jack Skinner and Miss Louise Whitfield, of Middleburg, Va., spent a day with Mrs. Charles Skinner."

Ki-Moid granules were advertised to bring quick relief for indigestion and (in a refrain which remains partially familiar) the copy for a product called Nujol read: "The doctor can't help it. He knows that the man has hard arteries, high blood pressure, and the beginning of kidney and heart disease, due to long neglected, chronic constipation."

The news on Saturday, October 6, 1923, included word that the first

American designed Zeppelin aircraft would be named Shenandoah, certainly a point of pride in these parts.

S.W. Washington was the president of the Bank of Charles Town, which was established in 1871. Their ad informed readers of $50,000 in capital and a surplus of $70,000. It boasted that the bank never failed to give the same good service to the farmer as it gave to any businessman.

Other highlights included the sale of the 317-acre Green Hill Farm outside of town for the price of $100 per acre. (The 2018 price for farmland averaged around $7,500 per acre.)

Bertha's father, Charles Snowden, forty-nine, was one of several local Negro men waiting at the Norfolk and Western Railway station. He inherited the trade and this particular franchise from his father. He earned a living delivering shipments destined for the local shops: Isaac Herz Co. clothing, W. Ralph Burns plumbing supplies or Riddleberger's dry goods in the St. George Building on Washington Street, where street lights were lit by gas.

Weather was mild that October as a train belched thick black fumes and screeched to a halt on the west side of town. Deliveries included everything from chickens to caskets. Cattle were offloaded at the far end. Snowden pulled his horse and wagon up to the platform. His hard work paid off, and Snowden had been able to purchase four lots for fifty dollars each on Davenport Street in Potato Hill. Barefoot children loved to race up and down the hill, with neighbors cheering them on from the front porches. The streets were in transition from crushed limestone to pavement. Davenport Street was dirt and crushed rock.

Prohibition was in high gear. Dennis Butts of nearby Martinsburg was charged with possession of 100 gallons of cider in 1924. The case became a question of whether it was a violation of the prohibition statues.

The *Farmers Advocate* newspaper also reported on sixty-eight-year-old "Joseph Reed, colored," who was arraigned and charged with having a copper still with coils in June 1928. He told Justice Willey he'd always "worked for a living" and the forty gallons of mash were just going to be used for "a little moonshine for refreshments."

Eleven months after Sylvia was born, the Rideoutts welcomed twins Edgar and James on September 5, 1921. One year later, Robert Lee Rideoutt was born on September 12, 1922. That added up to seven children in the family, but not for long.

Sadly, there soon was unfathomable grief, first with the whooping cough death of fourteen-month-old Edgar on November 18, 1922. Records noted his age as one year, two months and thirteen days.

The winter weather in early January 1923 was clear and cold with temperatures in the high thirties. It also was around this time that the sleepy northwest Florida black community of Rosewood was destroyed in a racially-laced massacre that left eight dead.

For the Rideoutts, there was another unspeakable death. The other twin, James Rideoutt, Jr., died at age one year and five months on February 5, while sitting in his high chair. The cause of death was noted as pneumonia. "They were tough times," Sylvia said.

By November 21, 1923, Bertha gave birth to a baby girl, Lucille, and Irma Rideoutt followed on June 4, 1925. These sisters remained close all their lives and later married the Berry brothers, two well-known local horse trainers.

The Ku Klux Klan fueled the fears of the Rideoutts and every other black family in the area. Originally founded in 1866, by former Confederate soldiers opposed to Reconstruction, the white supremacists began to flourish nationwide in the early and mid-1920s. They adopted a standard white costume and code words and conducted numerous cross burnings and mass parades, also stressing opposition to the Catholic Church.

In January 1923, in Brastrop, Louisiana, a district court heard testimony linking the Klan to the torture and murders of two black residents and also descriptions of other terror-filled activities—whippings, floggings, night riding and cross burning. On December 1, 1923, the Klan struck in Charles Town, setting fire to a cross in the public square.

"The cross blazed brilliantly for a few minutes and attracted much attention," Millard Kessler Bushong wrote in his 1941 book, *A History of Jefferson County, West Virginia*. "As the perpetrators of this act were masked and drove away soon after they started the fire, their identity was not revealed."

A.M.S. Morgan II (known as Buddy) was a white child in a family of some affluence. He grew up in the same era and authored a booklet, *Charles Town 1912-1924: A Boy's Eye-View of Charles Town and Its People*, published in 1987. "I never knew of any (racism) in Charles Town," he wrote.

"White and black seemed to get along as one. Maybe the 'help' situation made things so peaceful. The blacks weren't servants, but help. Everybody had help.

"It usually was a lifetime association. Lilly Watters and her daughter Bertha, worked with us for some 35 years. They brought their children to work with them and I played with them all day. Sometimes I would go to their house to spend the night. This was a big treat because they entertained me so well and I loved their little house down by Evitts Run.

"The food they carried home was not leftovers, but food purposely prepared for the help's entire family. The husband was waiting for his dinner when the 'help' got home and he had a regular dinner. Part of the pay. Also clothing, doctor bills, and unusual expenses were usually paid by the employer. Socially they seemed to have more distinct categories than we did. The bottom of their social scale was the 'poor white trash' and the colored would have nothing to do with them, and looked down on them as unfit to associate with."

On Monday and Tuesday, August 16 and 17 in 1926, the Charles Town Colored Horse Show took place on the grounds that would eventually become the racetrack. James Rideoutt was an active member of the show's committee. The first ever of its kind, the show began in 1913 and continued for fifty years. It was advertised as "Bigger, Better and Grander Than Ever." The schedule of events included a cakewalk, steeplechases and "amusements of all kinds to please the most refined."

A note in the paper added: "Suitable accommodations have been secured for all who may attend." Of course, all knew this meant they were not welcome at the local all-white motels and boarding houses.

Sylvia settles again into her lounge chair at the Charles Towers, pulls out more old photos, and begins to pull up her memories eight decades after the spring of 1929. The devastating October stock market crash was still to come.

As the country teetered on the edge of the catastrophic economic woes, Charles Snowden purchased a washing machine for ninety-five dollars in May 1929. He paid in installments and completed his obligation by November that same year. Perhaps he was helping his ever-expanding family keep clean clothes on hand. By this time, Bertha had given birth to nine children in nine years. He also paid seventy-dollars cash for a radio, perhaps to drown out the seemingly endless sound of happy babies, or those in need of changing and not-so-happy.

These days, pockets of housing predominately populated by black residents still remain in Charles Town, with their own evocative names: Dog Town, Potato Hill, Gibson Town, Mill Lane. Some of the homes are mostly unchanged, except they now have indoor plumbing.

Sylvia's family lived on Potato Hill. They raised pigs and planted a garden each spring. "We never had anything frozen," Sylvia recalled. This tiny community remains on the far western edge of town. The limestone-rich soil has always lent itself to raising cattle and horses, harvesting corn and growing apples. The Blue Ridge Mountains are to the east and the Potomac and Shenandoah rivers converge seven miles away in historic Harpers Ferry. But for many black residents, the luxury of wide expanses of land and rich soil has never been possible.

Charles Snowden purchased four lots on Davenport Street on Potato Hill in 1930 for fifty dollars. In 1936, he deeded Sylvia's parents, the Rideoutts (his daughter and son-in-law), one of the houses. There was no running water, and an outhouse served the eventual nineteen family members.

"Pig Chow Makes More Hog at Less Cost" a Purina ad in the *Farmers Advocate* newspaper boasted. Once a Rideoutt hog was slaughtered, one of the kids went uptown to Wilson's Butcher to have the fatback sliced for bacon. The rest was hung to cure, surely one reason Sylvia came to love ham.

With a house bulging with infants and toddlers, the not quite two-year-old Sylvia was sent to live with a childless couple, Lavinia and William Payne.

It was a mysterious and complicated set of circumstances. Bouncing between two homes was a routine she never questioned until later in life, and it certainly shaped her character.

"Those were tough times," Sylvia recalled as she lit up one of many Winston cigarettes.

Up on Potato Hill on Davenport Street, the Rideoutts butchered one of their hogs and prepared a pork roast for Easter dinner. It was cloudy and the temperature almost reached fifty. They ate home-preserved peaches, too. The family gathered at picnic tables outside. "We always had big pots of food," she recalled. Her father had served as an Army cook during World War I and later worked as a private cook for a well-to-do white family.

In Washington, 125,000 people flocked to the Tidal Basin to see the cherry blossoms. The traffic was reported to be very heavy. Some even took an airplane ride to view the blossoms from above. The *Washington Post* reported two sisters were injured when they were knocked down by a taxi cab driven by Moose Kent, "colored of 1339 V street northwest." He was arrested on a charge of reckless driving and later released. The President and Mrs. Herbert Hoover attended the very simple services at the Friends Meeting House with only a piano as accompaniment for a few hymns.

For Sylvia, there was a sweet combination of adventure, bliss, and magic on that Easter Sunday so long ago. Sunrise came at 5:54 a.m. The local *Spirit of Jefferson* newspaper reported that "Breaking over the Eastern hills in a blaze of glory the sun and nature seemed to sense the Spirit of the Risen Christ on Easter morning."

Hallelujah.

CHAPTER 5

MA PAYNE

Humpty Dumpty sat on a wall,
Humpty Dumpty had a great fall,
All the King's horses and all the King's men...

- Author unknown, circa 1797

Sylvia's life at age two immediately took a defining turn when she went to live nearby with Lavinia and William Payne. Friends and family insist this was not an unusual occurrence for the times; money was scarce, and feeding another child was never easy.

Yet, the question lingers as to why, out of an eventual brood of seventeen children, Sylvia was the only one sent to live elsewhere.

"My mother was sick and I was the baby and the Paynes were very good friends," Sylvia recalled. When she was baptized on April 1, 1923, Lavinia Payne and William Baylor were listed as sponsors and godparents. In the end, it was a blessing for her in many ways. "They didn't have any children, but they were very good friends. They stood up for my mother and father when they got married."

"She always felt her mother had given her away," recalled Sylvia's cousin, Shannon Hull, who maintained and shared a family diary. Generations later, loose ends to the story linger. One family member claimed Sylvia reported her birth mother had her ears pierced and had blood poisoning. She was too ill to properly take care of three toddlers.

Photo by Vicky Moon

Charles Town, with a population of close to 6,000, was the type of place where children of all colors could run barefoot, although rarely together. Bouncing between two homes was a routine Sylvia never questioned. Yet, she also was never truly able to reconcile the situation.

Friends spoke of the lifelong emotional weight she seemed to carry, including a suppressed fear of abandonment. That also bubbled to the surface later in her life after two unpleasant divorces.

"Abandonment fears typically stem from a loss in childhood, such as the loss of a parent through death or divorce, but it can also result from inadequate physical or emotional care," according to Good Therapy. "In adulthood, these early childhood experiences result in fear of being abandoned by the significant people in one's life. While some degree of abandonment fear may be a normal part of being human, when the fear of abandonment is severe, frequent, and impossible to comfort, it can cause significant impairment, particularly with regard to developing healthy relationships."

Psychologist Ann Reilly of Wellington, Florida, works with horse people and equestrians of all levels. She also spoke about filling the void of abandonment with her clients.

"I've found that there are two types of women who get involved with horses," she notes. "There are those who strive to fill maternal needs and others who seek to fill achievement, self-worth, control, escape from reality, safety, stability, identity, relationship, and at times, happiness, joy, and freedom needs.

"It sounds to me like this trainer (Sylvia) may have been in category two," Reilly continues. "She was also working in a primarily male dominated business. Most maternally, classically-feminine women would not survive in the men's world. This woman's drive for acceptance would keep her in the game."

Whatever the underlying issues, from an early age, Sylvia was able to fill the lifelong void. It began on that long ago Easter Day when she discovered what became a lasting love of horses.

Sylvia's godmother, Lavinia Strother, was twenty-three when she married her first husband, Richard Wilson, twenty-one, on October 15, 1904. Birth records reveal a daughter, Hazel Schuyler French Wilson, born on March 7, 1906. Shortly after that, she was baptized at St. Philip's with minister Joseph Livingston officiating. But there is very little mention of her after the Wilsons divorced.

However, ten years later, when Lavinia married twenty-five-year-old William H. Payne on June 17, 1914, her daughter Hazel was listed with them on census records. The Rev. W.M. Craven performed the marriage ceremony. Records reveal Lavinia as divorced, but her age was listed incorrectly as twenty-nine. There is no way to tell if that was a mistake, or intentional. She was actually thirty-three and had no children with Payne. That may well explain why the Paynes took Sylvia into their life.

One has to wonder: did they try to have children and fail? Was Sylvia's mother Bertha, a mid-wife, privy to reasons behind all of it? Did something happen in childbirth?

A chill blew in through an open window as Sylvia spoke from the comfort of her favorite recliner. She had no qualms in confiding the duality of her circumstances. Perhaps, at age eighty-four, it was cathartic; after all, it was no secret.

She described how "Ma Payne" worked as a cook and William Payne was employed as a chauffeur for the Braziers, a well-to-do white family. He also had a part-time job at a stone quarry—the nearby Keystone Lime Plant. And while Sylvia's heart felt broken at the rejection from her birth mother, she did fall into caring hands. She was raised by loving, hard-working folks who also were generous with their hard-earned money. She eventually inherited a large home and many furnishings from the Paynes. Eighty years later, her sister, Lucille, remained envious: "She had a bike."

Each winter, Sylvia looked forward to returning to her birth parents' home while the Paynes traveled to Florida with their employers.

When the Paynes returned to West Virginia each spring, Sylvia was indulged as the center of attention and showered with toys and dresses. Friends and surviving family members repeatedly point out that the Paynes had no children and were thrilled to spoil little Sylvia.

For her entire life, Sylvia bounced between the two families almost on a daily basis. On the surface, she seemed happy. But decades later, long after her death, friends say it always haunted her.

"Each time this little girl went to visit her birth family, I'm pretty sure she most likely felt some shame and fear of disapproval," Reilly said. "She was critically abandoned and emotionally injured, and with each visit, she was reminded she just was not valuable enough for this family to keep."

While love and affection from her birth mother and family did not make up for giving her away to another family, it may have sporadically eased her pain. It did teach her not to trust people who love you, because you could lose them and they might reject you. This little girl most likely presented in one of two ways: as "shy" and hard to get to know, or like an over anxious puppy, trying too hard to get the approval of others and appearing very needy.

On Easter Sunday, March 31, 1929, the temperature reached a high of sixty-seven. Following the Rideout family's Easter meal, little Sylvia once again headed back to the Paynes, to a plain two-story clapboard house on Congress Street.

By the next day, Sylvia's search for love and self-worth would take a profound turn.

Targa

Photo courtesy of Lucille Rideoutt Berry

CHAPTER 6

TARGA

*There's something about the smell of a horse
that does something to my nose. It don't smell
like any wildflower or any rose.
It has a smell all of its own.*

- "The Smell of a Horse," Don Ohman, cowboy poet

Eight-year-old Sylvia saw the man with a piebald pony in the distance as she was skipping up the street on Easter afternoon in 1929. He was going house to house, selling a two-minute ride for ten cents. A photo, which she cherished for life, was an extra quarter.

Horses were very much a part of the fabric and rhythm of the town. Her grandfather, Charles Snowden, sometimes used a horse to transport freight off the train to haul supplies to the rear doors of the Lorenzo grocery store, Brown's Ice Cream Parlor or Clarence Eby's grocery. At other times, Charles Snowden trudged on foot with a handcart with freight from the railroad station.

Heavy, large-boned workhorses lugged carts and plows and were not used for a leisurely trot. Nor were they employed in the sport of Thoroughbred racing, where Sylvia eventually spent a life filled with triumph and tragedy.

The town had riding horses and carriage horses and a livery stable offered food and shelter, not to mention hiring out a horse-drawn buggy for an afternoon outing. Many of the stately homes in town had carriage houses out back, and the remnants of some can still be seen today serving as sheds or garages.

Several large lots were reserved for parking horses while their owners went about their business at the butcher shop owned by the Johnson family, Dr. Light's drug store or Pete Brooks' fish shop. All those businesses were owned by whites and only patronized by whites. (The one exception to the white business owners was black barber Jim Thompson, who charged a nickel less than the competition for children's haircuts.)

Customers at the men's clothing store co-owned by Frank Jones thought nothing of his attire; he wore his 1st Virginia Cavalry Confederate uniform to work, with no complaints from his patrons. For many years, a dozen Confederate veterans would congregate near the courthouse each day.

As the automobile began to make its appearance in Charles Town, horses spooked as cars backfired. They took off running, surely a similar reaction from modern day horses exposed to the same noise. In the early 1920s, there were a number of serious injuries as horses bolted and carriages flipped, scattering occupants on the limestone-covered roadbeds.

While Sylvia no doubt witnessed several of these panicked horses running away, her passion for horses had its roots from the moment she sat on Targa, and stayed with her forever. It ultimately competed with her two failed marriages and may well have cost her quality time with her only daughter.

Life was mostly carefree for eight-year-old Sylvia. She had a new pair of shiny black patent leather shoes and a crisp new dress thanks to Ma Payne, her "second mother." The itinerant entrepreneur hawking pony rides steadied his camera in preparation to take a picture. Sylvia was instantly smitten, she never stopped thinking about the ecstasy she felt as her little hand reached down to pat the pony named Targa.

Goosebumps erupted as she leaned over and threw her arms around his neck.

"Oh, I want one of my own," she squealed.

At the time, for Sylvia, it was only a dream. The cost of any horse—pleasure, show jumping or Thoroughbred—was and remains an expensive, risky, and even frivolous expenditure. But those who cannot shake away the intoxication of a horse find a way to pursue the passion.

In her first ride on Targa, she felt a connection to the pony that made her feel happy and may well have eased her pain and loneliness. It was an experience she had without her siblings, one that was "special" only to her and left a huge hoof print on her heart and soul. It also led to a feeling of accomplishment, as in "I rode a pony!"

She also had a sense of control over the pony, a feeling she likely had rarely sensed before. Later in her career, her drive for recognition may have been the motivation when training more difficult Thoroughbred racehorses.

The fuzzy Targa felt soft against Sylvia's face. She never failed to remember his name. And, she never forgot his sweet smell, an intoxicating mix of sweet grass, newly-mown hay, carrots, apple drool, molasses, peppermint, grasshoppers and leather. For many, it's a life-addicting aroma, and not just a simple smell. Horse lovers of all levels have various takes on what a pony smells like. One little girl said, "applesauce."

Applesauce?

Not everyone sees it that way. One tough long-time Irish steeplechase rider said, "Those answers are a load of bollocks. I've never smelled a pony like any of their descriptions. They usually, especially pony ride and fair ponies, smell like horse shit, but one must be a horse person to appreciate that wonderful, soothing aroma.

"Truth is, it's like walking in the middle of New York, where this country boy is totally out of my depth, then walking past those horse carriages near Central Park, smelling the poop, feeling at home and suddenly realizing 'I own this city.' The problem is that it's not a smell, but more of an emotion."

Meanwhile, after her pony ride, Sylvia scurried back to join her birth mother, father, brothers and sisters. The next afternoon, Monday, April 1, 1929, the Rideoutt family of Potato Hill would dye eggs, which cost forty cents a dozen.

They dressed up for church and took part in an egg hunt at the white-frame St. Philip's Episcopal Church on South Lawrence Street. It was the same church where Sylvia's parents were married, where she went to nursery school and later married for the first time. Family members continue to worship at St. Philip's to this day.

In Washington, President and Mrs. Hoover welcomed over 47,000 to the White House grounds for the annual egg roll, including 18,000 children. Seventy-one kids got lost during the festivities. Following the egg roll, the Marine Band performed, as did a quartet from Harvard and the Earlham College Glee Club. A Maypole also was set up for the first time. One little girl brought her own rabbit, and others left the property weighed down by candy and dyed eggs.

In Charles Town, Sylvia couldn't have cared less about candy. She was still giddy from the pony ride and couldn't stop talking about the black and white pony.

Targa.

Hallelujah.

CHAPTER 7

READING, WRITING AND THE STRAP

*The board of education of Charles Town district
has purchased from Mr. George Washington for the sum
of $500, a half-acre lot for a Negro school site.*

- Virginia Free Press, August 8, 1894

From her own recollections, Sylvia was a busy little three-year-old from the moment she popped out of her bed by seven in the morning. She'd willingly dress herself for nursery school with her first teacher, Miss Nethersole Ross. No hand me downs for baby Sylvia; she was constantly lavished with new dresses by Ma Payne. Those dresses, in turn, were passed on to others in her Rideoutt birth family, which continued to expand.

In addition to learning her ABCs and numbers, Sylvia also was exposed to plenty of music in the basement of St. Philip's church. The weekly nursery school tuition was forty-five cents.

As Sylvia started first grade, she had a bike, the only member of her constantly swelling family to own such an extravagance. Every day, she pedaled one mile each way to the four-room Eagle Avenue School, also known as the Charles Town District Colored School. Her route took her right past Davenport Street, where the rest of the Rideoutt family lived.

Mrs. Cerelle Craven was her first grade teacher. "She was very nice, her husband was a preacher and she had one son, Adam," recalled Sylvia, well into her eighties. "We went to school together."

Sylvia's aunt, Irma Snowden Hull Patrick, taught fourth grade at Eagle Avenue and kept an eye on all of her nieces and nephews. Mrs. Patrick went on to become the school's principal, earning seventy-five dollars a year.

The school was built on a lot purchased by the Charles Town District Board of Education for $500 from George and Emily Washington in 1894. It was located next to the railway station where Sylvia's grandfather, Charles Snowden, worked. The soot from the coal-fueled trains often overwhelmed the students.

In 1929, the year of Sylvia's first pony encounter, a new school with six rooms and an auditorium was built on the same lot. Each day, some Eagle Avenue children went home for lunch. A teacher pulled a rope to ring the lunch bell and the doors to the classrooms swung open. Before departing for the forty-five-minute break, the entire school would sing: *"Thou art grace, thou art good. Lord, we thank you for this food. By thy hand, we all are fed. Give us Lord thy daily bread."*

The reference to "thy daily bread" had major significance when the Wall Street bubble burst on Black Thursday, October 24, 1929. Stock prices began to slide for what became a total loss estimated at $5 billion. Four days later, the stock market crashed and the Great Depression was about to cripple the nation. Unemployment was rampant and many were forced to their daily bread lines.

James Tolbert lived around the corner from the Rideoutt family on Harewood Avenue. His mother made jelly sandwiches, or sometimes tomato and mayonnaise sandwiches on white bread, which cost about eight cents per loaf. Lunch literally provided a breath of fresh air for the children. Tolbert also recalled the stench from the school's septic tank, which was constantly backing up. There was no sewer line. "It was rough and running over all the time," he recalled, decades later. "It was by the grace of God no one got sick."

On weekends, the school served as a community center where children gathered for baseball games, rounds of tag, and picnics after church. The subjects listed on report cards included reading, writing and spelling. They put on plays and music shows, including an Indian operetta. They studied history, civics, agriculture, drawing and home economics.

Although the racetrack had not yet been built in Charles Town, a wagering boom broke out during the Depression era, according to an article by Brian Field first published in the *Saturday Evening Post* in 1935. "With everything in life feeling like a gamble, these Americans began taking chances that they never would have considered in prosperous times," writer Jeff Nilsson recounted in a 2011 online review. Back at the little local schoolhouse, Tolbert recalled, for science class, the older students had a textbook called *Our Environment: How We Adapt Ourselves to It.* They studied the solar system, weather, water (including how to make soap), as well as receiving useful lessons on gardening and intricate details about soil, crop rotation and making cold frames to grow vegetables.

There were English lessons in poetry. Edward Lear's "The Owl and the Pussycat" and George A. Strong's "The Modern Hiawatha" were included in a textbook called *Prose and Poetry Journeys.*

Students were evaluated for "personal characteristics of courtesy, self-control, reliability, industry, punctuality, speech habits, health, leadership and cooperation." The marks went from A for superior to E for unsatisfactory. There was little coddling. Teachers were strict, often employing a ruler to rap the occasional knuckle. More serious discipline included the use of a dreaded leather strap. It had been crafted at Hiram Goetz's Harness Factory (billed as "The Largest in the World") in the adjacent town of Ranson, by the father of a student.

"They wanted you to keep clean," recalled eighty-year-old alumnus Russell Roper, who, decades later, purchased the land where Eagle Avenue School once stood until it burned to the ground in 1966. "They tried to make something out of you."

One of Russell Roper's classmates recalled how Roper and Adam Craven shared a desk. When they started to push and shove each other one day, Russell Roper reported the incident to Mr. Braxton, the mathematics teacher.

"You should get Adam for pushing me," a fellow student recalled about Roper's snitch.

Braxton let loose with "the Strap" on Russell Roper's rear end.

"Don't tell me what I should do," Braxton snarled.

Another teacher constantly warned the students, "Don't take any tea for the fever. You can cut up if you want, but I'm going to whip your butt."

"We behaved out of fear," Shannon Hull recalled.

"The teachers demanded respect," James Tolbert added. "If you didn't behave, the teachers told the parents and you'd get it at home. All the teachers knew the parents. You'd get the stick at home."

The same punishment was meted out if anyone played hooky. Teachers informed parents of any unexcused absence and "if not, your classmates would carry the story home."

There is no record of a science class where one might have even seen a drawing of a horse with all its parts—withers, hock, cannon bone, hooves—now standard in tack rooms at most riding school stables. That instruction would come much later for an eight-year-old girl named Sylvia.

Each year with the first snowfall, industrious young black boys armed with snow shovels headed up to George Street. They could earn at least twenty-five cents cleaning up the sidewalks of one of the big homes. Several times a year, kids of all colors pulled their sleds up to Dixon Hill, a street in Potato Hill. They'd race down and trudge back up all day. If there were any broken bones or serious sledding injuries, it became separate and unequal, because the hospital on Congress Street was segregated.

During the summer, most children went barefoot. The same industrious boys who shoveled snow again headed up to George Street. This time, they pulled weeds and mowed lawns, again at the going rate of twenty-five cents. The white boys set off for a special spot on the Shenandoah called the Big Eddy. The black kids cooled off at Evitts Run, a stream leading to the Shenandoah, or to Mitchell's Bottom behind Happy Retreat.

Buddy Morgan's father built the first swimming pool in Jefferson County. "It was eight by twelve feet with brick walls covered with concrete," he wrote in his memoirs. "We filled it with a garden hose with city water and the word quickly got around, so it was soon filled solid with bodies—both black and white-all splashing around so much that we had to constantly keep filling it. Small as it was, many kids learned to swim in it."

Children helped pick apples, cherries and strawberries. When the Rideoutt family frequently gathered on Sunday afternoons, Sylvia couldn't wait to visit. She happily pitched in, cranking the ice cream freezer set inside a wooden bucket lined with ice and salt. Then, she'd sneak a taste as they all took turns turning the dasher. No need to even think about going uptown, where the white kids could purchase a soda or a double-dip cone

STRAWBERRY ICE CREAM

2 cups sugar
6 eggs
1 gallon heavy cream
1 quart milk
2 cups mashed strawberries

Beat eggs with sugar and then mix in the cream real well. Put in the inside freezer and then pour milk on top and close the lid tight. The ice and salt packed are around the outside. Crank until almost done and then add the strawberries.

at Brown Brothers Ice Cream Parlor.

Sylvia cherished many of her mother's recipes.

The Rideoutt family continued to grow during the early 1930s. A fifth son, Donald Morris Rideoutt, was born March 11, 1931.

In early 1932, local banker J. Richard Russell announced his intention to run for mayor of Charles Town, and America's secretary of agriculture, Arthur M. Hyde, visited West Virginia, urging famers to attend Farmer's Week at the College of Agriculture at West Virginia University in Morgantown. That same year, iconic trumpeter Louis Armstrong popularized the song "All of Me."

Plans were underway for the annual George Washington Social at the parish house of the Zion Church, where members of the black church, including the Rideoutt family, would be serving the white members of St. Mary's Guild. The newly developed low pressure Firestone Air Balloon Tire made news and prices were slashed. And Sylvia's favorite Florida grapefruit was three for ten cents at the A&P.

Just as Sylvia entered sixth grade, Rideoutt daughter number seven, Veda Marie, was born on September 23, 1932. And curiously, six months later on March 3, 1933, along came a baby girl named Imogene Rideoutt.

The B & O Railroad and the N & W Railway Company announced that two night trains would now be making stops in Charles Town, perhaps cutting down the soot at the Eagle School.

On December 2, 1933, came the biggest news since they hung John Brown. That memorable day, the racetrack opened with abundant fanfare on a cloudy, frigid Saturday afternoon.

Charles Town Grain and Feed Co. advertised Over the Top Laying Mash. And, the following poultry notes would have been of interest to all those raising chickens in their backyards, including the Rideoutts. Dirty eggs are costly. Oyster shell is probably the best source of lime for poultry. All breeds of poultry with white earlobes produce white-shelled eggs. This includes Leghorns, Anaconas, Minocaras and Andalusians. All breeds of poultry that have red earlobes produce brown or tinted shell eggs. This includes all Plymouth rocks, Rhode Island Reds, Orpingtons, Brahmas and Langshank.

CHAPTER 8

THE HOITY-TOITY AND THE HOI POLLOI

There was horse racing-and everything
that goes with it.

- Walter Haight, *The Washington Post*,
Sunday, December 3, 1933

The baby girl named Imogene Rideoutt was born on March 3, 1933, less than six months after Veda Marie Rideoutt had emerged on September 23, 1932.

Sometimes spelled as Emma Gene, she was actually the daughter of the Rideoutts first-born daughter, Elaine Rideoutt, who was seventeen at the time. The father was unknown, and the baby girl died on August 1, 1935.

Photo courtesy of Jefferson County Black History Preservation Society, Inc.

Govenear Paige Rideoutt, the sixth son, took his first breath on October 28, 1933, several months before the racetrack opened. News of the same day included word that President Franklin Roosevelt would soon address the Federal Council of Churches to defend his controversial policy on gold buying intended to increase commodity prices.

The racetrack was built on land once owned by the Charles Town Horse Show Association under the name of the Shenandoah Valley Jockey Club and Joseph B. Boyle of Baltimore. The cost was $160,000, much of which was funded during the Depression. The facility included twelve stables and forty-four betting windows and a heated grandstand. Between races, live music echoed from a nearby covered bandstand. Ironically, "Gold Diggers' Song" from the film *Gold Diggers of 1933* starring Ginger Rogers was a chart topper. It began, "We're in the money…"

On opening day, a total of $44,175 was wagered on seven races. Odds were calculated by slide rule under the supervision of Baltimore-based Mortimer M. Mahoney, who held similar pari-mutuel positions at several other tracks.

According to the *Shepherdstown Register*, "This is the first time that legalized racing has ever been conducted in West Virginia." It became reality because of recently passed racing legislation, under the direction of Commissioner J.B. McCaughlin of the State Department of Agriculture."

The race meet was to continue for twenty days, through Christmas. Charles Town was the lone northern track to operate during the winter. Joseph B. Boyle, the brother of track founder Albert Boyle, and Thomas K. Lynch, who also operated the Maryland tracks in Bowie and Marlboro, served as administrators. The grandstand overflowed, trains unloaded customers from Baltimore and Washington onto a platform 100 feet from the track's entrance. Attendance reports fluctuated from 3,000 to 10,000 over the twenty days.

The Spanish-inspired architecture of H. Harold Riggins, with a stucco-over-concrete clubhouse, was envisioned to resemble the grand Hialeah, Florida racecourse. Riggins was involved with that stately facility, which included red barrel tile accents and Moorish details.

Katherine Elkins Hitt was the hostess up in the VIP section of the hoity-toity clubhouse. Her late father was Senator Stephen Benton Elkins (1841-1911), the founder of Elkins, West Virginia, and a Republican senator from 1895-1911. Well-known socialites and racing royalty, Liz and Jock Whitney, were among the guests.

John Hay "Jock" Whitney was best known as a financial backer of *Gone with the Wind*, the classic film starring Clark Gable. He also was publisher of the *New York Herald Tribune* and ambassador to the Court of St. James. When he married the stunning Mary Elizabeth "Liz" Altemus in 1930, he also purchased the Upperville, Virginia estate known as Llangollen, where they raised many successful Thoroughbred racehorses. She would carry on the tradition after they divorced ten years later.

Charles Curtis, a racing aficionado and former vice president (1928-32), also was on hand. He had ridden as a young jockey in races in his native Kansas. Other sparkly clubhouse notables included police court Judge Isaac R. Hitt of Washington and Virginia Senator Harry F. Byrd's daughter, Westwood Byrd.

Hotels and private rooming houses were overflowing with guests. Eight state troopers were hired to be on duty throughout the entire racing meet. The *Martinsburg Journal* reported that "Four and possibly five of the detachment are coming from posts in Central and Southern West Virginia, it is understood."

There was one other little-known distraction that afternoon. Adjacent to the grandstand, a fire broke out, reportedly caused by defective wiring. Charles Town firemen were quickly on the scene and extinguished the blaze, which caused less than $1,000 in damages.

Meanwhile, down with the *hoi polloi* in the general admission area, fans were shoulder to shoulder, with one exception; black race-goers were confined to a small area and required to use separate bathrooms. According to a *Time* magazine article, there were "pockets bulging with Mason jars of moonshine," with "Shenandoah farmers huddled over their tout sheets."

Bill Bennings, a handicapper for the *Washington Post*, reminded readers, "If you are out here, remember that the name of this town is Charles Town, not 'Charlestown', which is farther across the state. I'm going to try to christen this track with seven winners. I said I am going to try."

The track surface was defined as "slow" on that long ago opening day. The weather was defined as clear. The first race, five furlongs with a purse of $400 for maiden two-year-olds, went to the post for a walk-up start at 1:17 p.m. The starter was Marshall Cassidy, whose grandson went on to become a much-admired announcer at big-time New York tracks like Belmont Park and Saratoga.

As for that first race, Mint Mission in post position six, owned and trained by G. L. Alvin, was "strongly urged in the final drive, [and] just lasted long enough" to win. The horse was ridden by jockey Harold Thurber and paid fourteen dollars to win at 6-1 odds. The trainer and jockey also won the fourth, an allowance race worth $500, with Luck In. In a full page coverage of the historic event, the *Washington Post* featured a photo of Luck In with a blanket presented by the Jockey Club for his win in the "stake."

Writer Ann Hilton's father, Jim Bell, was a horse trainer and entered Electric Gaff in the third race on opening day. A plow pulled by two massive Percheron horses lugged the starting gate into position. Electric

Gaff ran next to last.

And, for the record, Bill Bennings picked one winner out of the seven races.

Around this time, teenager Sylvia Bishop began to show up at the track. Sneaking off long before the opening school bell rang, she was mesmerized as horses worked out at dawn, leaning over the railing as they came by prancing and snorting.

She watched the trainers (all men) with stopwatches clocking their charges breezing at three furlongs (3/8 of a mile in thirty-six seconds) four furlongs (half mile in forty-eight seconds) or five furlongs (5/8 mile, just over one minute factoring in one or more of the sweeping turns). In horse racing lingo, this is known as "a minute and change" because of the turns. The basic rule in calculating times is that ideally, one furlong should be equivalent to twelve seconds.

And, beyond a doubt, Sylvia also knew a career in racing might just be her future calling.

ACCORDING TO THE DAILY RACING FORM:

BREEZE- Working a horse at a moderate speed; less effort than handily.

GALLOP- A type of gait, a fast canter. Also, to ride a horse at that gait.

CHAPTER 9

HONEYSUCKLE ROSE, DON'T YOU KNOW THAT ANYTHING GOES?

I don't want to explain to somebody what pollen is. That is the secret and the beauty and the power and the potential of all this.

- Wolfgang Laib

Walter Haight was a highly respected racing writer for the *Washington Post* from 1932 until he died in 1968. He covered the Kentucky Derby thirty-seven times. On March 3, 1951, he wrote: "Charles Town, where somebody's forefathers raced horses before the birth of this nation." Indeed, racing in Charles Town, which continues to this day, actually goes back to George Washington's brother Charles, who first staged races through the village streets in 1786.

On any given day following the 1933 opening of the track, the race program would not start until a daily train filled with betting passengers arrived from Washington. Elwood Heironimus (1921-2004) worked at the track for fifty-five years in all manner of roles, from a groom on the backside to racing secretary and later as a steward. He recalled that the trains usually ran on schedule.

The racetrack ran in the red for those first two years, and owner Albert J. Boyle put up money to keep it going under the name of the Charles Town Jockey Club.

Sylvia started to work at the track as a teenager just after it was built in 1933, not long after she finished eighth grade at the Eagle Avenue School. During this era of overt segregation, there was no high school for Negro students.

A convenient alternative existed on Fillmore Avenue in nearby Harpers Ferry overlooking the confluence of the Potomac and Shenandoah rivers. Storer College was founded just after the Civil War on six acres in 1869, eventually expanding to a thirty-acre campus. It was founded by Dr. O.B. Cheney, president of the Free Baptist Missionaries led by the Rev. N.C. Brackett. Funds to purchase the land came from John Storer, a philanthropist from Maine.

Storer was located on a site known as Camp Hill, where abolitionist John Brown had staged his infamous 1859 raid on a federal arsenal and armory. Sylvia was enrolled at Storer as a ninth grade high school student.

Classes offered to freshmen included the Bible, taught by Prof. Saunders, so that students could become familiar with the contents and learn how the different "books" came to be written. Miss Church taught beginners' Latin. Mrs. McDonald

Photo courtesy and West Virginia University Libraries

drilled the students in the grammar and syntax of French.

English students used *Tanner's Correct English* book to further the "ability to command pure, strong language with which to clothe his thoughts," according to the 1935 catalog of classes. Mr. Winters' course on agriculture was required. Additional options in geology, chemistry, astronomy, sociology and commercial law were also listed.

The school had nine buildings along with housing for the school president—"the Waterman House"—and numerous cottages for teachers and staff. The school was intended to educate freed slaves, their children, and other black students. It was mainly a teacher's college, and also offered courses in carpentry, gardening, blacksmithing, cooking, sewing and drawing. A memo to incoming students asked them to bring "Your bible. A tooth-brush. Three towels, brush and comb. Three table napkins, bedding, if you do not wish to hire it."

President Franklin Delano Roosevelt had just been elected to the first of his four terms president in 1932. The *Spirit of Jefferson* newspaper said his election "is the keynote to business and economic recovery in the United States." Three cans of Campbell's Tomato Soup cost nineteen cents.

Sylvia entered Storer College in Harpers Ferry in 1933. To help pay tuition, Sylvia peeled potatoes in a school kitchen and lunchroom. "I still lived with the Paynes," she said, adding that they had purchased a 1929

Chevrolet car for her so she could drive herself to school. "I had others in the car and they helped pay gas. If you didn't go there (Storer), you didn't have anywhere else to go in Charles Town." Although Sylvia was only fourteen, historian Catherine Rakowski, a research librarian at West Virginia University, said, "It wasn't unusual to drive without a license at that time. There was not a lot of enforcement."

With Sylvia at the wheel and classmates often riding with her to school, they left Charles Town and headed east toward Harpers Ferry. They often stopped at Woody's Filling Station to get gas for ten cents per gallon from owner John Eagan before heading east onto Washington Street in Charles Town. Little did Sylvia know that the property next to that gas station would soon play a huge role in the rest of her life.

On January 16, 1934, the Paynes purchased Woody's Filling Station, fronting thirty-five feet on the east side of West Street to the corner on Congress Street. A note for a total of $150 was payable in two parts to the Farmers Bank and Trust Company. Lee Bushong, Jr. served as trustee and the notary on the document was F. L. Bushong. And just hold that thought.

It was a seven-mile ride on Rt. 340 over to Storer in Harpers Ferry. Along the way, Sylvia and her girlfriends listened to popular songs on the radio, including Fats Waller's "Honeysuckle Rose," which earned him a belated Grammy in 1999, fifty-six years after he died from pneumonia in 1943.

Just outside Charles Town along the north side of the road, the girls passed by the early bones of the racetrack that was under construction for the December 1933 opening. Across the road from the track, Dutrow's Orchard was in full swing for the fall apple season. The two-lane road continued on through Halltown, a mill town that is still the site of the Halltown Paper Board Company. Just after Halltown, at Allstadts Hill, the Cliffside Motel offered cabins to rent. It's now a Clarion Inn.

They passed on to tiny Bolivar, West Virginia, which originally was named Mudfort until the then-Virginia General Assembly renamed it in 1824 in honor of South American leader Simon Bolivar. Once into Bolivar, the girls would soon pass Harpers Ferry High School on their left. When they got through the intersection of Union and High Streets, the Storer campus loomed close by at the top of a hill. Many of the school's stately buildings, such as Anthony Hall, can still be seen today, though it has since been renamed Wirth Hall. Conrad L. Wirth had been the National Park Service director in charge of Mission 66, a $1 billion, decade-long project to improve National Park Service facilities for the agency's fiftieth anniversary in 1966. The old campus is now the Stephen T. Mather Training Center. Anthony Hall, a Romanesque Revival building, served as the college's administration offices from the time it was built in 1881 until Storer shut down in 1955. The Free Will Baptist Church is nearby.

In the spring of 1934, a local paper noted in a column called "At Random" that, "For a few days last week, especially Friday, everyone enjoyed a taste of Spring. Charles Town was a picture of contentment as people…with smiles on their faces and minus their overcoats, went happily about their business."

To supplement her tuition and earn extra gas money, Sylvia also walked horses after their early morning workouts at the track. Racetrack people call this "walking hots." Sylvia arrived at her job that delightful April morning just after five. In the middle of the month, a new moon glowed and dawn temperatures were in the high fifties.

It was also the peak of allergy season as pollen from great ragweed (Ambrosia *trifida*) and rape (Brassica *rapa*) permeated the air, causing horses and humans to suffer with watering eyes and sneezing fits.

Sylvia greeted some of her co-workers one morning. "Hey there, Spud," she said. She nodded to Junior, who worked as a groom, and waved to exercise rider Sam, who had just come back from galloping his horse around two turns on the track.

Depending on how far the horse had galloped or breezed, they all returned to the barns covered in a messy mix of mud and sand. The old horse show grounds had been chosen to house the track because of superior soil and the grade of the land surface.

"Take him over to Sylvia," the head man in the barn might say. "She can help take off the saddle and bridle, hold him for a bath and walk him."

Sylvia immediately noticed the bay horse she held was breathing quite heavily. There was thick goo coming out of his nose. "He's coughing like crazy," she said to anyone who would listen. As she helped take the saddle and bridle off, she noticed the horse's nostrils flared and he shook his head.

"Let's get him washed and walked and get him back in the stall with a fan," the barn manager said. This was Sylvia's introduction to horses and their pollen-induced allergies. She also learned pollen could cause horses to have hives.

Sylvia's horse education these early mornings extended to "plants that can poison." She was not in charge of one horse who decided to grab a breakfast bite of an intriguing trumpet-shaped pale blue morning glory (*Ipomoea*) that was winding its way up a nearby fence. This colorful vine in various shades of blue, pink, white and purple can be toxic if a horse takes a few too many bites of the flower and its seeds. The results range from mild gastrointestinal discomfort to liver issues and occasionally can be fatal.

So much for Morning Glories.

Sylvia quickly learned botanical and horticulture danger lurked everywhere, with hyacinths, iris, hydrangea, and lily of the valley, as well as black locust and horse chestnut trees.

Sylvia's pre-dawn labor also resulted in a new love, in the form of Pinkie, a lead pony. A surviving vintage photo of a teenage Sylvia shows her riding him on a Western saddle. She rode him at every opportunity and he eventually lived in a stable on Congress Street near her home.

"The pony lived with her there," her sister Lucille recalled more than six decades later. "She fell into it with the Paynes."

The teenage Sylvia gained a priceless equine education working at the track. As the horses returned to the stables each morning, all manner of curious conditions and situations surfaced.

One morning, as Sylvia was cooling her down, a chestnut mare started to make a frightening sound, like a series of giant hiccups almost fifty times per minute, in sync with the heartbeat. "We had all kinds of things back then and still do today," she said. The horse's problem was a contraction of the diaphragm that is known around the stables as "thumps." The technical term is "synchronous diaphragmatic flutter," and it is caused by dehydration. Just like human hiccups, it usually can be curbed with plenty of water.

Azoturia is also called "tying up," and is a somewhat common situation often referred to as "Monday morning disease." According to the *Horseman's Veterinary Encyclopedia* published by Lyons Press, it's "a condition associated with forced exercise after a period of rest during which feed has not been reduced." When this happens, a horse becomes inflexible, sweaty and anxious. The horse must stand still and not be moved until a veterinarian is called. Horses also can suffer from heatstroke. And in extreme heat, some will stop sweating.

Sylvia did not need a book to recognize any of these conditions, and all that knowledge came into play throughout her career as a trainer.

As a twelve-day race meet concluded on Christmas Day in 1934, a total of $578,000 had been wagered at the track, with the state pocketing $17,340 as its three percent take.

Sylvia was forced to quit her studies at Storer after three years and did not graduate from high school. "I had to work," she recalled. "Yeah, Ma Payne was sick, a complication of age."

For the record, the 1954 Supreme Court ruling on Brown v. Board of Education technically ended school segregation as well as state funding for the college. Instead, the West Virginia legislature decided to fund other public colleges, schools that would now admit black students. Without its annual $20,000 a year state funding, Storer College closed in June 1955.

"No plans for future use of the school buildings have been made by the board of trustees," said L. F. Terrell, Storer's president at the time, according to the Jefferson Republican publication. He went on to suggest, "that the school be used for care and training of maladjusted children." In 1962, it became part of Harpers Ferry National Historical Park, and is now used as one of four National Park Service training centers.

On New Year's Eve, the nation's capital rang in 1935 in a mood the Washington Post described on the front page as "gayer than ever before in recent years…" The city was covered in a "magic palette of snow."

On May 30, the Charles Town racetrack opened for a thirty-one-day meet, with Genie Palatine winning the feature race that day. Up on Potato Hill on the western edge of Charles Town, the Rideoutts welcomed their thirteenth child on June 13, a baby girl they named Shirley. In August came a sad report that the two-year-old girl known as Emma Gene Rideoutt died.

In the larger world of big-time horse racing in New York and Florida, the Milky Way Farm owned by Ethel V. Mars was listed in the American Racing Manual as the leading owner in 1936. Back in Charles Town, Elizabeth "Betty" Rideoutt was welcomed into the world (as the fourteenth member of the family) on May 23, 1936.

On June 20, two lucky Charles Town bettors won the daily double that paid $2,284.20. The train that summer day brought 1,000 racing fans from Washington, with a crowd estimated at 8,000 betting just under $100,000. The Washington Post reported that "The day was warm enough to stimulate the sale of beer and pop and the good customers were three deep on the rail all afternoon."

Miss Norma G. Darr was crowned the queen of the October fall festival, celebrating 150 years of the 1786 founding of Charles Town. She and the eight all-white members of her "court" were featured on the front page of the Spirit of Jefferson newspaper.

There was an ad at the bottom of page five in the newspaper for the Trump Contracting and Improvement Company to announce they were giving away free calendars.

Melvin Talbott Strider (1880-1962) was an RFD postal carrier who owned the funeral home and a furniture store. He also served as vice president of the Jefferson County Board of Education and taught Sunday school at the Methodist Church. He was named president of the Kiwanis Club in January of 1937.

Bayer aspirin cost a penny a pill (by 2018, it was nine cents), and A. F. Rees, Inc. of Berryville, Virginia offered to humanely destroy and remove diseased animals—horses, calves, hogs or sheep—"quickly without any trouble to you."

On the other hand, Hyman Viener & Sons in Charles Town offered to buy legally caught furs, including skunk pelts for two dollars and muskrats for $1.50. Creamy Wisconsin cheese was twenty-five cents per pound and coal was selling for twelve dollars per ton.

On June 12, 1937, Madge Virginia Rideoutt, number fifteen of the family, was born in Charles Town. A month later, a mid-July heat wave hovered over Washington, with one reported death and four prostrations. A West Virginia miner drowned while out fishing. And in an all-too-familiar subject during the Donald Trump presidency, a front page Washington Post story reported that "President Roosevelt's eldest son, James, agreed yesterday to disclose his income tax returns in response to a Republican demand."

Sylvia's cousin, Shannon Hull, penciled a note in his diary that Yvonne Devon Snowden, age twenty-four in August of 1937, was operated on by Dr. Morison and Dr. Porterfield at Charles Town hospital. (Whatever the medical concern, the surgery was obviously successful because Yvonne lived until November 15, 1981.)

Washington Post society columnist Dudley Harmon observed that many would escape to Florida, Bermuda and Jamaica in early January 1938. The Post's society editor, Hope Ridings Miller, covered Mrs. Edward Beale McLean's New Year's Eve dinner party for 900 guests.

The hostess, best known as Evalyn Walsh McLean (1886 –1947), wore a gown ranging in shades of blue "to blend with tones of her famous Hope diamond." The family had once owned the Washington Post before it went bankrupt and was sold at auction.

The society orchestra Meyer Davis played dance music later that evening and the playlist no doubt included many Cole Porter songs, including "Anything Goes," that featured lyrics referring to Mrs. McLean's well-publicized trip to Soviet Russia.

Nearly fifty years later, Sylvia, now eighty-four, was sitting with a visitor in apartment number 5-P at the Charles Towers, when the phone rang.

"Bill," she said curtly. "I'll call you later."

THE 1935 STORER COLLEGE CATALOG

WEST VIRGINIA LAW AS TO TUITION OF STATE STUDENTS

The state law requires boards of education not supporting high schools to pay the tuition of pupils of high school grade directly to the school attended. No absolutely accurate statement of the expenses of a student in Storer College can be given. That depends upon the indulgence of parents in furnishing spending money and the tastes and inclinations of students. The following is a reasonably accurate statement of the necessary expenses of a student for one school year. *The fee was listed as five dollars per month.*

CHAPTER 10

SOMEWHERE OVER THE RAINBOW

I am in the bad news business. Seldom do I get to report on puppies,
rainbows, or the sounds of children giggling. Well, never.

- Gwen Ifill

In March of 1936, the worst flood ever to hit Jefferson County swamped Harpers Ferry and Shepherdstown to near oblivion from the rain-swollen waters of the nearby Shenandoah and Potomac rivers. A circa 1889 bridge across the Potomac and another highway bridge at Harpers Ferry were obliterated. It took three years for the demolished structures to be rebuilt. Sylvia's studies at Storer College in Harpers Ferry came to an end, partly due to the bridge collapse as well as a lack of funds to pay her way.

On New Year's Day 1939, the twenty-fifth Rose Bowl was played in Pasadena; Southern California defeated Duke, 7-3. That year, Marjorie Kinnan Rawlings was awarded the Pulitzer Prize for her novel The Yearling. And, on September 1, Nazi Germany invaded Poland, an opening salvo leading to World War II. In October, Albert Einstein wrote a letter to President Roosevelt about the possibility of building a nuclear bomb.

A fire broke out in downtown Charles Town and did $1,000 in damage at J.A. Engle's store. There was huge news affecting West Virginia when the Security and Exchange Commission approved a new track in the northern panhandle. Al Boyle was to serve as president and manager at Waterford Downs, named in honor of his ancestral family home in Ireland.

Bing Crosby's rendition of "Pennies from Heaven" could still be heard on the radio, and a young actress named Judy Garland sang "Over The Rainbow" as she portrayed Dorothy Gale in The Wizard of Oz.

The waters of the Shenandoah and Potomac rivers continue to captivate visitors in Harpers Ferry, West Virginia. Ruins of a circa 1889 stone bridge at the confluence can still be seen. *Photo by Jacob Fleming*

Washington Post racing handicapper Bill Bennings wrote that "It felt nice to return" for the May meeting at Charles Town. Brother Boyle is here to take care of the managing." Once again, he promised to name a few winners. "After all a buck is a buck, whether you get it in pennies or a crisp bill."

Bertha and James Rideoutt welcomed their final child, Macgruder Rideoutt, on September, 6, 1939.

The population of Charles Town in the 1940 census was 2,926, the largest in the town's history. Al Boyle traveled to Florida over that winter to visit the tracks at Hialeah and Tropical Park. He was preparing for Charles Town to open for a forty-six-day meet in May and had 700 stalls available. According to the Washington Post, "Several new barns, to be located south of the grandstand, are already under construction. A water tank holding thousands of gallons will be installed, so that the plant's sanitary conditions will be improved. The racing strip is being re-soiled and the turns graded and banked."

That same year, the first transmission of FM radio was clear and static-free. Richard Wright's novel Native Son was published, and the ninety-ninth Grand National steeplechase in Aintree, England, was won by Sgt. Mervyn A. Jones aboard Bogskar. A horse called Gallahadion, with jockey Carroll Bierman, captured The 66th running of the Kentucky Derby.

The 1940 Olympics, first scheduled in Tokyo, then moved to Helsinki, were eventually cancelled as a result of World War II. And in Charles Town, a four-year-old filly named Palkin won the Montani Semper Liberi, a six-furlong feature in honor of West Virginia Day.

Fire units from three companies in Martinsburg, Shepherdstown, and Harpers Ferry and two from Charles Town, raced to the barn area at the track engulfed flames in mid-January. They used over a mile of hose to fight the fire and one 100-stall stable went up in flames, though only one horse died.

Forty-year-old Leslie Combs II, best known as the owner of the famous Spendthrift Farm in Kentucky, was named a steward at Charles Town for the December meet. Racing writer Bill Bennings noted he had never missed a day of racing since the track had opened. He fondly recalled the time when a 10-1 shot he had bet on was leading around the final turn and "disappeared as if by magic, having slid under the inside rail and into the infield."

"But," Bennings wrote, "Charles Town has come a long way in a few years."

Indeed.

Around town that year, two runaway boys from Washington, D.C., ages twelve and sixteen, were picked up by the Charles Town police and kept until their father came to retrieve them. It turned out they had relatives in the area and no harm was done. Racing continued as usual at the track, where the National Horsemen's Guild also met to support a "victory meeting" from June 15-July 4 for Army-Navy Relief and West Virginia Charities. Track employees were paid seventy-five percent of their wages in war bonds and stamps. Horsemen also took part of the winnings in war bonds. And jockey fees, above their regular rates, also were paid in war stamps, a first for America's racetracks.

As 1943 dawned, Negro League baseball star catcher Josh Gibson suffered a nervous breakdown, and eminent black scientist George Washington Carver died at age eighty-one. In the Orange Bowl, Alabama defeated Boston College, 37-21. And by June, Heinrich Himmler ordered the extermination of all Jewish ghettos in occupied Poland.

In Charles Town, thirty-year-old Wilton Buckner, a groom at the track for the Everhart Stables, fell from a second story window of a restaurant adjacent to the track and died. And Sylvia's paternal grandmother, Maria Elizabeth Harris Rideout (it was spelled with one t when she was born March 7, 1873) died at age sixty-three from tuberculosis. William "Daddy" Payne, Sylvia's beloved occasional father, also died as the result of a ruptured gastric ulcer, eleven days short of his fifty-fifth birthday on December 31, 1943.

The Army and Navy relief victory meet was again part of the racing program. A new West Virginia Merchant Marine Endowment Fund was established to provide college tuition for men wounded at sea.

In 1944, the parents of Marine Charles F. Reininger, Jr. received the devastating news that their son, a star high school athlete in Charles Town, had been killed in action.

On December 2, another fire broke out in the barn area of the track. This time, fifty-five horses were rescued and were not injured. There was extensive damage to the structure and many saddles, bridles and other tack were burned. Still, racing went on as scheduled.

In early June, a short one-paragraph notice in the Washington Post reported that "President-General Manager A. J. Boyle of the Charles Town Jockey Club announced today 'Upon official announcement from Allied headquarters of the long awaited D-Day invasion of Europe, the Charles Town Jockey Club's program for the day will be canceled.'"

All eyes were on news reports as an Allied Expeditionary Force of 150,000 landed in Normandy, France, on June 6, 1944. It marked the beginning of the end of the war the following year.

In mid-December, the track was closed because of heavy snow, and racing resumed a few days later with the James Saeger and Art Brown races as co-features. It also was announced that over the three years of victory meets since Pearl Harbor, $186,672 had been raised for returning veterans.

On Thursday, April 12, 1945, President Franklin D. Roosevelt died while sitting for a portrait. He was serving a never-to-be-repeated fourth term as president, and was replaced by a former haberdasher named Harry S. Truman.

Long-time Washington Post racing writer Walter Haight had a horse named after him and continued to report from Charles Town. "To many turf fans in this section, the little West Virginia track supplies a part of the yearly racing show that is important. They don't go up where 'John Brown's body lies a-molding in the grave' expecting to see any Kentucky Derbys or Preaknesses, but they do get the feel of the homey, down-to-earth sport that Charles Town provides. And lest we forget, they pay off in the same old United States dollars as they do at fashionable Belmont Park."

Post time was 1:15 p.m.

CHAPTER 11

I GET IDEAS

*Dear Folks, Cumberland's track
opens on Tuesday.*

**- Bill Bennings,
The Washington Post, July 1951**

As World War II raged on in Europe and the Far East, a dashing John Bishop (1919-2006) and his brother, Morris Norvell Bishop (1923-2014), were in the thick of the fighting. They had signed up to serve their country after the Japanese surprise attack at Pearl Harbor in Hawaii on December 7, 1942.

John was in the Army's Quartermaster Corps in the Pacific Theater when he sustained an injury falling off a truck. He ended up at the Newton D. Baker General Hospital in Martinsburg, West Virginia, named for Martinsburg native and attorney Newton Diehl Baker (1871-1937). Baker was the former mayor of Cleveland and later served for five years as secretary of war under President Woodrow Wilson. The hospital, built in 1944, is now known as the 449-bed Martinsburg Veterans Administration Medical Center.

On August 24, 1945, Sylvia Rideoutt and John Bishop were married at St. Philip's Episcopal Church on South Lawrence Street in Charles Town.

The Bishops immediately added to their "family," but it was not a baby, or even a horse. Sylvia and John had a Dalmatian they called Tank. He strolled the streets with them each evening after dinner.

Charles Town police officers also were out walking in the evenings and the young couple, as well as many other black residents, recalled being warned repeatedly to "watch your step."

In 1946, three hundred horses were on the grounds of the Charles

August 24, 1945 from left: Lucille Rideoutt, John E. Berry, Jr. , bridegroom John Bishop, father of the bride James Rideoutt, the bride, Sylvia Rideoutt, officiant Rev. Winston, Irma Rideoutt and Cecelia Green at reception at Payne's Tap Room.
Photo courtesy of Lucille Rideoutt Berry

Town racetrack preparing for the opening on May 29. This included a string of horses from Mexico's Hipódromo de las Américas. A day-at-the-races junket for members of the National Press Club in D.C. was also on the schedule.

John Bishop was working a maintenance job at the hospital in nearby Martinsburg. He always liked to "play the ponies," he said years later while traveling along West Virginia Rt. 9 through Kearneysville and Shenandoah Junction towards Charles Town. One night more than fifty years later, he spoke about how after picking up his paycheck, he took the same road to get to the track to bet on a horse called Bouplay that his wife Sylvia owned.

The horse won and John Bishop never went back to work at the hospital. He joined his wife in the horse business, but his interest was at the betting windows, not getting close to the horses. He also understood there were lines blacks knew not to cross while at the track. "We all knew to keep our place," he said. "It was not just to keep your place but, to know your place and stay in it."

Just one year after they were married, Sylvia and John sold two lots to Emilio Garrillo that Sylvia had purchased from her grandfather, Charles A. Snowden, in October 1943. The lots were at the intersection of

Kimball and Roger Streets, which later became Harewood Avenue and Davenport Street, just around the corner from Sylvia's childhood home on Potato Hill. The sale provided some much-needed start-up money for the newlyweds.

In 1947, Army veteran and star college athlete Jackie Robinson became the first African-American to play in Major League baseball when he joined the Brooklyn Dodgers. That year, Edward W. Brooke married his wife, Remigia Ferrari-Scacco, a union that ended when they divorced in 1979. Brooke, then living in Massachusetts, became the nation's first popularly elected African-American United States senator in 1966. He also maintained a residence in the horse country of Warrenton, Virginia, and in 1973, had an affair with television personality Barbara Walters. Also in '47, singer Ella Fitzgerald wed bass player Ray Brown. And, a horse named Colored Boy turned in a reported "sparkling performance" to win the Harpers Ferry Purse during the May meet at the track.

On February 17, 1947, the Bishops dressed in their Sunday best clothes to go over to the Old National Bank of Martinsburg to sign papers for a loan to purchase a 1937 Buick Sedan for $604.08. (The original price in 1937 would have been approximately $959) Their agreement with the bank called for monthly payments of forty-three dollars after a first payment of $36.08. They paid it off ahead of time on January 23, 1948.

Family members recalled John's fondness for Buicks and how he preferred to travel in style. He was a smart dresser, as well, but it soon became clear he did not share his wife's passion for the horses. "He was scared to death of horses," one family member recalled, as did several other friends. His main interest was at the wagering windows. He also had a burning ambition to become involved in the entertainment business, specifically in what was referred to as the "Chittlin Circuit" catering to black audiences and featuring black performers. The circuit weaved from its starting point in Baltimore on to the traditional southern states of Virginia, the Carolinas, and West Virginia, reaching all the way to Texas.

From 1950 to 1965, John Bishop became known as a prime mover on the circuit's music scene after he produced summer events at abolitionist John Brown's farm in western Maryland, only five miles from Harpers Ferry. The 254-acre farm had been purchased on April 28, 1950, by a chapter of the Improved Benevolent and Protective Order of Elks of the World (IBPOEW) as a national shrine. The group, the largest national organization of blacks, is also known as the "Black Elks."

During its first year, the property had been renovated with a large auditorium, barn, and a cottage with plumbing. Bishop was an extraordinary promoter. His friends, family and co-workers defined him as composed, classy and very skilled. They also described him as a lady's man with a wandering eye.

This also was the very same swath of land where Brown and his ragtag group of twenty-one followers attacked the federal armory in Harpers Ferry on October 16, 1859. Brown wanted to distribute munitions to slaves and spark an uprising for their freedom.

Brown was captured two days later. He was tried for treason, rebellion and murder in Charles Town and found guilty and sentenced to death on November 2, 1859. Brown rode atop his own coffin to his execution by hanging just up George Street from the jail. A historical marker stands nearby on this street still lined with stately old homes

More than a hundred years later, thousands of music fans flocked to the very same farm from Washington, D.C., Virginia, Maryland and West Virginia. John Bishop oversaw the entire operation, from making sure the food stand was stocked (a fried chicken sandwich was very popular), the performers were comfortable, and the stage was set with the instruments positioned perfectly in place.

Each weekend, the farm shook with music and shimmied with dancing. Little Richard put in an appearance, as did James Brown, Ray Charles and Tina Turner. One attendee later told the Herald Mail in Hagerstown, Maryland, he'd never forget the night Chubby Checker showed up and did the twist. Other well-known performers, including Cab Calloway, Duke Ellington and Big Joe Williams, also appeared.

John Bishop also fulfilled a yearning to run his very own nightclub when, in September 1947, he and Sylvia purchased an old inn just outside of Charles Town on Rt. 340. The structure, known as the Orchard Inn and previously owned by Charles E. Spinks, cost them $4,000, with a $2,000 down payment and a $2,000 promissory note. The payments were $100 each month for what was later known as the Rainbow Inn.

It was here that Mr. Bishop, often referred to by his middle name of Vernard, presented an all-girl band called the Sweethearts of Rhythm. "They had played at the Apollo," he recalled in a later interview as he drove through the countryside. "And then, they broke up." He also presented an all-female show called "The Coppertone Review."

A late-1950s ad for the Orchard Inn in the Spirit of Jefferson Farmers Advocate offered "dancing every Saturday and Sunday night," with music by Tom Kat and His Kountry Kittens.

Their business and financial interests expanded on March 17, 1948, when Sylvia and John served as "accommodation makers" for Lavinia Payne for her property on South West Street. Following the death of William Payne in 1943, Lavinia purchased full interest in the property from his two children George Payne and Rebecca P.Johnson from a previous marriage to Rebecca Williams. The note was for $5,000 from Homer W. Wagely, payable to the People's Bank of Charles Town at five percent, and released on August 21, 1963.

In the basement of the Paynes' old home, known as Payne's Hotel and Rooming House, the Tap Room was born. It was recognized throughout the area as a welcoming retreat for blacks to eat and spend the night. "I created an Afro-American club," Bishop recalled. "It was membership only. But I did have one white, Mr. Bloom from the hardware store."

Guests are said to have included the legendary entertainers Billie Holiday and Dinah Washington. The Bishops' daughter, Laverne, told writer Ed Maliskas in his book John Brown to James Brown, that, "When Ray Charles (1930-2004) stayed at the hotel, my mother would fix his dinner, and he'd eat two whole fried chickens at one sitting."

On September 13, 1948, Sylvia and Lavinia Payne borrowed $367.13 from the People's Trust Company for the forty-five-foot lot on West Street. The loan was released April 17, 1967.

Also in 1948, Sylvia and John Bishop teamed up in the racing business to purchase a chestnut mare named Bouplay. She was a two-year-old with one fruitless start. Foaled on January 1, 1946, Bouplay was sired by Head Play out of a mare called Beauty by Claptrapat. Thomas E. Heflin was listed as her breeder. In 1949, the horse ran eighteen grueling races and never won. She did finish in third place five times and posted $1,150 in earnings.

In 1950, at age four, Bouplay had not yet been in the winner's circle after five starts. A total of fifty dollars in earnings were posted so far that year for one distant fourth place finish.

The first record of this shining chestnut mare running under the ownership of Sylvia came on the afternoon of June 25, 1951, in the third race at Charles Town. The three-quarter mile claiming race was for four-year-olds and up, with a $1,000 purse. Bouplay finished a dismal eighth out of ten horses. Ridden by jockey N. Griffith, he was four pounds over the allotted weight of 113 at 117 pounds.

The grandstand at the Cumberland Race Track
Photo by Vicky Moon

Five days later, Bouplay ran at Charles Town on June 30, 1951, and finished last. On July 7, the mare finished sixth. At hard times like this for owners and trainers, Sylvia surely was asking herself:

Should I continue to put money and effort into a horse that is now five years old without coming in first?

What can I do to help this horse along to the winner's circle?

Should I just give up on her and find

Cumberland, Md.   July 18, 1951
Mrs. S. Bishop's - "BOUPLAY" - H. McKinney, up

someone to buy her?

In mid-July 1951, Sylvia and John drove ninety miles northwest from Charles Town to Cumberland, Maryland, just as the sun was coming up at 5:58 a.m. There was some early morning fog as the Bishops lumbered along in their Buick sedan. The fog lights, which sat just above the front bumper, cast a yellow glow.

They were headed to the first half-mile racetrack in the state. Many deemed the setting of the track, with the backdrop of the Appalachian Mountains, as one of the most pleasing tracks in "the Old Line" state. If they had to stop for gas, the price was twenty-three cents a gallon.

Sylvia and John rolled along as the song "I Get Ideas" came on the radio. The saucy opening stanzas of the popular tune streamed across the radio. John leaned over to finetune the reception and put the volume up two notches.

The first three notes pealed out in G…

Originally written for the tango as "Adios, Muchachos" in 1927, by Argentinian Julio Ceasar Sanders, the lyrics by Cesar Felipe Vedani were in Spanish at that time. American Dorcas Cochran wrote the English lyrics, and with Tony Martin singing and Louis Armstrong on the trumpet, it was on the Billboard charts from May 25, 1951, for thirty weeks. Peggy Lee also recorded the same song in 1951. Still in the early blissful stage of marriage, the Bishops hummed and sang along as they made their way to Cumberland.

The windows were rolled down and the nippy early-morning fresh air held some promise. John rested his left arm on top of the driver side door and smoked a Salem menthol cigarette. He maneuvered the triangular vent at the front of the window to a perpendicular position to block the wind and air so smoke would not come inside the car. They were oblivious to the news swirling in Washington.

Some of that news is startlingly familiar six decades later. Headlines in the Washington Post included "Harriman Hits Blank Wall in Iran Oil Talks," "Beef Price Rollback Sustained by House as Coalition Crumbles," and "Seemingly Happy 12-Year Old Found Hanged in Attic."

There was one insightful article on page A1 that might be a revelation years later: "Pollen Can Affect Hearing, Doctor Warns Allergy Victims."

And then there was this item on the bottom left hand corner: "Revenue Finds Still on Property, Suspect Jugged."

In the sports section of the same edition, racing handicapper Bill Bennings wrote: "Dear Folks, Cumberland's track opens on Tuesday. The Western Maryland oval, like Charles Town and Santa Anita, has a mountain backdrop and a scenic setting. Industrial troubles in Cumberland held down betting and crowds in recent years, but this season everything is ship-shape."

Indeed, things definitely were ship-shape for the Bishops on the afternoon of Wednesday, July 18, as the temperature rose to a mild seventy-five. Winds were calm and a late afternoon shower passed through, leaving the track surface "heavy," according to the Daily Racing Form. It was the "Royal Order of the Moose Day" at the Cumberland Fairgrounds where the track was located. "Showers muddied the racing strip," racing writer Walter Haight wrote in the Washington Post, "but served to make it a cool afternoon at the races for a crowd of 6,000."

The Cumberland Fair, also known as Fairgo, was positioned on 100-acres along the Potomac River in the shadows of the cliffs of Knobley Mountain. The track had originally opened on Tuesday, October 9, 1924, and cost $150,000 to build. It was an annual gathering spot for a mix of carnival rides, agriculture exhibits, and a whirlwind of horse racing each summer for a two-week meet.

There were several exhibit halls and a caretaker's residence along with tennis courts and a skeet shooting range. There was a jockey house for the riders to dress and prepare to ride. The outsized grandstand loomed in the distance as the Bishops pulled through the gates and on to the fairgrounds.

The track also had a clubhouse with an open air dining area on the second level that featured crisp white tablecloths occupied totally by all-white patrons. The ladies wore stylish dresses and hats and the men wore suits. The ground level below was dotted with multi-colored umbrellas and shaded picnic tables.

The grandstand area was fenced off with a white Rivera picket fence. There was no shelter here, and these patrons definitely were not in suit jackets. Yet another section was set-aside for "colored."

When the Bishops arrived, Sylvia headed straight to the barn area to find her horses. There were seven stables and sixteen open-air barns. As she heard Sylvia approach, Bouplay stuck her head out of the door and looked around. Her legs were bandaged tightly in gray flannel wraps with cotton batting underneath. The mare was not hurt or lame; it was standard for horse's legs to be covered while traveling in order to avoid injury. Sylvia opened the bottom half of the door and ducked in to remove the bandages.

The mare was relaxed and stood still as Sylvia walked around and checked her legs. She glanced at the water bucket that was half full. "Don't worry, big girl," she said. "I'll fetch you some more."

Bouplay was entered in the eighth race, the last claiming race of the day, for a price of $1,000 at 1 1/16 mile. The horses were saddled in the paddock and made their way onto the track for a parade to the post. The gray limestone cliffs provided a striking backdrop as they walked in a single file to the gate.

At 6:04 p.m., 4,500 spectators watched as Bouplay jumped out of gate six with jockey H. McKinney. The mare was in fourth place at the first quarter mile by a head and continued in the middle of the pack. As the field of eight turned for home, Bouplay was on top. She won by six lengths. A horse named Goldbart was second, and Colored Boy was third.

The Bishops were ecstatic. Sylvia stepped onto the track for a win photo as if this happened every day. John's joy came from a two dollar win ticket in his pocket, which paid him $57.80. He headed to the windows to cash in.

The Daily Racing Form charts described Bouplay's victory as "easy." For Sylvia Bishop, nothing was easy. Still, the $625 winning share of the $900 purse seemed a heaven-sent gift. She headed back to the barn to bathe and take care of her mare.

Two days after winning with Bouplay, Sylvia and John took the $625 in winnings to make a down payment on a 1949 Buick. On July 20, 1951, they entered an agreement with Commercial Credit Plan, Inc. for $1,330.95. The paperwork stipulated the vehicle could not be used to transport liquor for personal or commercial use, and it had to be properly insured. (The same car was re-financed on November 21, 1951, for $1,441.80 from the same Commercial Credit Plan for eighteen installments of $80.10).

Meanwhile, Bouplay ran at Cumberland again on July 25 placed and was out of the money in fifth place. That two dollar win ticket was likely tossed on the ground.

The Maryland summer racing circuit moved on to Hagerstown, Maryland. On August 2, 1951, Bouplay placed fifth, and then fourth in what was her last race on August 10. She was awarded twenty-five dollars for that fourth place finish. The official record reflects Bouplay ran thirty-two times in her four years on the track, with her one and only win that day in Cumberland. Bouplay's total earnings in her final and only year with Sylvia were $650.

In November 1951, Sylvia borrowed $200 from Merchant Salvage Co. over in nearby Ranson for a half-ton 1941 Chevrolet truck, payable in weekly installments each Monday of ten dollars at six percent interest. With this vehicle, she could haul hay and feed and fill it with a variety of horse supplies, like feed and water buckets and pitchforks.

Still, at the beginning of 1952, the Bishops were in a financial slump, perhaps a result of John's betting or just a run of bad luck with the horses. There was a past due bill for $112.63 at Southern States for horse feed and hay. A judgment against John and Sylvia Bishop was issued.

A letter in January arrived from Jefferson Hardware informing them of another claim against the Bishops for $251.46, most likely for more horse supplies used in the stables.

John continued to be indirectly involved in the horse business. Another trainer, Mike Johnson, had recently died and "I took over training some of his horses," John Bishop said. But it was actually Sylvia who took care of the day-to-day details of feeding and training.

CIVIL RIGHTS TIMELINE

July 26, 1948: President Harry Truman issues Executive Order 9981 to end segregation in the Armed Services. And two years later, Elizabeth Simpson Drewry was the first African American woman elected to the West Virginia House of Delegates.

CHAPTER 12

TIME TO GO HOME

*Was all the meticulous preparation, the months
of planning to come to naught?*

- Jane McIlvaine, The Will to Win, 1967

The 1950s marked the arrival of trainer Robert R. Hilton at the Charles Town track. He saddled more than 2,500 winners over a four-decade career and was Charles Town's leading trainer at eleven consecutive meets. His filly, Turn Capp, was a track Hall of Fame inductee, as was Hilton. She was a multiple stakes winner and prolific broodmare. Hilton was married to writer Ann Hilton, whose father, Jim Bell, saddled the slow-running Electric Gaff on opening night back in 1933.

In other news, Washington Post handicapper Bill Bennings wrote in his 1950 Valentine's Day column that the first session of racing at Charles Town would be eighteen days, starting March 4. Anyone skeptical that racing would succeed at this time of year was soon proved wrong. By the end of March, it was reported that 60,000 fans went through the gates and a total of $3,220,815 had passed through the betting windows.

"The track will be closed while Laurel gets in its spring session, starting

March 25, but will reopen April 8 to oppose Havre de Grace for 18 days," Bennings wrote. "The summer meet was scheduled for July 1 for 15 days followed by its December session as usual."

Racing news covered almost a full page in the Post's sports section on April 8, 1950. It included entry charts from the Laurel, Gulfstream, Havre de Grace, Jamaica and Charles Town meetings. The Gold Cup steeplechase in Warrenton, Virginia, also was mentioned. The B & O Race Train to Charles Town advertised a schedule for three trains to the track, departing from Union Station in Washington at 11:30 a.m. with stops in Silver Spring at 11:45 a.m. and Rockville at 11:55 a.m. Arrival at the track was 1:10 p.m., with post time for the first race scheduled 1:30 p.m. The trains would return "promptly after the last race." Handsome Gabalier men's suits from the Hecht Co. were offered for thirty-five dollars, top coats for seventy-five.

The stables were filled, and Racing Secretary Leeds Riley told Bennings, "Horses have been working out every day since we closed in December. As far as thoroughbreds are concerned, we could open tomorrow."

Clubhouse admission was one dollar and grandstand seating was fifty cents. Black patrons were required to sit in a separate area. Some of the races were broadcast on radio station WGAY in Silver Spring during an afternoon show hosted by Ben Swort.

The fifteen-day summer meet in July at Charles Town was declared by the Post to have the "best grade of horses available in the 17-year history of the track." The racing strip had been resurfaced, and there were now ten horses in the field instead of the previous number of eight.

As 1950 came to a close, the December session of racing was interrupted by snow for one day. Track President A.J. Boyle said, "The thoroughbreds could have run. However, the hazardous condition of highways, particularly those leading from Maryland, led to the decision to delay racing. Reports tonight [Dec.11] were to effect that main roads have been cleared or sanded and that transportation was moving in a normal manner."

On June 26, 1952, Sylvia and John borrowed $250 from Jefferson Loan and Finance Co. in Charles Town for a thirty-eight-case Victor beer cooler, a four-piece bedroom suite, a studio couch, two large chairs, a Crosley range, Crosley washer and a radio table combo. Lee Bushong was the trustee/attorney, to be paid in fifteen monthly installments of $21.39.

But that year ended on a low note with a judgment against the Bishops for $48.26 from Adam Link and Sons on December 13.

In Maumee, Ohio, a one-mile racetrack called Fort Miami was run by the Toledo Turf Club. It began as Fort Miami Fairgrounds and operated as a harness and flat track. It was the first horse racing facility in the country to install lighting for night racing in 1929.

The Fort Miami racetrack became known as Maumee Downs; in 1958, it was called Raceway Park. The grandstand loomed large as John Bishop drove a load of horses out to Ohio to race. "My Uncle Eugene Smith worked as a trainer for the Funkhouser family and my dad drove the truck," daughter Laverne Purnell recalled.

As he bounced along the hills of West Virginia and into Pennsylvania, John headed toward the northwest corner of the Buckeye State toward Toledo. The 500-mile trip took eight to ten hours with horses. He stopped only to give them water, grab a snack, and take a bathroom break where "colored" were allowed to use the facilities. In those days, horses were supplied with bags full of hay tied up to keep them occupied and full. (Since then, this routine has changed and horses are no longer offered hay. The theory is that dust can get into their lungs and cause them to cough.)

Fog and light rain gave way to a drizzle and then clear skies with visibility of seven miles as May 5, 1953, unfolded. The temperature was a comfortable fifty-nine degrees as Sylvia, thirty-two, and John Bishop, thirty-three, watched their ten-year-old bay mare, Quick News, walk toward the starting gate for the second race, scheduled to go off at 2:33 p.m. (Horse people can watch a horse walk and, without taking a peek at the private parts, they can easily identify the gender.) The five-furlong claiming race for four-year-olds and upward of fillies and mares offered a purse of $700.

Quick News was just that as she jumped out of the gate from post position ten. She went to the front immediately and led all the way with jockey H. Craig. She paid $7.60 and brought home $525 in earnings. The Daily Racing Form reported the result as "won handily." It should be noted here that John Bishop was listed as the owner, but evidently did not have his trainer's license. G.R. Collins was recorded as trainer. "All I remember," their daughter related, "is that he was a friend."

Four days later, on May 9, 1953, Quick News was back for the third race. It was a five and half furlong claiming race for three-year-olds and up and non-winners of two races since October 10. This time, she finished fifth and out of the money. The Bishops also had Wise Bet, their five-year-old bay mare, entered in the first race that day. She finished tenth in a field of twelve in a five and half furlong race for four-year-olds and up.

Rain and fog and some early morning rain launched the day on Friday, May 15, 1953. Wise Bet was entered in a six-furlong claiming race. The cost to claim one of the eight entered would have been $800, not even a top-of-the-heap horse, even at this small venue.

Wise Bet won wire to wire and took home $525 of the $700 purse. The five-year-old bay mare's win was officially listed as "easy." The Bishops could celebrate again, with a two dollar win ticket paying $4.80.

A month later, the Bishops and their horses were 140 miles southeast of Maumee at Ascot Park near Akron for the fourth race on June 6, 1953. Built in 1923, it was billed as "The Biggest Little Racetrack in America" with a three-quarter mile track.

"Three-quarter-mile tracks are proving exceptionally popular in Canada, having the advantage from a spectator's standpoint that in races of almost any official distances, the start is mad near the grandstand," the Beacon Journal newspaper noted in 1933. "In addition, the three-quarter-mile track allows spectators to see the horses and jockeys clearly when on the backstretch."

The short track was a blessing for some, with the exception of the jockeys in the Ascot Gold Cup, the final race of the meet. Scheduled at a distance of two miles, it posed a mathematical dilemma to keep track of how many times they had to go around the racetrack. One report said some jockeys put peas in their mouth "and spit them out each circuit to keep track of the distance."

Steve Steinmetz, a local businessman, and twenty other investors had built the racing complex on sixty-eight acres of farmland along state Rt. 8. The cost was reported to be $262,000. It began as Northampton Park; during the Depression, the track closed from 1929 to 1935. It was renamed as Ascot in 1938.

Beacon staff writer Mark J. Price wrote in the same paper in 2009, that Ascot Park was "a park with a heart." He also noted the grandstands were "creaky" and the barns were "ramshackle." Those bygone days of racing were a far cry from the modern game, when the dwindling number of race-goers often look up at empty glass grandstands with blackjack tables and slot machines located in windowless adjacent gambling casinos.

Quick News came close to victory that June afternoon in 1953 at Ascot, finishing second and taking home $200 in winnings.

The Ohio circuit then moved one hour due south to Cranwood Park in Warrensville Heights and Thistledown in North Randall, as well as Randall Park racetrack.

Three days after running at Ascot, Quick News loaded into the starting gate at Cranwood on June 9 for the eighth race at 5:28 p.m. She ran fourth and gathered sixty dollars for her efforts. Four days later, she ran fourth again and banked sixty dollars. In studying the race charts, she appeared to be tired, obviously with good reason.

And yet, the very next day, the Bishops ran Wise Bet in the third race at Cranwood. She finished second and collected $240 for the effort, then earned sixty dollars for a fourth-place finish in a six-furlong race on June 18.

As the meet at Cranwood Park concluded, Quick News finished next to last on June 19, 1953, and ran last on July 15.

It was time to go home.

CHAPTER 13

A WISE BET ON A HAGERSTOWN HOLIDAY

The horses at the post! They're off and running neck and neck.
Ev'ry one's a nervous wreck! Who's showing all that speed?
What's that blanket that I see; Who else could it be.

- "Come On, Spark Plug!"
by Billy Rose and Con Conrad, 1923

After racing in Cumberland in the summer of 1953, the Bishops returned to Charles Town briefly before continuing around the circuit of half-mile tracks in Maryland, racing at Bowie, Bel Air, Marlboro and Hagerstown.

Hagerstown comes by its name quite simply. Jonathan Hager, a farmer and politician, is credited as the founder in 1762, though it originally was referred to as Elizabethtown, after his wife. Hager was a fur trader and gunsmith, which seems somewhat compatible with his other listed professions.

He also was a real estate tycoon. He owned more than 10,000 acres, some of them involved in planning the town located at a crossroad known as the north-south Warrior Trading Path. The town later became known as a "Hub City" with the arrival of the railroad in 1834. The lines included the Baltimore and Ohio (B&O), Western Maryland and Chesapeake and Ohio (C&O), all of which continue with freight service but no longer run passenger trains.

Founded as an agricultural society in 1807, the Hagerstown county fair, first held in 1852, was managed and operated by the Agricultural and Mechanical Association of Washington County, chartered in 1856. The now sixty-five-acre fairgrounds began with thirty acres purchased in 1880. Additional property was added in later years. A fence surrounded the land with spaces for competition horticultural and agricultural displays (some of which remain). There were individual flower specimens, massive floral parterres, vegetables, clothing, art, poultry and livestock. It became known as the Great Hagerstown Fair.

The fair was interrupted during the Civil War. Once revived, patrons flooded the gates each year in the last few days of September into early October. Former Confederate Col. Henry Kyd Douglas, the youngest officer on the staff of General Stonewall Jackson, booked the general's famous horse Little Sorrell, as a taxidermy mount, to be on display in 1884. He was shipped to the fair in an individual railcar. Douglas went on to become a lawyer and circuit court judge in Hagerstown.

The Norfolk and Western, Western Maryland and Baltimore and Ohio and several other railroad lines delivered passengers to the fair from all points. "The extensive network of railroads converging in Hagerstown was important to the success of the Fair," according to the Maryland Historical Trust report. "It enabled agricultural products and machinery to be shipped readily for exhibit, and also brought visitors and exhibitors from neighboring counties and states."

In 1908, a local paper reported a record number of 18,500 railroad fairgoers one Thursday. There were an additional 3,000 trolley passengers. Forty years later, in 1948 on the same Thursday, the crowd was estimated at 50,000.

There were other intriguing numbers in that 1948 story. "Up to date, twenty-four couples have secured marriage licenses, gotten married and spent their honeymoons on the fairgrounds." Attractions for the honeymooners might have included fireworks, stage acts, a dog show and a horse show.

John L. Cost, a Civil War veteran for the Union, initiated what became the largest poultry competitive fair show in the world. A large granite memorial remains on the grounds.

A rectangular wood frame with German siding building at 412 North Mulberry Street was constructed in 1913. There are six, two-story metal and wood fluted columns. According to a master plan report produced by Lampl Associates, Studio 27 Architecture and James M. Gross, Inc, in June 1999: "Architecturally, the entrance building is a fascinating example of exhibition architecture, retaining the materials that speak to the vernacular rural tradition while incorporating non-agriculture features (such as the columns and diamond-pane casement windows) to connote a building of higher import and more public character."

The entrance was renovated in 2001-2002 after the city voted in 1996 to save the grounds for use as a public park. More than twenty volunteers donned old clothing and showed up to help paint the structure in June 2002. The remaining stalls, grandstand and entrance are a revered reminder of the glorious days of the fair. They now sit majestically among baseball diamonds, a hockey rink, running trails and a nearby dog park.

Thoroughbred racing began at Hagerstown on October 1, 1929, just ahead of Black Thursday, October 24, when the stock market crashed. This was followed four days later, on October 28, by Black Monday. The market dropped by 22.6 percent that day, only to be followed the next day by another drop of 12.8 percent. By 1932, the stock market had dropped by eighty-nine percent.

According to Jeff Nilsson, writing a 2011 blog for the Saturday Evening Post, the ensuing Depression was something of a boon for the racing business. "With everything in life feeling like a gamble, these Americans began taking chances that they never would have considered in prosperous times…So it's not surprising to read, in a 1935 Post article, 'The Betting Boom,' that racetrack gambling had become one of America's few booming industries that year."

A larger grandstand in Hagerstown was built in 1939 with a seating capacity of 4,800 seats and space for 900 in the clubhouse. Photographs reveal yet another new grandstand and clubhouse that cost $750,000 when it was built in 1955. This structure held 6,500 in the grandstand, with room for 500 more in the clubhouse dining room overlooking the track.

Horseman and trainer Tony Bencivenga, a jockey in the early 1950s, said the track here "wasn't easy. Going into the first turn some of the horses ran wide and ended up along the outside rail and even further."

Exercise riders and jockeys of that era referred to the half-mile tracks as a "bull ring," meaning it was small and tight.

"We all used that slang term bull ring. It was like a kindergarten track for eight horses. Small," Bencivenga recalled decades later. Each little racing venue on the circuit with a half-mile track "had its own atmosphere. And the town people were happy to see everyone."

Hagerstown was strategically located near the Mason-Dixon line separating the North from the South in the Civil War, and as a consequence, it played an important role in four different Civil War campaigns. Both Confederate and Union troops camped in the area.--flickr.com-Hagerstown Race Track

It's difficult to calculate if John and Sylvia Bishop received that same warm reception as they drove north from Charles Town on a calm Wednesday, August 26, 1953. The race meet was held this year from August 18-29. They journeyed along Leetown Road toward Kearneysville, then went on to Shepherdstown and across the Potomac River into Maryland. Part of the thirty-mile trip took them on Sharpsburg Pike and then onto Hagerstown Pike.

Sylvia and John saw rolling hills, plenty of pastureland, some of it studded with shale outcroppings. They listened to "Crying in the Chapel" by the Orioles, the hit rhythm and blues song of the moment. They also passed weathered red bank barns, small apple orchards, grazing cattle and sheep, and fields filled with corn.

The White House had just announced that President Dwight D. Eisenhower was scheduled to meet with President Aldolpho Ruiz Cortinez of Mexico in October on the Rio Grande River to dedicate the Falcon Dam.

In the entertainment world, film director William Wyler's Roman Holiday starring Gregory Peck, Audrey Hepburn and Eddie Albert was a huge hit (and still fun to watch). The Bishops were having a Hagerstown holiday.

At the entrance to the Hagerstown fairgrounds, the circa 1913 carved wooded façade-
The Agricultural & Mechanical Association of Washington County-remains as a moving
statement of untroubled afternoons among flowers, horses, pigs and poultry.
Photo by Vicky Moon

In local news, phone workers of Local 2105 of the Communications
Workers of America in Hagerstown, Cumberland, Oakland, Frostburg
and parts of Baltimore went on strike at six that morning. It ended at
eleven that evening. It was referred to as a "wildcat strike" in the Daily
Mail newspaper.

Local real estate agent Samuel Sowers was celebrating his eighty-fifth
birthday and passing out to friends a six-page booklet with poems and
biblical passages. The A&P supermarket was having a grand re-opening
after being remodeled. The sports pages devoted six paragraphs to a report
of the previous day's races. And there was a mention of the Hagerstown
Pigeon Racing Club dates for the upcoming season in September.

The Bishops' hard-running Wise Bet had been in six grueling races
since winning in Cumberland. She had been shipped 500 miles out and
back to race in Ohio with no luck. She ran unsuccessfully in two outings
in late July and early August in Charles Town. And, though G.R. Collins
was listed as the trainer, let there be no doubt that Sylvia was calling all the
shots on this mare. She would soon be taking and passing her final exam
to earn a trainer's license.

Between her last time running at Charles Town on August 7 up to nineteen days later for the race in Hagerstown, Sylvia prepped Wise Bet first by walking her by hand without a rider around the shed row of the barn for three days. This allowed the mare to get any kinks out and at the same time, Sylvia made sure she was sound and uninjured.

On the fourth day, Wise Bet most likely went out on the track to jog once around. She was bathed after every trip to the track, occasionally including a rinse of a still popular mild liniment called Bigeloil. She was brushed and babied. Sylvia talked to her in her own soothing way.

Wise Bet went out more mornings for at least a light gallop. She then was breezed-a very strong gallop-three furlongs from the quarter pole. She most likely was hand walked the following day.

Sylvia was working Wise Bet to run back at the same six-furlong distance for the same price, $1,000. So, her methods did not change. There were no ready answers for her previous dismal finish in seventh place. Was the horse tired or unfit? Did the mare get boxed in by other horses? At the age of five, was she possibly in heat?

Or was it simply not her day?

That's horse racing. She could have pulled a shoe or been boxed between horses. It was time to freshen up. The magic in Sylvia's touch was what she got done between races. She had a vision.

"I can think of lots of horses I've had," said current trainer Don Yovanovich, who met Sylvia several times. "And people are sometimes shocked when they win. They ask me what I did, but I don't reveal what I did to get to the winner's circle." Neither did Sylvia.

The bay mare was entered in the third race, a six and a half furlong contest for three-year-olds and up, fillies and mares. The purse was $1,000. The starting gate sprang open thirty seconds after 3:15 p.m. Wise Bet jumped out of post-position number four with jockey Mike Sorrentino, Sr.

Sorrentino hustled Wise Bet to third place at the quarter pole. By the half, she was rolling along in second place. As the field of eight turned for home, the Bishops were anxious and imagining all they would do with the $700 for the winner. They hugged as she came across the finish line ahead of the entire field.

A winning two dollar bet paid a nice $9.20, and it's likely Mr. Bishop cashed a ticket or two. When he clicked on the radio, the "Going to the Chapel" music continued...

Sylvia was reading a study guide for her trainer's license. On what day of the year do all Thoroughbreds become one year older? What does 'also eligible' mean? What is a claiming race?

It's been over forty years since the sound of pounding hoofbeats around the track has been heard in Hagerstown. The grandstand, once packed with cheering fans, is now empty, fast asleep. It's now a silent, almost solemn reminder of those once glorious fall days of horse racing.

A BIT OF RACETRACK HISTORY

1870-Pimlico Race Course, home of the Preakness, opens in October

1873-The first running of the Preakness Stakes

1887-Timonium racetrack opens in September

1911-Laurel Park opens in October

1912-Havre de Grace racetrack opens in August and closed in 1950

1914-Marlboro racetrack opens in July and closed in 1972

1914-Bowie Race Track opens in October and closed in 1985

1921-Cumberland racetrack opens in October and closed in 1961

1929-Hagerstown racetrack opens in October and closed in 1970

CHAPTER 14

A PHOTO FINISH, OR FINISHED?

The horse I bet on was so slow, the jockey kept a diary of the trip.

- Henny Youngman, comedian (1906-1998)

ll athletes, from Little League baseball players to Olympic champions, experience the elation of winning and the agony of defeat. Training a fractious, fragile, unpredictable Thoroughbred racehorse is no different.

Sylvia experienced anguish throughout her demanding career. This was especially true early on as she struck out on her own, training horses under the radar without a license, that official endorsement of competence. She worked behind the scenes while her husband took the credit. He was a so-called "program trainer," listed on the official program, yet not at all involved with the day-to-day preparation and maintenance of the horse.

Such was the case when John Bishop was listed as owner and trainer for an eleven-year-old bay mare named Quick News when she won $700 in a 4½-furlong claiming race on the afternoon of March 20, 1954, in Charles Town. That year was her last in competition and she raced eight times in Charles Town, then traveled on to Fort Miami in Ohio and back to Cumberland, Maryland. She won once and collected $750. Quick News obviously was on the tail end of a career 101 starts. And by July 3, 1954, Sylvia was finally listed as the official owner of the horse for the first race on the final afternoon of a ten-day meet at the Cumberland fairgrounds. Quick News finished next to last in seventh place, her final career race.

The horse ran for ten years between 1945 to 1954, and never more than fifteen times in a single year, which is about the average today. It's the disconcerting statistic of 101 total starts that catches an experienced eye.

"I'm stupified," trainer Diana McClure said while going over records of some of Sylvia's horses. "Did they have shoes on? Maybe they just wanted to pay for the shoes? It's a phenomenal record, and old man time just caught up. They should have bronzed her."

Forever Noble, foaled in Maryland on May 14, 1953, was by Noble Impulse out of Hope Eternal by Eternal and bred by J. Funkhouser. The brown gelding had seventy-eight starts. John Bishop was listed as owner and trainer from July 4, 1956, to October 11, 1957, when the horse ran at Charles Town, Hagerstown, Cumberland, and Marlboro. Two of Bishop's thirty-three starts were victories. At that point, everyone at the track knew Sylvia was totally responsible for those wins. A jockey named Joe Servis was listed as Forever Noble's jockey. He spent his riding and training career at Charles Town, and his sons Jason Servis and John Servis are both big-time trainers now. More on them later.

CIVIL RIGHTS TIMELINE

May 17, 1954: Brown v. Board of Education, a consolidation of five cases into one, is decided by the Supreme Court, effectively ending racial segregation in public schools. Many schools, particularly in the South, however, remained segregated for many years.

December 1, 1955: Rosa Parks refuses to give up her seat to a white man on a Montgomery, Alabama bus. Her defiant stance prompts a year-long Montgomery bus boycott.

Vanesian Bead, a dark bay horse, was foaled March 27, 1958, in Kentucky. His sire, Polynesian, was bred at Elmendorf Farm and was owned by Gertrude Widener. Polynesian won the 1945 Preakness Stakes, and as a sire, his most notable offspring was Native Dancer, considered among the greatest horses in racing. The legendary Man o' War also appears in Vanesian Bead's pedigree.

Despite its impressive genes, the horse had only one win in 1961. It came on October 12 at Shenandoah Downs in a 3½-furlong claiming race. Sam Palumbo, one of Sylvia's all-time favorite riders, came out of post position

MRS.SYLVIA A.BISHOP   SAM PALUMBO - UP
OWNER-TRAINER   **VANESIAN BEAD**   WYCHING WIND   2ND
3 1/2 FURLONGS :40:2   VAGUE STAR   3RD
SHENANDOAH DOWNS   OCT.12,1961

two and led all the way over a fast track in 40 2/5 seconds. The winning purse of $715 went to Sylvia, the owner.

Vanesian Bead had two more wins in 1962 under Sylvia's ownership and training. A win ticket on the longshot horse on Flag Day, June 14, 1962, at Charles Town paid $36.20 in a 4½-furlong claiming race. That win also triggered a Daily Double payoff of $230.60 as the second part of the wager. The horse won driving with jockey Charles McKee, the very same rider who broke his left thighbone in a 1958 starting gate accident. As Vanesian Bead's owner, Sylvia collected $650. Later that summer, at Shenandoah Downs, he won a 3½-furlong claiming race with jockey J. French. Sylvia took home another $715, and a two dollar wager paid ten dollars.

Sylvia owned and trained the five-year-old mare, Myrtle W., for four months and five starts in 1959, with no success. Laura Benedict's filly Lou was trained by Sylvia and ran forty-six times over her career with only one win, on June 4, 1963.

Cosmic Dust had a hard knock career with 128 starts. Trained and owned by Sylvia for five races in 1962, his best finish was third place for $110 in earnings.

"Well, there's one phrase that I use," said McClure, "Even if you're second in a photo finish, you have to tell a client they didn't win, but at least they were in the photo finish. I always say, at least in my head, 'but there is NO win picture for them to put on their wall for finishing second, no matter how close they were.'"

MARLBORO

Sylvia traveled to Upper Marlboro, Maryland, in Prince George's County across the Potomac from the nation's capital to race some of her horses. The 5/8-mile track was known simply as Marlboro. It opened on July 1, 1914, and also included an agricultural event. The open grandstand and clubhouse held 2,600 and there were stalls for 475 horses.

Marlboro closed on September 30, 1972. At the end, controversy reigned supreme. It involved the purchase of the 150-acre track by a group that had ties to Maryland Governor Marvin Mandel, who then added more racing days (from thirty-six to ninety-four) to the calendar. This increased the value of the track.

The group then sold the track at a profit. It dominated the state and national news in 1977. Mandel and five others (Ernest N. Cory, Jr., W. Dale Hess, Irvin Kovens, Harry W. Rodgers III, and William A. Rodgers) were tried and convicted of mail fraud and racketeering under federal law.

That decision was later reversed. According to law.jrank.org, it "signaled a limit on the ability to attack state crimes through federal statutes."

When a fire destroyed the old Marlboro grandstand on September 3, 1980, the Washington Post reported that arson was suspected. Thirteen firefighters were injured, with damages estimated to be $750,000.

Ward Caddington, a Prince George's County Fire Department official supervising the arson investigation, told the Post, "Most major fires that occur in abandoned, vacant buildings are the work of arsonists."

In its place, an equestrian center for horse shows was built, and in 1988, there was a two-day revival of racing in October. This continued until November 1993, when the meet was canceled. A horse named Purely Irish won the last race.

CHAPTER 15

LAVERNE AND MR. R.C.

The West Virginia legislature approved holding a referendum election for Jefferson County in 1956, so that residents could vote on having another track in Charles Town. The measure was approved.

The Charles Town Raceway, Inc. had a piece of land adjacent to the existing track. The organization wanted to have harness racing during the day and flat racing at night. At first, the West Virginia Racing Commission turned them down. However, the Raceway group won their case with the West Virginia Supreme Court the following year. The harness track was named Shenandoah Downs.

By 1958, the annual amount bet at the original Charles Town track was more than $23.5 million, up from a meager $37,000 in their inaugural year of 1933. There were now eighty-six racing days, up from twenty at the start. The owners enclosed the clubhouse and added new heating and air-conditioning systems. Four new barns now offered stabling for more than 2,000 horses.

The two tracks alternated racing dates and were off and running and vying for first place. Shenandoah Downs was in the lead for the first decade. Charles Town battled back, and also started racing at night after installing new lighting on the track.

As for Sylvia, on Sunday, January 5, 1958, she had the same familiar pangs of labor her mother, Bertha Rideoutt, had experienced when Sylvia was born thirty-eight years earlier. Sylvia was lifting a saddle onto a horse when her water broke.

It was sixteen miles west from Charles Town to the hospital in Martinsburg. A bone-chilling northwest wind was sweeping across the region, and the temperature was expected to drop to a low of ten degrees and then hover in the twenties. R. Lyle Criswell, a weather observer for the Martinsburg Journal newspaper (a one-year subscription was $10.20) reported from the airport the temperature was thirteen degrees. The announcement of the birth of Laverne Augusta Bishop at Kings Daughter

Hospital was listed in the afternoon newspaper published Monday through Saturday. Her name was a derivation of her father's middle name, Vernard.

Due to the freezing temperatures, several chimney fires were reported in the Charles Town area. The news out of Washington was eerily similar to something one might read six decades later: "Stormy Weather Ahead for Congress" along with deep concern from Senator A. S. Mike Monroney (D-Oklahoma) over Vice President Richard Nixon's proposal to convert a Strategic Air Command KC-135 jet tanker into a cross-country tanker.

Cultural news in the Washington Post came from the feisty New York-born soprano Maria Meneghini Callas, who had walked off the stage during a performance of Norma at the Opera House in Rome. A holiday portrait of President Eisenhower and his family at the White House appeared on page three.

"I went and saw Laverne in the nursery," John Bishop recalled. "I think we thought we wouldn't have children. It was late in life, and I remember she took some stuff to conceive."

As new and clearly loving, concerned parents, the Bishops took some time off from the track to be with their daughter. Sylvia stayed home, and racing records indicated she took six months off.

Laverne had a nanny, Sara Eliza Jones, who lived with the family until she died in the late 1970s. There were other babysitters as well—Laura Bell and Mary Berry.

From time to time, Laverne went to her Aunt Lucille's home on South Lawrence Street next to St. Philip's church. That's also where she attended pre-school with teacher Genevieve Bradford Baylor. Known as BeeBee, Laverne described her as "a wonderful sweet lady."

With the blessing of a new child also came the agony of a death in the family. Three months after Laverne's birth, Sylvia lost her father, James Rideoutt, on April 7, 1958. He was sixty-six.

Later in April, there was plenty of buzz about the upcoming Kentucky Derby on the first Saturday in May. Some of it focused on a new mode of horse transportation. Trainer Gene Jacobs informed officials at Churchill Downs that Martins Rullah, recently third in the Wood Memorial, was traveling to Lexington on an overnight train and then by horse van into Louisville. He would be ridden by jockey Conn McCreary.

Today, horses are equine frequent flyers, traveling by FedEx air. While Sylvia never had the occasion to ship a horse on a plane, many other trainers took advantage of the John J. McCave Agency, Inc. With offices in Los Angeles, Miami, Lexington, and Laurel, Maryland, the company boasted "For the 'Fastest Route' to the winner's circle, ship with the leader in horse air transport." Derby winners Count Turf (1951) and Needles (1956) were early flyers. And when Gallant Man, second in the Derby and winner of the Belmont Stakes in 1957, took a one way charter flight from New York to California in '58, the price of his flight was $8,200, which included his groom. The small yet mighty brown Irish horse paid for his ticket by winning the $150,000 Sunset Handicap and the $100,000 Hollywood Gold Cup at Hollywood Park racetrack with iconic jockey Bill Shoemaker.

For the record, Tim Tam, the 1958 Kentucky Derby winner, traveled by van when he won that race for Calumet Farm. He again took the overland route when he won the Preakness. In his bid for a Triple Crown, Tim Tam finished a heart-wrenching second to an Irish horse named Cavan in the Belmont Stakes. Tim Tam was neck and neck with the Irish horse as they turned for home, but suddenly broke the sesamoid bone in his ankle down the stretch and had to settle for second. He went on to have a successful career at stud for twenty-one years.

Sylvia always watched the big race results on television, but she was mostly focused on the horses she had in training for many owners. On Saturdays when Sylvia went to the track, Laverne stayed with her grandmother up on Davenport Street in Potato Hill. Known as "Mom Bert," she watched little Laverne until she was old enough to stay home and sleep in.

Sylvia was something of a frequent flyer herself. John Bishop would drive her to a small airport on Flowing Springs Road to get on a private plane to fly to another track for afternoon racing. He returned later in the afternoon to pick her up so she could get back to Charles Town in time to saddle a horse for night racing. She kept busy with her stable and he kept busy at the nightclub.

As the family had expanded and expenses mounted, the couple put up their 1954 four-door Ford station wagon in June of '58 in order to borrow $1,290.63 from the Blakely Bank and Trust Company on Mildred Street in Ranson. There were twenty-four installments of $53.77.

The Bishops also had a full-time cleaning lady, Gladys Harris, and her husband, "Mr. Cliff," did odd chores around the house and cleaned the bar downstairs in the Tap Room. By the time Laverne was three, Sylvia put her on top of a horse to get a feel for it all. The love her mother felt for horses never took hold with her child, though Laverne's first husband, Millard F. Dotson, also was a trainer.

As Charles Town's 1958 summer season was off and running, general admission to the track cost only fifty cents. Admission was one dollar for the clubhouse, which also boasted being the only track in the world to be fully air-conditioned in the box seats, dining room and the betting area. That racing season, nineteen-year-old Bobby Cherel was the youngest trainer on the grounds, and eighty-four-year-old Leo Crist was the oldest.

By July 1958, Sylvia again was up before dawn and toiling at the track. She left her seven-month-old daughter at home with the nanny. At the stables, she dictated the morning workouts to riders: "Take the chestnut horse, jog him back up (in the opposite/clockwise) direction to the half-mile pole and turn around and gallop a turn a half," or "Take the grey filly back up (in the opposite direction) to the finish line, turn her around, let her look and stand in and then go a nice easy [breeze] from the half-mile pole."

Henry Allen is very familiar with the language of morning training. Now in his late seventies, he began his racing career as a trainer and is now the official track clocker at Charles Town. Henry Allen knows the saddle towels, colors and initials of every trainer on the property, and sometimes the color of their horses. During the races, he's in the press box with the stewards, helping to record the fractions of the race. He vividly remembers Sylvia.

"She did real good training horses and she did really good for a lady trainer," he recalled. "They have 300 or 400 empty stalls and they didn't give women stalls. Why they didn't let them in, I don't know. There was no washing machine to wash bandages at the barn and just six stalls. You had to go in and out of a certain door. Racing commissions rules, and no couch for a nap or a comfy chair."

"I remember old stories, they didn't like women back then," said Mark Munden, a former Charles Town jockey.

In spite of the roadblocks Sylvia faced as a woman, she dutifully went about her daily routine of feeding horses and mucking out stalls. It should be noted that even some current women trainers feel the same bias.

Sylvia had a half-dozen horses in training: a five-year-old chestnut gelding named Mr. R.C., her beloved and now five-year-old chestnut mare, Chalkee, and several others.

Charles Town's summer season began June 6. Mr. R.C. ran third, going seven furlongs to earn $120 on July 5, and was second on July 9 at six furlongs, a $240 payoff for his effort. Trainers today would cringe at such a short time of three or four days between races; the norm now is three to five weeks between outings.

The sun was up just before six with calm winds and scattered rain and a thunderstorm expected in the afternoon of July 12. Bobby Darin's "Splish Splash" was climbing the charts and reverberated around the barn from a radio. One groom sang along as he gave his charge a soapy bath.

Mr. R.C. was foaled in 1953 and started racing as a two-year-old. He was bred in Maryland by Mrs. R.C. Williams, which may account for his name. As a five-year-old, the chestnut ran eight of his 115 lifetime starts with Sylvia listed as owner between July 5 and August 16 of 1958.

Mr. R.C. came out of post-position one for the fourth race on July 12 just after a ferocious flash rainstorm washed out the third race. Eight horses jumped out of the gate at 3:35 p.m. under cloudy skies for the seven-furlong claiming race. Jockey Juan Soto was third for the first call,

Charles Town,   July 12,1958
Winner Owned By "*Mr. R. C.*" Helen's Hope(2nd)
Sylvia Bishop,   Camp Out(3rd)
John E.Berry,Trainer   (J.Soto,Up)   About 7 Fur;1:29 Flat

fifth at the quarter pole, and fourth at the half. As they came down the stretch, Mr. R.C. won by a nose over Helen's Hope. Sylvia got a welcome check for $780.

Mr. R.C. ran again on July 18 with Joseph Servis aboard for a mile and a sixteenth. They finished out of the money in fifth place. Only four days later, on July 22, Mr. R.C. walked into the starting gate at post-position seven. Sylvia was listed as the owner for this 1 1/16 mile contest in the ninth race. The temperature was a tolerable seventy-six degrees under cloudy skies as the horses burst from the gate at 5:30 p.m. Her brother-in-law, J.E. Berry, was listed in the program as Mr. R.C.'s trainer.

Despite the short time off after his previous race, jockey Juan Soto brought Mr. R.C. home first. Sylvia collected $780.

Many long-time Charles Town track denizens recall what they generally describe as a peaceful coexistence between white and black grooms, trainers and spectators, although there were designated areas for each. This did not exist outside the track gates, or around the country. As Mr. R.C. was running his heart out, there was troubling news of racial conflicts from nearby Virginia.

A headline on the front page of the Washington Post on Tuesday, July 22, 1958, read, "Eleven Negroes Boycott Tests in Charlottesville." Black students seeking admission to the all-white Lane High School were asked to take achievement tests in order to be admitted. On page fifteen of the same day's paper, a story reported that a segregated school in Arlington, Virginia was not allowed to open.

Meanwhile, Mr. R.C. appeared to flourish in the longer races at a mile and a sixteenth. He was third on July 31 ($120) and second on August 11 ($240). In seven races over six weeks, he had earnings of $2,280, with two wins.

Arthur Godfrey, the popular radio and television personality who lived in nearby Leesburg, Virginia, was among the spectators and owners when his horse, Lord Culpeper, ran in the Shenandoah Series at Charles Town in late July. The big three-year-old chestnut was trained by Shirley T. Payne.

Mr. R.C. was loaded in the starting gate on August 16, once again at the longer distance. Juan Soto was up, but this time they never got closer to the front than fifth place. As Sylvia walked to the finish area, where the jockeys wave their whips to the officials to indicate they have no foul to claim, she saw someone walking toward Mr. R.C. with a halter in hand. The jockey jumped off and walked to the scales to confirm his weight as 122 pounds. Trainer R. S. Gilbert had, no doubt, been watching the success of the horse and made a $1,250 claim on behalf of new owner W.V. Shilling.

Those eight races were the only time the gelding was with Sylvia. He ran thirty-six times before she trained him. He ultimately ran 115 times over the course of twelve years, with earnings of $23,105. He was what might be called "very durable."

Indeed.

CIVIL RIGHTS TIMELINE

September 9, 1957: In Washington, D.C., President Dwight Eisenhower signs the Civil Rights Act of 1957 into law to help protect voter rights. The law allows federal prosecution of those who suppress another's right to vote.

CHAPTER 16

TATTOO ARTIST

In 1894 The Jockey Club was born, an organization without parallel in American history in terms of political power.

- Bernard Livingston, Their Turf, 1973

Throughout Sylvia's career, all Thoroughbreds who raced were required by individual state racing commissions to have a tattoo on their upper lip on or before their first start. There were occasional rare exceptions when a horse was allowed to have one race before getting the tattoo. The Association of Racing Commissioners International (ARCI) recommends the use of tattoos to identify horses, in addition to their other markings.

As each horse enters the paddock at the track, the official identifier has a list of each horse and their tattoo mark. The tattoos begin with a letter of the alphabet, which corresponds to the year they were born, plus their Jockey Club registration number. Two-year-olds born in 2017 have a tattoo beginning with the letter U. The program began in 1947 and was designed to protect the integrity of the sport. It is overseen by the Thoroughbred Racing Protective Bureau (TRPB), a part of the Thoroughbred Racing Associations of North America. Thoroughbreds who do not race are not required to have a tattoo.

Mark Munden, a former jockey who rode several times for Sylvia, was the tattoo artist at Charles Town from 2017 to 2019. He recalled Sylvia as "a classy lady. She carried herself well and was as nice to ride for as anybody." Munden is a third generation horseman. After riding races, he worked in the racing office at Charles Town for twenty-four years. He then moved on to identifier, and adding the art of tattoos to his resume was a natural next step.

Mondays are set aside for the procedure because it is a "dark day" (no racing) at the track. Munden commutes thirty miles one way from Stephens City, Virginia. He arrived at nine to begin his tattoo work on nine horses signed up for tattoos on Monday, October 22, 2018.

The horse is led into a stall and backed into a corner. Munden is assisted by Laura Carson, an exercise rider and pony girl. The top lip is held

Photo by Vicky Moon

in the up position with a bar, which strongly discourages any horse from rearing or objecting to just about anything, including the strong wire brushes used to imprint the tattoo. Wearing disposable blue medical gloves, Munden dips the wire brush in the form of the letter T into a tray of ink. He presses it into place on the top lip. As he continues along the lip with each imprint, the wire brushes are dipped into a strong disinfectant of Cetylcide.

T07159…from start to finish, about three minutes.

And yet, it's not really that simple these days.

The very same organization (TRPB) that mandated tattoos in 1947 revised the system with "digital" identification, scheduled for implementation by January 1, 2020. The Jockey Club now requires horses to be microchipped prior to being registered. Munden now handles the microchip procedure.

The TRPB issued a statement, which said in part: "With modern technology, specifically the use of microchips, scanners, wireless technology and tablets, a digital tattoo will clearly provide a superior and more robust form of identification."

Over the years, there have been notorious cases of "horse swapping"— entering a ringer in a race in spite of the tattoos.

The chip, the size of a grain of rice, is implanted in the middle third of the horse's neck on the left side. A scanner is used to detect the chip, much like the successful technology used for dogs and cats.

Another objective of the microchip is to save no-longer-useful, retired racehorses from "the kill pen" of livestock auctions, where horses are sold cheaply and sent to slaughter for their meat.

"Nobody wants to see that," Munden said.

Yet, all that has to happen is the person at the auction house operating the chip scanner simply does not turn it on. This makes it seem as if there is no chip and the horse is not registered. So, no tattoo and no chip and they go right into the auction kill pen.

CHAPTER 17

NEXT STOP: CAMELOT

For the record, unprecedented votes in state after state,
clearly show that the American people do not want
four more years of Republican indifference and neglect—
that they do not want Mr. Nixon in the White House—
and they do want a return to the dynamic
and creative leadership of the Democratic Party.

- John F. Kennedy, Charles Town Race Track speech, April 27, 1960

As the summer of 1958 came to a close, racial tensions continued in nearby Virginia. It was two steps forward in Norfolk, when federal district judge ordered that "fifteen Negroes" were assigned to white schools. Then it was one step back on the same August 25 day, when the Virginia Pupil Board in Richmond rejected all applications for transfer to white schools in Newport News and Arlington.

Sylvia continued on her path as a trainer with a win for Chalkee on August 26. She also had an eight-year-old chestnut gelding named Hylo Son in training for owner J.G. Gardner. On September 26, 1959, Hylo won going a mile at Shenandoah Downs and again on October 3 at one mile and seventy yards, on a day when far bigger sports news was focused on Game Two of the World Series between the Los Angeles Dodgers and Chicago White Sox. In Hylo's seventeen starts with Sylvia in the only year she trained him, he won twice, placed second once, and was third twice for total earnings of $1,800.

The Morning Telegraph brought front page news on May 21, 1959, from New York City that "The one and only Ethel Merman stars in the new musical Gypsy, a David Merrick-Leland Hayward production opening tonight at the Broadway Theatre."

In Camden, New Jersey, jockey Bill Hartack remained suspended at Garden State Park. Apparently, the horse he rode on May 8 named Star Ice had been given some sort of an amphetamine. At the track in Bel Air, Maryland, Tin Lassie "charged along the inside" to win the Kingsville Purse by a nose.

"Charles Town Track Is Purchased by Pimlico" read one headline. It was the second time in two weeks the track was sold. The first sale came on May 8, when a Texas syndicate led by Clint W. Murchison, later to become the owner of the Dallas Cowboys, and Billy Byars paid Mrs. Albert J. Boyle, widow of the founder, more than $5 million.

The Texas syndicate immediately donated the property to the New Orleans-based Ochsner Clinic. They, in turn, flipped the property two weeks later for an undisclosed sum. The new owners of the track, Ben Cohen, Herman Cohen and Louis Pondfield, had been leasing the track

Image courtesy of the Jefferson County Museum, Charles Town.

for four years under the Maryland Jockey Club banner. They also owned and operated Pimlico in Baltimore. The newspaper noted: "Pondfield declared that Charles Town will open its 54-day summer meeting on July 13, as previously scheduled. He added that he'll take personal charge as general manager."

Meanwhile, charismatic Massachusetts Senator John F. Kennedy was running against Hubert H. Humphrey for the Democratic presidential nomination. The party's convention was set for July 1960, in Los Angeles.

On Wednesday, April 27, Kennedy and his elegant wife Jacqueline, a lifelong horse lover herself, made five stops in the key state of West Virginia at Bluefield, Princeton, Ronceverte, Martinsburg and Charles Town. The senator flew into the Martinsburg airport from Washington around 6:30 p.m. Earlier in the day, he had been in D.C. to vote on a bill pending in the senate. Mrs. Kennedy met him at the rural airport on a flight from Bluefield, where she had been campaigning on his behalf.

Senator Kennedy jumped in a car to get to the radio studios of WEPM for a thirty-minute question-and-answer broadcast, taking listener questions by telephone. He emphasized his strong support, as evidenced by a great number of write-in votes he'd recently received in the Massachusetts and Pennsylvania primaries.

"The question of Kennedy's Catholic religion was not brought out by any of those telephoning the radio station," the Martinsburg Journal reported the following day. "Most of the queries, which numbered approximately ten, were concerned with his position on various matters of legislation and national policy."

From the radio station, Kennedy stopped at Rose Hill Farm in Leetown on his way to the racetrack rally in Charles Town. He met with the Right Reverend Robert E. Lee Strider, the former and then retired Episcopal bishop of the West Virginia diocese. They discussed the issues of religion.

Band music, solo and group singing preceded the introduction of the senator to a boisterous Charles Town crowd of 3,000. As Kennedy stepped up to speak, he received a standing ovation. "I greet you at the beginning of a great Democratic march to victory—a victory for a Democratic president, a victory for a Democratic Congress and a victory for the American people who, after eight gray years, to use F.D.R.'s phrase, need and demand the leadership of the Democratic Party. And I am so confident that the state of West Virginia is going to head that march."

Jacqueline arrived mid-speech to a "flurry of excitement" according to the Martinsburg Journal, which included a description of her wardrobe— "a three-quarter length off-white wool, with hair long and full." There was no mention if the "three-quarter length off-white wool" was a suit or a coat.

That day, Kennedy also spoke of mechanization as an overlooked topic in the state and the nation. "We must make machines serve us, not replace us," he said.

A reception and dance followed the speech. The Kennedys returned to the airport in Martinsburg and flew back to Washington around midnight. The following morning, Bishop Strider announced his endorsement of Kennedy. The pre-Twitter method of communication came from his son-in-law, Ray Niblack, the news director of a Charlottesville, Virginia radio station.

All of this conjures up future images from the Kennedys' 1036 days in the White House. In a tale made famous by writer Theodore White for a December 6, 1963 piece he wrote for Life magazine, he mentioned Jacqueline Kennedy's reference to the mythical place called Camelot and how her late husband adored the Broadway production.

Back in the stables in Charles Town after the Kennedys' news-making campaign stop, the horses in the stables would be up and out on the track in five hours as the sun rose at 5:46 a.m., and Sylvia was there with them to greet the day.

A lifetime later, we have no way to know if Sylvia saw the future president and his horse-loving wife when they stopped at the track. But the lilting melody as Richard Harris sings Alan Jay Lerner's title tune of the musical Camelot is forever emblazoned in many memories.

But, we do know this,: when JFK was assassinated in Dallas on November 22, 1963, like so many grief-stricken Americans, Sylvia was deeply upset. She and four-year-old daughter Laverne watched it all unfold on television. "He was a good man," she told Laverne, then added, "now sit still."

They were mesmerized, watching three pairs of matched gray horses pulling a caisson carrying the president's flag-draped mahogany coffin. The Morgan/Quarter horse cross with Army serial number 2V56 branded on the left side of his neck jogged down Pennsylvania Avenue. Pfc. Arthur A. Carlson of the Army's 3d Infantry led the caparisoned horse. The boots were secured tightly in the stirrups backwards.

The riderless horse's name was Black Jack.

CIVIL RIGHTS TIMELINE

August 28, 1963: Approximately 250,000 people take part in the March on Washington for Jobs and Freedom. Martin Luther King gives his "I Have A Dream" speech in front of the Lincoln Memorial, stating, "I have a dream that one day this nation will rise up and live out the true meaning of its creed: We hold these truths to be self-evident: that all men are created equal."

CHAPTER 18

DON'T LOOK A GIFT HORSE IN THE MOUTH

To tell the age of any horse, inspect the lower jaw, of course.

- Author unknown

To the casual observer, a horse's teeth might seem like a danger zone... all the better to bite a passing human. That's true, but just like their owners and trainers, they also require dentists. Horses must be able to properly chew their hay, oats and grass. Regular dental visits now cost as much as $100 or more per horse.

Theodore Togans Sr.   *Photo courtesy of Theodore S. Togans, Jr.*

Equine dental care dates to the late 1800s, when horses were a vital element in transportation and agriculture. The sharp edges on a horse's molars create pain in the mouth. According to MacKinnon Equine Services in Prince Albert, Saskatchewan, Canada, a horse indicates pain "by tossing his head, pushing away with their head, pulling back, nosing out through the bit, and becoming difficult to catch, bridle or halter."

Theodore Togans, Sr. worked six days a week for thirty-five years as a veterinary assistant at the Charles Town track tending to the teeth of many racehorses, including Sylvia's string. Back then, he earned fifteen dollars per horse. Born in 1920, he was the same age as Sylvia. He also worked for local veterinarian Donald "Doc" Master (1918–2013), Charles Town's mayor from 1968 to 1990.

Today, equine dentist Graham Alcock of Philomont, Virginia, charges $120 per horse.

A large float speculum (which now costs the equine dentist from $500 to $2,500) is placed inside the horse's mouth in order to keep it open. An alternate method is to use an equine dental halter and a dental wedge. The outside of the upper teeth and inside of the lower molars are filed and aligned. There are wolf teeth to deal with along with the molars, canines and incisors. Some dentists now use a power float. Either way, there is no pain for the horse. However, it's crucial the examination and procedure should be done by a professional, the better to avoid being bitten.

Max Brown wrote a sports column for the Spirit of Jefferson Farmers Advocate in Charles Town on July 27, 1972, recognizing Dr. Togans as a distinguished local. He quoted an item that had originally appeared in the Daily Racing Form describing Togans as "the horses' dentist." It was estimated he tended to the choppers of about ten horses a day, "give or take a few Sundays and some vacations." It was calculated that over the course of his career it came to "something over 10,000 dental jobs."

The newspaper reported Togans, a native of Charles Town, "rarely ventures out of the community except on business." He was married to Emogene Daisy Braxton Togans (1921-2002). They had four sons: Theodore S. Togans, Jr., C. Larry Togans, Paul W. Togans and Keith V. Togans. He died in 1992.

"I think he had a relative that came to the track and he tagged along," his son Larry recalled when asked how his father became a horse dentist. "It just caught on and it was a way to make money. He went to work at 16."

As a teenager, Larry said he had no urge to work at the track, yet vividly recalled a trip with his father to the training track in nearby Middleburg, Virginia. "He was pulling a tooth out," Larry said, "and he had a hold of the horse's ear and asked me to hand him a bucket. I'm thinking 'I'm not going in there,' but I did and then I dropped the bucket and ran out."

Larry himself had a distinguished forty-year career commuting one hour from Charles Town forty-two miles southeast to the U.S. Geological Survey offices in Reston, Virginia. He served on the Jefferson County School Board for eight years and also worked at the Bank of Charles Town for sixteen years in addition to serving on the bank's board of directors.

"My father would sit and read the racing form," Larry recalled. "He just loved animals. You could see it, how he handled them."

Sylvia shared the same love of animals and horses. Early on, she often watched and was mesmerized as the trainers checked each horse's legs, feeling the temperature for any heat that might indicate a possible injury. She scrutinized and deliberated as they put bandages on them, tacked them up and administered medications—some good and some questionable.

As she proved her value, walking hots for twenty-five cents each (the rate now is between five and ten dollars per horse), Sylvia was soon ready to move up to cleaning stalls. She was well aware that if she mastered that task, the next step would be working as a groom.

Sylvia cleaned the stalls at dawn while the horses were working out on the track. She and everyone else used burlap from feed sacks that had been sewn together to form a square. Once the manure was placed on the bag, she took hold of the four corners and carried it over her shoulder to the muck pile.

Those muck sacks weighed between thirty-five to 150 pounds, according to trainer Don Yovanovich, who frequently runs horses in Charles Town from his Middleburg, Virginia barn. "Baskets for droppings can be up to forty pounds, if it's just manure, not much straw. It also depends on who is mucking. An experienced groom just takes out the manure. A young inexperienced groom throws out more straw than poop, if you know what I mean."

Speaking from firsthand experience decades ago at the Middleburg Training Track, even when wheelbarrows were available, this muck sack tradition remains at certain stables.

Even though it takes longer to walk a horse than to clean a stall and bed it down with fresh straw, young Sylvia got fifty cents to clean stalls.

In 1959, Dwight Eisenhower was in his first of two terms as president, gas was twenty-five cents a gallon, a loaf of bread cost twenty cents and ladies' stockings were one dollar. Alaska and Hawaii became the forty-ninth and fiftieth states. The movie Ben Hur, starring Charlton Heston, premiered, and the price of a ticket was about one dollar.

When Sylvia finally took the exam to become a licensed race horse trainer that year, her trainer brother-in-law, William S. "Wash" Berry, had been ruled off of training by track officials. This provided an opportunity for Sylvia to manage his horses if she passed the test.

One might assume any possible obstruction for her to take the training exam might be a racial issue. In reality, it had far more to do with her gender.

"It just wasn't a thing for a woman to do," Danny Wright, a steward at the track in Charles Town, said in 2017. "It was a tough life for a lady." Wright is also a former jockey who rode 23,684 horses during a twenty-seven-year career. He said that nowadays, for a young woman embarking on a new career at the track, the notion of racial or gender prejudice seems remote. Then again, the #MeToo movement, an anti-sexual harassment hashtag and catch phrase, shone a light on an issue that is still pervasive today.

Anyone who has followed the history of horse racing from the South Florida winter high spots of Gulfstream, Hialeah, Tropical Park and Calder, to the magical August mecca of Saratoga Springs, New York, to the horse hub of Keeneland, Kentucky, knows that even now, a woman saddling a horse as a trainer of record is rare indeed. The same holds true at celebrity-filled tracks in California at Santa Anita or the surfside equine enclave of Del Mar.

Reviewing the thousands of pages of racing records, charts and past performances of Sylvia's horses, one would be hard-pressed to find the name of another woman.

Seldom, then or now.

Women trainers today tell stories of subtle methods of gender discrimination. Space is not available when making a request for permanent stabling at a track. Male administrators in key racetrack offices are too busy to answer questions: "Can you come back later or tomorrow?" might be the reply. Many potential clients turn to a man for what they incorrectly perceive to be a man's job.

Racing rules in West Virginia dictated that applicants must hold a state occupational permit for three straight years in another racing job before they can apply for a license. Those occupations might range from being an owner to a horse transport driver. Other possibilities included blacksmith, clocker, starter, jockey, steward or even tip sheet vendor. More on that later.

Sylvia's husband, John Bishop, surely qualified to apply for a training license. But it was and remains an open secret that he really had no use for horses. He didn't like them-other than to place a bet-and was actually fearful of them. He was in the entertainment business and it was merely a formality for John Bishop's name to be printed as the horse's owner in the program or newspapers. In reality, Sylvia was backstage in the barns cleaning out the stalls, wrapping legs and scheduling crack-of-dawn training sessions for the few horses they first owned.

To become a trainer, Sylvia first had to pass that pesky test. She presented herself to the steward's office to take the exam, picking up a no.2 Ticonderoga pencil to begin.

Some incorrectly believe it was not a difficult test during the 1950s. Not true, according to Dickie Moore, who worked at the track for fifty years starting in 1964. Long before the computer age, he toiled at the pari-mutuel windows, where payouts on winning bets were calculated on scrap paper. Later on, he also served as racing secretary, and finally as general manager of racing operations.

"It was much tougher back then," Moore said. "If you didn't pass the test back in her day, they made you wait and wait to retake it, sometimes six months or even a year later." About half the applicants taking the exam today do not pass. And the same six-month wait to retake it remains in place.

The trainer's test is administered in two parts: written and practical.

The first section of the written test focuses on basic horse care. They must know that the normal resting heart rate is thirty to forty-two beats per minute, the resting respiration rate is twelve to twenty breaths per minute, the rectal temperature is 99.5 to 101.5 degrees. There is a question many can't even guess the correct answer: after a work or race, fit horses will regain normal vital signs within how many minutes?

Five.

A thorough knowledge of required and recommended vaccinations, from tetanus to flu to rabies or the deadly and highly contagious Streptococcus equi (commonly known as strangles or distemper) is mandatory.

The bacteria for strangles can be ingested or inhaled and remains in the environment for three months. It can be spread by shared water buckets or contaminated tack, stalls and trailers. Infected horses show a severe inflammatory response to the bacteria, causing upper respiratory discomfort, anorexia, and copious nasal discharge. Fever can reach as high as 106. Most horses recover, but some may develop internal abscesses with devastating consequences.

The written test also includes the topics of deworming, and internal and external parasites. Anemia, dull coat and even colic can be the result of damaging internal parasites such as tapeworms, small strongyles, large strongyles (blood worms or red worms) and ascarids (round worms). Caretakers and trainers must be constantly vigilant for symptoms. A veterinarian will test for worms by taking a fecal sample and sending it to a lab for examination on type and extent of worm eggs. A protocol of how often and what type of deworming is then recommended. This can be administered by paste or liquid about every three months. According to experts, the majority of harm from intestinal parasites is due to the larvae as they pass through the body.

Other internal parasites include lungworms, pinworms, bot eggs (tiny specs on the skin that horses tend to lick) and threadworms, which can lead to diarrhea in foals. All of the above were a constant concern for Sylvia, not to mention a necessary expense to treat their maladies.

Disease-spreading flies, by far, pose the greatest threat in a horse barn. Controlling them has always been a challenge. That long yellow sticky tape that traps flies as well as automatic fly spray can reduce the problem. There are now fly masks applied over the horse's head, as well as full body coverage in the form of special outer wear. Not only do flies cause disease, but when a horse is constantly stomping their legs to shoo flies away, lameness issues can ensue.

For the practical part of the exam, part of which involved working on a real live horse, Sylvia was asked about the use of blinkers, a hood with eye cups used when a horse races. As part of the tack a horse wears, they come as a full half, quarter and a semi-full in three-quarter size. In rare cases, if a horse is missing an eye, a full cover is used.

"The hood's effects are varied and not always easy to predict," Marcus Hersh wrote in the Daily Racing Form in July 2013. "They can turn an anxious horse docile, a docile horse anxious." The idea is to keep a horse focused on the race. "Blinkers channel their vision, cut down on the scope of their sight," leading trainer Todd Pletcher told DRF. "Some horses see everything out there, from the bushes on the track to the grandstand and the poles. Some are distracted. Some are scared. Some are scared running next to horses. It's all instinct. You look at a bush by the eighth pole, and to you it's a bush by the eighth pole. To a horse, it's a panther."

Sylvia often used blinkers on her horses. In the practical exam, she also had to demonstrate that she knew how to pick up each foot on a horse in order to "pick out the feet." That's horse talk for cleaning out the nooks and crannies filled with mud and manure. If left untouched, it can cause thrush, a stinky discharge in the underside of the foot. The problem is usually easily relieved with specific treatment. A pebble also can cause a bruise, which then turns into an abscess, which also must be treated.

There are several locations for taking a horse's pulse, including under the jaw; for the record, there's only one location for taking the temperature. During the practical test, Sylvia demonstrated a tongue tie. She reached inside its mouth and took a strong hold of about six inches of the tongue, which varies in total length from ten to sixteen inches. She pulled from her pocket a fourteen-inch length of white flannel strip about an inch wide. She spoke to him, "Whoa now, steady," in a hushed, protective tone. She wrapped the strip around the tongue, then crisscrossed the ends under the chin and tied it snuggly two times.

To the uninitiated, this may seem somewhat harmful or even cruel, yet it's a time-honored safety measure to keep an excited horse from swallowing its tongue and possibly choking. She double checked the steps to make sure all parts were in place.

They say never to look at a gift horse in the mouth. But Sylvia's gift after completing the exam was this: she passed and earned her trainer's license.

CHAPTER 19

THE HOLY LAND

*There is a place for what is called 'half-mile' racing
in Maryland. Many fans prefer it inasmuch as they can see
the horses and the jockeys without binoculars.*

- Gerald Strine, The Washington Post, April 16, 1975

In September 1954, as Sylvia crossed the state line out of West Virginia into Maryland, Catoctin Mountain loomed in the distance, the 134-acre Camp David presidential retreat hidden in the hills not far away. She was on her way to the racetrack in Timonium for the Maryland State Fair, passing into what some considered "the north."

"But let's not forget it was still south of the Mason Dixon line," said one long-time Maryland horseman.

White trainers and owners were embraced warmly in nearby motels and restaurants, places like the Knotty Pine Restaurant, one of the few commercial establishments on York Road. But, for this humble black woman, finding a place to sleep and eat was a constant frustrating succession of stress and strategy. Her living accommodations during the eleven days of racing would be a room in a boarding house run by a black family three-and-a-half miles north of the track in Towson.

Underground word-of-mouth lists detailing which eating establishments served customers of both races existed. Their locations often were exchanged among blacks working in the stables. Small roadside stands, variety stores, and sometimes a drugstore lunch counter were noted as "friendly." After working all day with her horses, the last thing Sylvia wanted was a hostile environment at a diner. The owners of her boarding house likely would keep a home- cooked evening meal warm until she arrived not long after sunset.

One extremely informative traveling reference back then was The Negro Travelers' Green Book. It was first published in 1936 as The Negro Motorist Green Book and written by Victor H. Green (1892-1960), a former mailman who expanded his New York-based publishing business into reservation services. The small booklet offered listings of friendly restaurants, barber and beauty shops, taxicabs, hotels and tourist homes. It was sold by mail order and at African-American friendly Esso gas stations as well as by the American Automobile Association.

At the track, Sylvia's reception was "chilly," according to Coley Blind, who regularly attended the fair as a boy and later worked at the Maryland Jockey Club. "That was a given for the era. In the mid to late '50s, you just didn't see too many blacks at all. As a kid you didn't see that many blacks at the track beyond the grooms and hot walkers."

"There were a few blacks scattered around," according to Maryland native Gordie Keys, who started going to the fair showing pigs and cows and watching the races in the 1940s. He recalls very little difference between the legendary Deep South intimidating atmosphere toward blacks in Virginia and the unreceptive atmosphere in Maryland. "Even though it was on the edge of Baltimore, there was no way blacks would be welcome unless somebody knew them." Historical photos of the era confirm his recollections.

"After they worked all day as grooms, they tended bar at the parties at night," recalled Alex Speer. She's a life-long Marylander from a well-to-do family of horse owners who lived in the nearby posh area known as the Green Spring Valley. "I remember my parents definitely believed that whites were superior."

Though octogenarian Carol Hackney didn't realize she shared the blatant, bigoted views of Speer's parents, it bubbled up in a telephone interview in late 2011. Also a horse lover, Hackney began riding ponies at age three, showed her family's cattle at the Timonium Fair each year, and now raises Morgan horses. She attended the exclusive Garrison Forest girl's boarding school near Baltimore, where riding still holds as much importance as courses in English and history. Well-known in certain circles, the equestrian program was then run by alumni and noted equestrienne Maud Dulany Barker Jones.

"There were never any blacks at Garrison," Hackney said, adding that when she attended the exclusive Bryn Mawr Women's College on the Main Line outside of Philadelphia, there was only one Jewish student—"and she had to leave because it was so unpleasant."

Growing up, Hackney recalled that her family "had black servants, a black nanny and black farm workers, but we didn't discriminate. My father was a judge and many blacks came in front of him in court and he would scold them. I think he was very fair. It's just too bad we have to lower our standards. I blame the parents. They can't help them because they can't read."

Hackney wanted to add that she is totally against horse racing and considers it cruel. And, she insisted, she does not discriminate. "I have a broken leg and I have a black girl who helps me with the shower."

Against this sort of bigoted backdrop, which sadly still exists, Sylvia struggled to carry on as best she could.

"Probably the greater resistance was against women," Lambert Boyce, the son of Maryland-based horse trainer Lambert Gittings "LG" Boyce, recalled five decades later. "All of my father's generation did not feel the racetrack was any place for a lady."

The Baltimore County Agricultural Association was formed in 1879 when the first six-day fair was held at the Timonium Mansion, once known as Belle Field. Eight years later, the first Thoroughbred races took place during the 1887 fair and have remained part of the program, with one exception. In 1943 during World War II, the grounds were altered for military vehicle repairs and cargo space while leased to the Army.

Located on thirty-seven acres along the York Turnpike, fourteen miles from downtown Baltimore, the half-mile oval has forever been praised for the unobstructed views of the entire track.

During the 1890s, officials of the Baltimore County Agriculture group butted heads with the Maryland Jockey Club, which held races as part of the Pimlico Fair. In 1894 and again in 1897, each association held races before they eventually joined forces and formed the Maryland State Fair and Agricultural Society.

In the 1950s, the organization mistakenly agreed to sell the precious tract of land for possible development. Evidently, they did not factor in the ire or the power of local farmers, horsemen, and others who helped purchase the land for more than $600,000. According to horseracing.com, that "ensured that the Maryland State Fair at Timonium would continue to be Maryland's premiere event at the end of each summer."

Almost.

Yet another threat came up during the 1970s, when a move was made to hold the meet at the other big-time Maryland tracks—Bowie, Pimlico and Laurel. But cooler heads in the form of the Committee of Friends of the Maryland State Fair prevailed, and the fair and racing at the venue continues to this day.

By 1975, all of the classic old Maryland half-mile tracks of Sylvia's career—Cumberland, Bel Air, Hagerstown and Marlboro—were but a wistful memory. Only Timonium remained, a gem once called "the Holy Land" by Washington Post racing columnist Gerald Strine. "Timonium, a five-furlong track, seems to be sacrosanct ground," Strine noted in his column on April 16, 1975. For the record, the oval is technically considered a half-mile in length, but when the starting gate is placed in a chute on the grandstand side, it covers five furlongs, or five-eighths of a mile.

The September racing also takes place at a venue featuring all manner of fattening, funky food stands, wildly nauseating spinning rides, and a chance to win a stuffed bear on the midway. In another section of the fair, there are contests for farming and gardening, featuring fruit, thick honey, flowers, Christmas trees, wool and fleece and even wine.

In the highly competitive vegetable division, the rules state that "exhibits will be judged on the basis of quality, condition, uniformity and trueness to variety. In order to rate highest in quality the product must be in the best edible stage. It should be free from blemishes caused by disease, insects, or other factors. The term 'uniformity' applies to size, shape and color as representative of the variety. The average size from the commercial standpoint, rather than the largest specimens, should be exhibited."

There are four categories of beans: snap green flat podded, snap green round podded, snap green wax podded or any other kind, and long green beans. Add to this: five varieties of cabbage, eight classes of onions, eleven types of peppers, every imaginable form of squash, pumpkins, watermelons, and tomatoes. But it's hardly a surprise that okra, parsnips, and turnips stand alone.

The Home Arts Department includes handmade dolls, baskets and jewelry in crafts, baking (this includes a Chocolate Championship), sewing (quilts, knitting, hooked rugs), photography, woodworking and pottery. Other distractions include pig races, a 4-H livestock auction, musical concerts such as the U.S. Navy Commodores, Cruisers and Sea Chanters, "Masters of Chainsaw," jousting, and cow milking lessons sponsored by the Maryland Guernsey Youth Association.

The Livestock pavilion is home to dairy, beef, sheep, swine (the four legged variety), a personal preferred pet of goats and, of course, horses, including adorable Shetland ponies and huge huggable draft horses.

Still, best of all for many fair-goers is the opportunity to wager the week's rent over at the track.

On Friday, September 10, 1954, the tenth day of Sylvia's presence at the eleven-day Timonium meeting, District Court Judge Henry Schweinhaut refused a plea to delay integration in District of Columbia schools. And back in West Virginia, sixty mothers kept their white elementary age children home because thirteen "Negro" children had been enrolled.

The civil rights movement of the 1960s was starting to simmer. In May 1954, the Supreme Court ruled in Brown v. Board of Education of Topeka that school segregation was unconstitutional, a watershed decision that was not popular in many areas of the country. Coley Blind recalled the racial scene at the track of black hot-walkers and grooms and white spectators and racehorse owners as "self-segregation."

Members of the International Society for the Scientific Study of Race Relations were making arrangements to set up offices at Howard University, Washington's historic black college founded in 1867. Reporter Joe Shephard of the Baltimore Sun reported on the American Legion parade on the mall in the nation's capital. The headline was "Mall a Riot of Color During Big Parade." He was referring to the colorful uniforms of the soldiers, not the color of their skin. His mention of "one of the most roundly applauded units—the Tom Powell Post 77"—ignored the fact that this was the first "all-colored unit to appear before the reviewing stand" as accurately reported by Trezzvant Anderson in the Baltimore Afro-American.

"As the thousands upon thousands of marchers came up to give their salute to national Commander Arthur J. Connell, colored faces were few and far between," Anderson wrote, noting there was not a "colored face among those which packed the official reviewing stand." The headline in the Afro-American read "Legion's Segregation Pattern Hasn't Changed" and his story said it was "just as marked now as it was 20 years ago."

The temperature hovered at a mild seventy degrees, with scattered showers in the forecast later in the day. The two-plus hour drive was a leisurely and scenic outing past vast swaths of farmland and fields soon to be harvested from the summer's final planting of corn.

Admission to the fair was $1.50, but Sylvia did not have to pay since she had horses in the stables set to run that afternoon. Her trainer's license allowed her inside the gates. Post time for the first race was 1:30 that afternoon. The sweet fragrance of cotton candy intermingled with the scent of sizzling popcorn and a whiff of horse you-know-what wafted in the air.

Sylvia had two horses entered on September 2, 1954: Wise Bet placed third and won $100 in the second race and Happy Yuletide placed seventh and next to last in the third race with no earnings.

Eight days later, on the showery afternoon of September 10, Wise Bet was locked in to post position number four of the starting gate for the third race. Washington Post handicapper Bill Bennings picked the mare to win.

As the eight horses in the field warmed up and headed to the starting gate, jockey Mike Sorrentino was perched atop the horse when the gates clanked open. The mare settled into second place all the way around the final turn into the stretch. Then, she lost momentum to fourth and finally faded to fifth place, with no purse money awarded.

During the next two races, Sylvia would have followed Wise Bet back to the barn to make sure the mare came out of the race uninjured. She may have grabbed a hot dog and taken a deep breath before she prepared Happy Yuletide for the sixth race.

Her hunger would have been satisfied at a food tent set up in the stable area. Blacks didn't much hang around the old wooden grandstand, according to Coley Blind. "They went to the track kitchen to eat because it was, number one, cheaper and, number two, more accessible."

Still, heaven help any black fair-goer who dared to go to a white-only water fountain, as Lambert Boyce recalled five decades later. "I remember being there when a black man—I think it was Joe Joyce—went to drink out of a fountain spigot in the square. It was supposedly white only. He asked Pop if he'd mind if he took a drink, and Pop said go ahead.

"The security guard who was normally at the incoming gate took note and said Joe couldn't because it was white only. My father told the guard that he said Joe could drink from it and to leave him alone. Pop insisted that Joe go ahead and drink. The guard protested a bit more but my father said that was just BS and not right. Being that Pop was six-foot-four and 200 plus pounds and the guard shorter and lighter, my father's reasoning prevailed."

As Sylvia watched the fifth race, she witnessed an appalling accident. As the field of eight horses began to glide down the backstretch, no. six, Hi Buddy, suddenly stumbled, catapulting twenty-three-year-old jockey Joe Snyder close to the inner rail. As Lace Ruffles and rider Eddie McIvor came up behind, they were unable to avoid the accident, and Snyder was trampled.

One of the most well-known and successful jockeys on the half-mile circuit, Snyder was taken to Bon Secours Hospital in Baltimore and would live to ride again…but only for four more years.

When all the others crossed the finish wire, none other than Wise Bet's jockey, Mike Sorrentino, won the race by four lengths on T.J. Evans' Chicle Sador.

Sorrentino went on from Timonium to gain fame and a bit of fortune while riding in the big-time races in New York. He won the 1963 Alabama Stakes on Tona and the 1965 Knickerbocker Stakes on a horse called Circus.

Before the sixth race at Timonium, the three-year-old chestnut mare, Happy Yuletide, circled the walking ring for what would be the nineteeth start of her career, which had only begun five months earlier at Wheeling Downs. She had not yet won a race and her earnings were a paltry $380.

Sylvia had owned Happy Yuletide since July 30, when she finished fourth at a Charles Town race, winning only fifty dollars. In her next five races leading up to this race, the mare finished fourth twice more for an additional $100. In three other races, she was near the back of the field.

Sylvia's hopes had to be high in a sport that is an endless barrage of "if onlys." She gave jockey Anthony Russo a leg up on the chestnut mare. The horses headed to the starting gate, and Happy Yuletide was loaded in to post-position number eight.

The mare finished fifth, eight lengths behind the winner and out of the money again in a seven-furlong claiming race worth $1500. There is no indication on the racing charts that Happy Yuletide was injured, but it marked the last time she ever raced. Six decades later, Charles Town trainer Diana McClure studied the results. Her comment about Happy Yuletide was simple: "She needed another job."

There are so many variables in horse racing. Sylvia was just beginning her training career that day, and would be in the winner's circle on many glorious afternoons to come. Her only consolation after a losing afternoon was the setting of the track, which remained enchanting. Gazing in the direction of the midway and the amusement rides surely had to bring a smile to her face. Now, more than sixty years later, visitors can still take a spin on rides such as the Tornado, Dumbo, Supershot, and Zero Gravity.

And perhaps, the elusive Baltimore reptile from 1954 might even be inside the much ballyhooed "Killer Snake" slideshow?

There are now food stands such as the bulk candy store ("the sweetest place at the fair"), pizza by the slice, turkey legs, corn dogs, onion rings, Maryland crab cakes, Greek gyros, and oh yes, a fair-goer's favorite: fried dough.

CHAPTER 20

CHALKEE

*Fine horses were kind of an expression of a man's ego
and the competition to own top horses was intense.
Some wanted beauty, some endurance, some speed —
much like automobile owners of today, however
no car ever came close to matching the affection
of a man and his horse.*

**- A.M.S. Morgan II, Charles Town 1912-1924:
A Boy's Eye-View of Charles Town and Its People**

For a woman who loves horses, her first "big" horse is close to that first human love. That first love sets the standard by which all others to follow will be held.

In January 1956, the winter sun glowed on a chestnut filly named Chalkee, and Sylvia tried to control her glee. The light illuminated the bronze filly's shiny coat as she sauntered out of the barn. Some horses seem to know they're pretty and often show off. Such preening leads to a challenge in training.

Chalkee was gorgeous, unpretentious and confident. More than fifty years later, Sylvia teared up as she recounted Chalkee's shimmering color, kind eyes and cooperative manner.

Sylvia performed a detailed inspection of the horse. She walked up to the filly and stood beside her on the "near" (left) side. The filly didn't flinch as she ran her hands down her front legs, feeling for bumps. Sylvia walked to the front and stroked the striking filly. A distinctive white blaze marked her face. She studied how she stood up.

"Walk her down and back," Sylvia asked the groom. The filly walked straight and did not toe in or out.

Sylvia inspected the hooves and picked up each foot. They appeared strong, no cuts or bumps. The filly did not have any shoes on, and Sylvia added another eight dollars into her budget for a blacksmith every four weeks.

"I'd be taking a chance here, and I don't have money to wash down the drain," she told the man holding the horse she was about to purchase. The price was a staggering $2,000.

Leaning forward from the overstuffed lounge chair in the Charles Town Towers, Sylvia recalled, "I knew immediately, I just had to buy this fabulous filly. I bought her 'on the cuff.' I gave the man $200 down and the rest to be taken out each time she won, only if she won money for first place. Even if she won money for second or third, they wouldn't take the money. I had to cover my expenses for hay and feed."

Since all Thoroughbreds officially celebrate their birthday on January 1, Chalkee had just turned three. The Jockey Club registration papers listed her foaling date as March 14, 1953. Her sire was a bay stallion standing in Maryland named Bar Keep. "He started twenty-seven times, won seven and had $8,175 in earnings," Chalkee's owner told Sylvia.

Sylvia did not respond. She stood back and took another walk around Chalkee. "You can put her back in the stall," she told the groom, as if to dismiss the young horse.

"I know she's already started three times as a two-year-old and hasn't earned one red penny yet," Sylvia said. "And this stallion hasn't sired any winners yet either. I'd be taking a chance."

She waited for a reply.

Still, it wasn't long before Sylvia was loading the chestnut filly in the back of a trailer and taking her back to the barn.

Sylvia and Chalkee immediately went to work together for Charles Town's thirty-four day 1956 winter meet, running from January 28 to March 7. Chalkee was one of 800 horses in training at the track.

Horsemen and members of the Charles Town Jockey Club backed by the Horsemen's Benevolent Protective Association had successfully lobbied the West Virginia State Racing Commission to open the track in January, not February. A wire was sent to Governor William C. Marland pointing out a possible conflict: "All records show that when Charles Town has run in opposition to nearby tracks, the mutual play has been off about 50 percent."

"Let her gallop the way she wants to go," Sylvia told the exercise rider, who got one dollar a ride each morning. Some of the other trainers only paid the riders fifty cents. One trainer, referred to as "The Greek," offered the entire payment in dimes.

"Keep her where she's comfortable. Not too fast, no use to fight with her."

Though Sylvia had all the responsibility of training her new filly, she still did not yet have a proper license. She was listed as the owner when Chalkee started in Charles Town for the first time under her ownership and off-the-record training. It was almost post time for the fifth race on February 20, 1956, when

Chalkee was launched out of post position nine in a four and a half furlong claiming race for three-year-olds. With John Bishop listed as trainer, longshot Chalkee finished second out of ten horses entered on a muddy track.

Sylvia was ecstatic and John Bishop, ever the bettor, likely also was elated. The payout for a two dollar place bet was a whopping $42.80. A two dollar show bet returned $16.40.

In 1956, Chalkee had nineteen races. Washington Post racing writer Walter Haight noted in his "Horses and People" column, "John and Sylvia Bishop are justly proud of their four-time winner, Chalkee, and are smiling."

For each outing that year, Sylvia was listed as owner in the program and on the racing chart results. John Bishop was the trainer of record on July 25 and 31 in Charles Town and her brother-in-law, J.E. Berry, was listed as trainer on August 31 and September 5 at Timonium.

MRS. SYLVIA BISHOP'S
OWNER-TRAINER
5 ½ FURLONGS 1-08

CHALKEE
SHENANDOAH DOWNS
JULY 7, 1959

T. MAEDA   UP
CAR HOP   2ND
FAST AND FAR 3RD

Photo courtesy of Sylvia Bishop

Sylvia and John also traveled to Wheeling Downs in West Virginia as well as Cumberland and Hagerstown in Maryland. Gas was twenty-two cents a gallon. At the end of 1956, Chalkee had three second place finishes and was third twice. Her total 1956 earnings were $3,480.

In 1957, a novelty toy originally developed by Walter Frederick Morrison reached the retail market in January. First called the Pluto Platter, the Frisbee has endured. The Bridge on the River Kwai was a hit movie, and the original

Perry Mason captivated television viewers.

Chalkee, still listed as trained by John Bishop, ran twenty-one times in 1957 and won one race on June 13, at Waterford Park in Chester, West Virginia. By this time, Sylvia was queasy from morning sickness while pregnant at the age of thirty-six. Chalkee finished out the year with four second-places finishes and six times was third, with earnings of $7,075.

Chalkee's first race in 1958 came on July 8. The eight and half months she had been off since running at Marlboro evidently paid off, as she ran wire to wire in first place in a six-furlong race for four-year-olds and upward. The purse of $1,000 offered $650 to the winner. Better yet, for Mr. Bishop, a first place two dollar bet paid $46.60. Mrs. Sylvia Bishop remained listed as owner, and Berry again was the trainer of record.

Chalkee won again under J. Berry on August 26 at Charles Town. She traveled to Hagerstown again, but this time was last on October 6, in a field of seven going five furlongs. Two days later, she finished fourth at six and a half furlongs.

How often were most horses raced during this era? For the most part, Sylvia's horses ran every week. Still, from time to time when a race was offered that had the potential for a win, most trainers would run their horses one day later, two days later and sometimes in the afternoon at one track and that same night somewhere else. Today, most horses run about once a month. Chalkee's record for 1958 included just two victories, with Berry still listed as trainer. After ten starts, total earnings were a meager $2,000.

Chalkee again had a winter rest and started back on May 5, 1959. Now five-years-old, she finished in an unremarkable sixth place going six furlongs at Shenandoah Downs. As the year progressed, racing moved next door to the Charles Town track in August and back to Shenandoah in September. Chalkee raced eleven times with several second places finishes and also a third, the rest out of the money.

Until the day for which Sylvia had been waiting.

On October 1, 1959, Chalkee broke out of post position number two and went right to the top in the five-and-a-half furlong claiming race worth $1,250 and flew across the finish line. She paid fourteen dollars for a two dollar win ticket. The track was listed as good. The winning time was 1:09 3/5, and there was $650 to the winner. The Racing Form reported, "Start good, Won driving. Trained by Mrs. S. A. Bishop."

Chalkee finished 1959 with two wins, two seconds and two thirds. Out of twenty starts, she earned $2,000. In 1960, she ran five times and earned fifteen dollars. Chalkee's career as a racehorse included seventy-eight starts, nine wins and $8,970 in earnings.

In 1961, the fine-looking chestnut was retired to become a broodmare and begin a whole new career. In a somewhat unusual twist of fate, Sylvia went on to train all four of Chalkee's offspring.

CHAPTER 21

MILLION DOLLAR BABY

*The thoroughbred business is now considered an industry
in the Old Dominion, involving millions of dollars annually.*

- Kitty Slater, The Washington Post, September 27, 1963

To breed a winning Thoroughbred racehorse takes a dash of serious pedigree knowledge, money, sheer luck and dumb luck. Add to this a nice mare, perseverance, lush grass and even more buckets of luck.

As 1961 began, Hillside Fuel and Barrett Coal listed competitive prices for lump, stoker or run of mine coal between $12 and $17.50 per ton.

Potatoes were seventy-nine cents for a twenty-five pound bag, whole cut-up chickens were thirty-three cents per pound, and an angel food cake, regularly fifty-nine cents, was on sale for forty-nine cents.

The feature Toney Betts stakes, named in honor of the racing editor of the New York Daily Mirror newspaper, was scheduled for Saturday, January 10, 1961. Sylvia saddled longshot Irish Dash in the first race on opening day in a six and a half furlong claiming race for four-year-olds and up. Following a claim of foul, the result stood and Sylvia took $650 from the total purse of $1,000 as the horse's owner and trainer. That was only part of a very successful day, because a two dollar win ticket on Irish Dash paid $119.40. When Way Lowe won the second race for part two of the Daily Double, that ticket was worth $884.20.

Then, there's this item: the same day Sylvia's horse paid off big-time, John F. Kennedy was having a high old time himself. Only ten days before his January 20 inauguration, he flew on a private plane with his real estate mogul friend Grant Stockdale from Boston to New York for a night on the town. They had dinner at the swanky "21" restaurant prior to taking in the Broadway musical Do-Re-Mi starring Phil Silvers. Press Secretary Pierre Salinger arranged the trip, and the opening curtain at the St. James Theatre was held up when the president elect and his entourage arrived late. Still, as Kennedy took his aisle seat in the fourth row, the audience applauded.

Meanwhile, Sylvia was engaged in a venture to team up with one of her owners, attorney Lee Bushong of Hedgesville, West Virginia, a town located twenty-five miles from Charles Town.

They planned to breed the next generation of racehorses with Chalkee, her bright, recently-retired chestnut mare, soon after the New Year. That's when the mare's cycle came in "season"—fertile for mating.

And yet, even as Sylvia dreamed about a future of sleek young Thoroughbreds romping in the pasture and winning races, there was another reality. Constant racial discrimination in the 1960s was never far away. On January 3, 1961, Bushong's local paper, the Martinsburg Journal, published an editorial with a headline that read "Boycotts by Negroes Effective."

All around the South, which of course included this area, there was a "campaign to bring about integration of restaurant and other facilities." This time, it was called the "Santa Claus boycott."

Holiday shoppers were encouraged not to patronize businesses known to "still draw the color line." The editorial declared the action made "quite a dent in the year-end trade."

As Kennedy was inaugurated on January 20, 1961, and inspired the nation with a moving speech that included, "Ask not what your country can do for you…" Sylvia and Lee Bushong continued to make productive deals in the business of breeding racehorses.

A year later, their first foray brought them a chestnut horse on February 3, 1962. He was named Acrakee. All Thoroughbreds must have a Jockey Club approved name by the time they race. On January 1, the following year, no matter when they were born, they all have a birthday.

Acrakee was sired by the stallion *Acramitis (the * indicates he was born in Australia). Lee Bushong is listed as breeder on the pedigree chart and the official Jockey Club registration forms.

In 1954, as a two-year-old in Australia, the stallion Acramitis (named for the second highest mountain in Greece) won the prestigious seven-furlong Sires' Produce Stakes, leading all the way, at Flemington. He also won the Craiglee Stakes later that season, also at Flemington. At age three, Acramitis began the season with a win, but was injured later that year.

Acramitis came to the United States in 1957 at Holly House Farm, owned by George and Elizabeth Howe in Fulton, Maryland. Located in Howard County, it remains a horse-friendly area, though housing developments have encroached and the original farm has been divided.

The stud fee for breeding was $500 if a colt was produced and $300 if a filly. At the bottom of an ad in the Maryland Horse Magazine, it noted "live foal," a term all horse people understand. If the baby stands and nurses, it's considered live, no matter what happens later that day. There is no charge when the gut-wrenching stillbirth occurs.

Acrakee made his first start as a two-year-old on July 21, 1964, at Charles Town in a Maiden Special at four furlongs, and finished fourth. The owners were further encouraged next time out on July 29, when he finished third.

Acrakee was well-traveled and ran the circuit of half-mile tracks and fairgrounds in Timonium, Hagerstown and Marlboro, Maryland as well as the two tracks in Charles Town. It wasn't until Monday evening, October 12, in the first race on the first night of the Shenandoah Downs meet that Acrakee, ridden by jockey Carl Gambarrdella, "broke his maiden" with a first victory.

Sylvia and Bushong were now able to celebrate, and pay some of the feed bills when he won first-place money of $910 in the five-and-a-half furlong allowance, which was officially recorded as "won driving."

Acrakee finished his first year of thirteen races with two wins and $2,630 in earnings. During his three-year career of forty-six starts, he had six wins and earned $11,123, worth more than $90,000 in 2020.

Meanwhile, Chalkee was bred back to Acramitis. And Sylvia continued to commute the twenty-five miles to the Bushong farm to visit the newborns before it was time to head back to the Charles Town track to train.

Racial issues around the country were always in the news. Kennedy's secretary of defense, Robert S. McNamara, issued a directive to military commanders to consider off-limits businesses operating near military bases that did not allow black patrons. He denounced the "relentless discrimination against Negros."

There was some good news. Arthur Ashe, a Richmond, Virginia native and star tennis player at UCLA, became the first black player ever named to the prestigious U.S. Davis Cup team. Black actors and behind-the-scenes workers in the film industry in California also were stepping up their campaign to become members in entertainment unions.

Sylvia and Bushong welcomed a new chestnut colt they named Acramight on March 29, 1963. He had a four-year, forty-five race career between 1965-1968, winning four races and $6,720 in earnings, more than $55,000 when adjusted for inflation in 2020.

There were two other "babies" out of Chalkee. The Shrew was born on March 12, 1964, fathered by a British stallion called *Dominate II. She won one race in sixteen starts and $1,958 in earnings. Trojan Kee, by Trojan Monarch, was a light bay mare foaled on January 1, 1966, with just seven starts between 1968-1970. She had no wins and a paltry $218 in earnings.

Sadly for Sylvia, Chalkee died on May 6, 1967, while giving birth to her fifth foal, a filly named Mon Kee. She ran six times between 1968-1970, with just $218 in winnings.

The experience of watching a baby horse stand up, romp around the paddock, and eventually start running out in the field is filled with pride, joy and great anticipation for any owner. The rigors of breaking a young horse to saddle and bridle can be both treacherous and tedious, requiring heaps of patience. Training them to walk, trot, canter and gallop is monotonously repetitive, sort of like potty training a toddler. Horses, like children, are creatures of habit.

Watching your horse race can be elating, even while teetering on the edge of a cardiac event. It can also be laced with crushing heartbreak. For Sylvia and all others—grooms, exercise riders, owners and officials—just getting a horse into the starting gate is often considered a miracle.

Thoroughbred racing has often been referred to as "the Sport of Kings." Today, it's a global enterprise that includes Hollywood types, sports figures, and celebrities from media, high finance, the dot.com world, and countless boldface names. British royalty has always had a soft spot for a fine racehorse. Consider the surprise and dismay Queen Elizabeth, the Queen Mother, experienced watching her horse, Devon Loch, in the 1956 Grand National Steeplechase in Aintree, England. Jockey Dick Francis was headed to fame and fortune near the finish line as his royal mount took an inexplicable leap and landed splayed in a heap and lost.

Francis had 350 lifetime steeplechase victories, then retired from racing. He went on to become a journalist and celebrated writer of racing-inspired mysteries with forty international best sellers.

Some involved in the Thoroughbred business opt to sell or buy their racing stock through the Fasig-Tipton horse auction sales company. Founded in 1898, it now operates in four states. They conduct more than a dozen Thoroughbred auctions each year at various locations, including the swish late summer haunt of old and new money in Saratoga Springs, N.Y. It was there, in 1918, that legendary Man o' War sold for $5,000.

In 2008, Synergy Investments, Ltd., a Dubai-based company headed by Abdull Al Habbai, purchased Fasig-Tipton. The owner reportedly is Sheikh Mohammed bin Rashid Al Maktoum, the vice president and prime minister of the United Arab Emirates, ruler of the Emirate of Dubai, and a lifelong horseman and owner. Their annual sales from fourteen auctions in 2019 were $380,751,000.

In the heart of the Blue Grass country near Lexington, Kentucky, there's a magical place called Keeneland. This is where prestigious races take place each April and October. They also hold four auction sales each year.

Horse of the Year and 2018 Triple Crown winner Justify was sold there as a yearling for $500,000. He completed his career with a perfect record of six times out and six victories. His earnings were $3,798,000, but there was more money to follow. Justify stood at stud for $150,000 per mating to about 200 mares during the February-to-June breeding season.

In Sylvia's day, women were not permitted into the breeding shed. Since then, it's become an exact science and women work in the breeding shed as managers. With large amounts of money at stake, the physical act is often videotaped for proof the mare met with the intended stallion. The cycles of the mares are also a consideration, so some stallions often couple three times a day with three different mares.

Back in Charles Town, Jeff Runco began as a jockey and has been a leading trainer since he began in 1984. He's trained twenty-one winners in the prestigious West Virginia Breeders Cup, which began in 1987. And also won the 2017 Sylvia Bishop Memorial Stakes with Moonlit Song.

Runco's most successful horse was a bay gelding named Researcher, purchased by Hermen Greenberg for $5,000 at a small auction in Middleburg, Virginia. The 2005 sale was a fundraiser for the Virginia Tech Foundation, Inc. In twenty-seven starts, Researcher went on to win thirteen races, including the Charles Town Classic in 2009 and again in 2010 after Lisa and Zohar Ben-Dov of Kinross Farm, also in Middleburg, bought the horse following Greenberg's death. Researcher retired in 2012, with $1,379,379 in earnings.

Finally, there's the story of the Green Monkey, a bay colt with accents of white. He had regal bloodlines and was auctioned in January 2006, by Fasig-Tipton at the Calder Race Track in Florida. The final bid was $16 million, the most ever paid for a two-year-old in the United States.

After three failed starts at the track, he was retired. At stud, the results weren't much either. He later had soundness issues and was stricken with debilitating laminitis. At age fourteen in 2018, he was euthanized and buried on a farm in Ocala, Florida.

So much for the million dollar baby.

The Green Monkey was sold at auction as a two-year-old in January 2006 for $16 million. He never won a race. *Photo by Adam Coglianese*

CHAPTER 22

IRISH DASH

Women have certainly proved they can do it now.

**- Danny Wright, former jockey and steward
at Charles Town racetrack, May 16, 2017**

Summertime in West Virginia was heading toward its predictable soaring temperatures on Wednesday, June 10, 1959 when the mercury hit close to ninety degrees in Charles Town.

United Press International reported that, "Postmaster General Arthur E. Summerfield held that the expurgated version of Lady Chatterley's Lover is an 'obscene and filthy work unsuitable for mailing in the United States.'"

Actress Elizabeth Taylor was being wooed by MGM for the film version of writer John O'Hara's novel Butterfield 8. Movie tickets were one dollar, a loaf of bread was twenty cents, and Fidel Castro stormed into power as the eventual dictatorial prime minister of soon-to-be Communist Cuba. And, the Guggenheim Museum, designed by Frank Lloyd Wright in New York City, was completed.

The latest news in Charles Town, according to the Spirit of Jefferson Farmers Advocate, was of a special election, scheduled by the town council for the second time in three months, for a vote on extending the town limits by 308 acres. The Charles Town Senior Woman's Club annual picnic was to take place at the home of Miss Louise Briscoe. And, Vacation Bible School's final ceremony was scheduled at the Baptist Church on Friday, June 12, at 7:30 p.m.

Shenandoah Downs was in the midst of a sixty-two-night run from May 1 to July 11. Over at the Charles Town track just across the street, workers were renovating the racing strip in preparation for a sixty-nine-

MRS. SYLVIA BISHOP—OWNER *IRISH DASH* A. GOODWIN UP
OWNER-TRAINER MARKETER 2ND
5 ½ FURLONGS 1-07 SHENANDOAH DOWNS DISCMONT 3RD
JUNE 10, 1959

Photo courtesy of Sylvia Bishop

day meet to begin July 13. "Some 4,000 tons of top soil and limestone will be used in rebuilding the racing strip," the paper reported. In addition, an "internationally known interior designer from New York" was hired to spruce up the clubhouse.

The sun went down at 8:36 p.m. as Sylvia saddled Irish Dash for the fourth race on that night's program. The claiming race was scheduled to go five-and-a-half furlongs for a purse of $1,000. Sylvia slipped blinkers on over the bridle and drew the girth up on the four-year-old dark bay and took him around the walking ring. She gave jockey A. Goodwin a leg up. As was her lifetime custom, she offered no specific instructions. She expected all jockeys could do their job without her help, just as she didn't want anyone to tell her how to train. She wished him well and found a spot on the rail to watch the race.

Irish Dash came out of post-position number one at 8:59 p.m. and led all the way. The charts in the Morning Telegram described it as "Won driving." His share of the purse was $650. The track was fast and the final time for Sylvia's first victory as owner and trainer was 1:07 flat. It was the horse's only win in sixteen starts in 1959. But it was the first of many for Sylvia Rideoutt Bishop.

CHAPTER 23

IF THE SHOE FITS

No Foot, No Horse

- Old horse saying

t's a late September morning in 1959, as Sylvia leads the first of three horses out of their racetrack stalls in Charles Town for a visit with the farrier for new sets of shoes. All three—Irish Dash, a four-year-old bay gelding; Hylo Son, an eight-year-old chestnut gelding; and her beloved chestnut mare, Chalkee—are slated to run in early October.

For non-horse types, a farrier shoes horses. A blacksmith works with iron on all manner of products. And being a farrier can be a back-breaking and exacting profession. It's been said that the average career for a farrier is twenty-five years, given the physical stress on the back, not to mention potential bites and kicks.

These days, after spending countless hours working in a bent-over position on a horse that weighs anywhere from 900-1500 pounds, many farriers turn to yoga. According to Linda Braus, writing for American Farriers Journal in 2017, "Yoga can be a key component to career longevity."

Some farriers prefer to form the shoe to fit the horse's hoof by heating it first

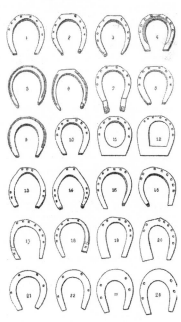

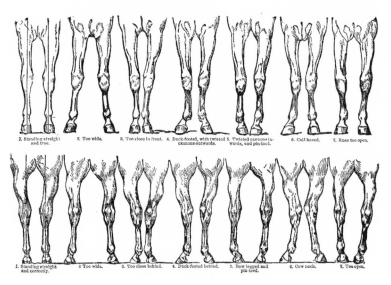

Illustrations from: Magner's Standard Horse and Stock Book Illustrated, 1887

in a forge and hammering its final shape on a large steel anvil. Others form the shape with the cold method—pounding the shoe without heat. Cold or hot is only a matter of preference between the farrier and the trainer.

As Sylvia held one of the horses for new shoes, she'd talk to the horse, always offering up sweet nothings. She was in a position horsemen call "on the head," a very important place to be if a horse becomes unruly. This also saved on expenses of paying someone to hold the horses. They don't normally act up with a farrier unless they're in fear or pain. Sylvia's horses were accustomed to the necessary routine.

The farrier starts by pulling off the old shoes, then trims the hoof and shapes the shoe. He stops periodically to tap the shoe on a portable anvil. Just like their human counterparts, the shoes come in various sizes. When a horse is not racing, a light steel shoe is used.

Four-and-a-half-inch nails are painlessly tapped in to secure the shoe. The next step is to clip the excess piece of the hoof's nail and smooth it over with a large rasp. Finally, just like at a human nail salon, a topcoat is applied, only this product for the entire hoof is pine tar, not nail polish.

A simple can of pine tar from the circa 1882 Bickmore Company based in Whitmore Lake, Michigan, could be found in most stables during her era. The purpose then and now is to maintain moisture in the hoof to prevent cracking. It can still be purchased from the company, which also manufactured leather-care goods. At one point during the early 1900s, the company also made human toothpaste, cold cream, and shave cream advertised by a young actor named Ronald Reagan.

Each horse comes with special issues. Some toe in, others toe out.

A few have weak hoof walls, and there's a conformation concern of a "club foot." According to Kentucky Equine Research, the "telltale signs of a club foot may include an excessively steep hoof angle, a distended coronary band, growth rings that are wider at the heels, contracted heels, and dished toes. Most horses only have one club foot, but it is possible to have multiple."

Toward the end of the new shoe session, the horse begins to fidget and wiggle. "Come on, horse," Sylvia coos, while a tabby cat winds his way around her ankles. For the record, many barn cats remain unnamed due to their elusive habits. To this day, the opinion on whether or not to name the stray cats is divided.

The most significant modification in horseshoeing from Sylvia's era involves aluminum racing shoes, which no longer have toe grabs. They were banned on January 1, 2009. This thin piece across the top of the front shoe was thought to be an advantage for traction. According to farrier Steve Sfarnas of Stephenson, Virginia, who now works on many racehorses that run at Charles Town, this is no longer the case.

"Studies found out that while running, the toe grabs acted as a brake and the horse's leg hit the ground dead (leading to numerous wounds)," according to trainer Don Yovanovich. "It causes injuries of bone chips and ligament pulls. There's no slide before the heel hits the ground."

However, the toe grabs still can be used on the rear shoes. "From behind, yes," Sfarnas said. "Because the horse pushes off and they need that kick and grip."

Today, the price for a set of four horseshoes runs between $125 to $165. Sylvia's handwritten notes listed expenses for shoeing during 1959 and into the '60s at sixteen dollars.

Many horseshoes are produced by the Victory Racing Plate Company in Baltimore. Founded in 1929, it's an independent, privately-owned enterprise committed to supplying "sport footwear for the equine athlete." Essentially, their shoes, made of ultra-light aluminum, are considered Air Jordans for horses. The great Secretariat, the 1973 Triple Crown winner, wore Victory plates.

When Hylo Son finished first in a one-mile, seventy-yard claiming race for four-year-olds at Shenandoah Downs on October 3, 1959, the winning purse money of $650 easily covered the cost of his shoes. In contrast, on that same day, Irish Dash ran sixth in a 3½-furlong claiming sprint for four-year-olds and had no income. He came home empty-handed again in sixth place on October 12 in a 5½-furlong claimer at Shenandoah.

And Chalkee, Sylvia's beloved and striking six-year-old chestnut mare, won easily at Shenandoah on October 1 in a 5½-furlong claiming race. The winner's share also was $650, and a two dollar win ticket on her nose paid fourteen dollars.

CHAPTER 24

CHANGING HORSES MID-STREAM

*The aim of teaching a horse to move beneath you
is to remind him how he moved when he was free.*

**- The Flying Change, Henry Taylor,
Pulitzer Prize recipient for poetry in 1986**

Sylvia was standing at the gap where horses step onto the track for a pre-determined morning workout to breeze, gallop or slowly trot around the outside in the opposite direction from where they race.

Jockey Charles McKee was the leading rider at Charles Town in 1957 with 151 winners. He was on his way to a second title until Monday, August 11, 1958.

The temperature hovered at a comfortable seventy-one degrees as the filly he was riding reared up behind the starting gate during an early

morning schooling session.

There is no other sport as treacherous or risky as riding a horse. It's one thing to dash down a football field or basketball court, skate the ice hockey rink at breakneck speed or sprint around a baseball diamond. In racing, it's imperative to factor in an unpredictable, irascible 2,000-pound Thoroughbred.

McKee, twenty-seven, who had forty-eight victories at this point in the season, was trapped under the two-year-old Bahati and suffered a broken left thighbone. Following surgery, he was out for the rest of the year.

The starting gate now used in racing is the ingenious invention of Hoyt "Clay" Puett, a seventh-grade dropout turned cowboy, groom and racehorse trainer. Born in Texas on September 14, 1899, he revolutionized the sport with a twelve-stall gate and V-shaped tubular steel front doors. Powered by a 12-volt battery, it was demonstrated first at Hollywood Park near Los Angeles and used officially on July 1, 1939, at Lansdowne Park in Vancouver, Canada.

Skeptics at the time declared a Thoroughbred would never stand still in the starting stall. The legendary Man o' War, who won twenty of twenty-one career races, including the Preakness and the Belmont in 1919 and 1920, was known to have demonstrable anxiety at the start. His owner, Samuel Riddle, did not like bringing Man o' War to the starting tape (it was twenty years before Puett's 1940 innovation was used). He kept away from any schooling or practice session with the 16.2 hand chestnut known as "Big Red."

Puett told the Daily Racing Form, "I knew that with the proper treatment, you could make a horse do whatever you wanted him to do. Horses are like people. You get along with them better with kindness than with anything else."

The new gate was first used for the Preakness in 1940 and in 1941 for the Kentucky Derby. He sent Charles Town trainer Robert F. Duffy to Greece in 1954 to demonstrate the gate. Various models of Puett's ingenuity and entrepreneurship kept him making the gates into his nineties.

Puett died in Phoenix on September 23, 1998, at age ninety-nine. Twenty-two years later, Churchill Downs acquired a new custom-made, twenty-stall starting gate from Australian-based Steriline Racing for the 146th running of the 2020 Kentucky Derby. The new gate is intended only for the Kentucky Derby, where the large number of entries has created horse traffic concerns.

Two United States manufacturers now claim a connection to Puett. United Puett-Electrical Starting Gate Corporation operates out of Connecticut with workshops in Vermont. Their website boasts they are "the leading supplier of starting gates to every major racing venue in the United States, including the nation's oldest tracks and most prestigious racing events." This includes Charles Town, which has also used one made around 1939 by C.N. McMillan at the Alamo Iron Works in San Antonio, Texas, and another from the Bahr Starting Gate Corporation from August T. J. Bahr in St. Louis, about 1932-1937.

True Center Gate in Phoenix also boasts of a connection since 1958, to "our founder, Clay Puett," whose "revolutionary design stills play an integral role in design and operations." The cost of a new twelve-stall gate from either company today ranges from $150,000 to $190,000.

When Charles Town opened in 1933, the walk-up gate did not have electric doors and was pulled open by horses. When a flash of lightning hit the starting gate in 1954, starter Harold Holland was knocked out, along with the two heavy draft horses that were hauling the gate into place. Today, the gates, with all their bells and whistles, are pulled by tractors.

The starting gate also is now where track veterinarians such as Dr. Jay Joyce keep a keen eye on the process of loading frequently fractious horses to a mobile stall, which is surrounded on all sides by metal. At the gate area, a horse can immediately be dismissed from the race for being unfit, unsound or not ready to race.

The jockeys need help to keep their mounts' heads straight and looking forward and to restrain them from rearing up and perhaps flipping. Once in the gate, jockeys are tossed side to side and up and down. They are constantly concerned about safety in the gate and are always begging for more assistant starters. Their mantra: "The horses are only going to stand for so long before they begin to get anxious."

Riding racehorses with jockeys has its roots in the South, when slaves were given the opportunity to ride in exchange for possible freedom. Slaves and free blacks relegated to farm duties of cleaning stalls and grooming who exhibited a natural aptitude with their horses were offered the opportunity to race a Thoroughbred in competition.

On May 17, 1875, in the first running of the Kentucky Derby, thirteen of the fifteen riders were black. Nineteen year-old Oliver Lewis won on Aristides, trained by a former slave, Ansel Williamson.

James Williams, a black trainer, won the Derby with Vagrant in 1876, as did Edward Brown with Baden-Baden in 1877, Raleigh Colston with Leonatus in 1883, William Bird with Buchanan in 1884, Alex Perry with Joe Cotton in 1885, and Dudley Allen with Kingman in 1891.

Jockey Isaac Murphy won the Kentucky Derby in 1884, 1890 and 1891. Willie Simms won in 1896 and 1898. Jimmy Winkfield won in 1901 and again in 1902, when he was the last black jockey to win a Kentucky Derby.

Those early black trainers and jockeys endured constant racial indignities, as did Sylvia many years later. They all heard the vulgar word "nigger" spewed by angry bettors when a horse did not live up to wagering expectations.

Today, it's not at all unusual to see an African American trainer saddling a horse at Charles Town. However, that is rarely the case at larger tracks like Gulfstream, Churchill Downs, Saratoga and Santa Anita.

Nearly a century after that first Kentucky Derby, female jockeys made more history. Following a court battle in Maryland, Olympic equestrian Kathy Kusner, born in 1940, was the first woman in the United States to be granted a jockey license, in October 1968. A broken leg prevented her from racing that year, but she rode in Charles Town a year later.

Meanwhile, in Miami, a horse-crazy Barbara Jo Rubin, born in 1949, overcame a childhood bout of polio and started riding in horse shows. She then went on to exercise racehorses.

At Tropical Park near Miami, Rubin, then nineteen, made an unsuccessful effort to ride in the races in January 1969. The male jockeys threatened a boycott.

She traveled north to West Virginia and was granted a jockey license. And, on Saturday, Feb 22, 1969, she rode Cohesian in the ninth race, a six and a half furlong allowance, at Charles Town. As 9,359 fans watched, she was escorted to the paddock, and shortly thereafter she became the first woman to win a horse race at a pari-mutuel track.

It's still rare to see a woman jockey today, but plenty of women work as grooms and hot walkers. Many women are "pony girls," who lead the horses to the starting gate. Laura Carson is one of many at Charles Town. She charges twenty dollars per horse, and says the worst part is when the horse acts up and "has no manners."

Jockey Barbara Jo Rubin had to withstand newspapers reporting her hair color (brunette) in their stories, and she was bombarded by questions about when she planned to get married. A guard stood at the door of her temporary dressing room inside the track's infirmary. A race at Charles Town was eventually named in her honor.

Jockey Sam Palumbo showed Rubin around the track on the day of her debut. Savino "Sammy" Palmumbo (1909-1985) rode many horses for Sylvia, including Bright Gem, which triggered that $10,733.80 payout on the twin double on June 26, 1962. It was Sylvia biggest victory—the Iron Horse Mile.

After traveling to Cuba and all around the country to bigger tracks, Palumbo rode on opening day at Charles Town in 1933. He settled in racing on the half-mile circuit, winning more than 2,000 races at Hagerstown, Bel Air, Cumberland, Marlboro and Havre de Grace. Seven hundred of those victories came at Charles Town. Often referred to as "the king of the half milers," Palumbo earned $1.5 million along the way.

A native of Flushing, New York, where his father, Nickolaus Palumbo, an Italian immigrant, was a barber, Sammy got his start six miles from home at the track in Jamaica. He earned twenty-five dollars a month walking hots and grooming. He eventually worked his way up to riding and once said he was just thrown up on a horse and told "you're a rider, go at it." He won for the first time in May 1927, in the second race on J.J. Murphy's Outstep, trained by Frank Bray.

When not in his jockey silks, Palumbo often wore a handsome tailored tweed, plaid, or windowpane jacket with a turtleneck and a sweater. He had an angular face, punctuated by a prominent nose and what one person described as "generous ears."

His life took a grim turn on the morning of August 2, 1950, as he was traveling on Route 40 east of Grantsville, Maryland. He was heading to the Waterford Park racetrack near Wheeling, West Virginia.

Perhaps it was due to Palumbo's fearlessness as a jockey, accustomed to speed and risk, that he tried to pass another car, much as he might do on a horse in a race—at the peak of a hill. Five miles west of Frostburg, his car drifted into the oncoming traffic and had a head-on crash. Noah Frazee, a passenger on his way to a produce stand, was killed immediately. Tossed against the gearshift in the middle of the floor, Frazee sustained grave chest damage, a ruptured lung and numerous hemorrhages. His body was taken to a nearby funeral home.

Palumbo and Walter Fearer, the driver in the other car, were uninjured. Both cars were totaled and towed away. Palumbo was described in reports as "a highly rated jockey of the minor racing tracks from Charles Town, W. Va." Charged with manslaughter, he posted a $1,000 bond, and was ordered to return for a hearing the following month. He got in another car and drove away.

On Monday, September 4, 1950, Palumbo plead guilty to manslaughter by automobile in front of Magistrate J.U. Stanton in Grantville, Maryland. He was fined $500, equal to $5,322.73 in 2020, and his license was revoked. There was no appeal filed. There was no word on when or if his driver's license was reinstated.

It's been estimated Palumbo rode 10,000 horses. He retired in 1965, then worked as a patrol judge at the track. In 1982, the Sons of Italy honored him at the Federico Tesio Dinner in Baltimore. He was inducted into the Charles Town Hall of Fame in 2010. And a race was named in his honor.

Sammy Palumbo was John Servis' godfather. Sylvia's daughter, Laverne, was a friend of Servis, and they both graduated from Jefferson High School, by then fully integrated, in 1976.

John Servis went on to train racehorses and won the Kentucky Derby and the Preakness with Smarty Jones in the spring of 2004. As of

September 2019, his horses had $59 million in earnings in 10,000-plus starts.

John said his father, Joe Servis, came to Charles Town to ride and never left. "My father always said, 'This is where I want to raise my kids.' We lived in a trailer and had a great childhood."

Another brother, Jason Servis, is also a trainer. His horses have won more than $47 million in over 5,000 starts. He won the Kentucky Derby in 2019 with Mary and Gary West's then undefeated Maximum Security, only to watch as the bay colt was disqualified for interference.

Vince "Jimbo" Bracciale, Jr. lived in the trailer next to the Servis family. His mother, Jeanette Bracciale, often cooked large Italian meals for her family as well as the Servis family and others from the track.

Jimbo followed his trainer father, Vince Sr., into the horse business and became a jockey. He rode in local horse shows, worked as a groom, exercised horses in the morning, and started at the small tracks before going off to the big time.

Braccaille became a top jockey and rode the great mare Ruffian. He retired in 1970 after nineteen years. He raced 20,291 horses, with $37.8 million in earnings and 3,545 wins.

Braccaille's neighbor, Joe Servis, won more than 500 races during his twelve-year career as a jockey from 1949 to 1961. Now retired, Servis and his wife, Delores, live in a house on the outskirts of Charles Town. He was born in Philadelphia on August 3, 1931, and grew up there. As a boy, he ran through the streets to ride horses at Juniata Park in the northeast part of the city. "It was a buck an hour," he recalled, "I absolutely loved horses."

At age sixteen, just before his junior year of high school, he managed to get a job walking hots for fifty cents per horse at Garden State in New Jersey. In order to get to the track, he took a train to Second Street in Philadelphia, then hopped on a ferry across the Delaware River, followed by a bus to the end of the line and then a two-mile walk to the track.

Servis eventually came to Virginia to break and gallop young horses and also to the track in Laurel, Maryland. He also went to Camden, South Carolina, where he learned to ride steeplechase horses.

Arriving in Charles Town, he recalled, "When I came here and went through the gap where the Shenandoah and the Potomac meet, I thought I'd died and gone to heaven. It's an awesome site near Harpers Ferry."

Armed with an exercise rider's license, Servis wore a colorful helmet cover so that the stewards could identify him as he galloped and breezed horses in the mornings. He also was required to break some of the horses out of the gate and had to be approved by the starter as being capable to handle that tricky task.

After that, Servis needed the endorsement of a trainer as he worked his way toward his jockey's license. There is no written test for this license, as required for a trainer's license. He passed, of course, and won his first race in 1949, in Cumberland, Maryland, on a horse called Smart Start.

As for Sylvia, Servis recalled that she never gave him specific orders on how to ride. "All the trainers told you about the idiosyncrasies of the horse…'be here at the quarter pole.' But when you left the gate, it was still up to you. It was your horse, you got off good, went on and I tell you a good thing about Charles Town, a key thing. In races that went 6½ furlongs or 7/8 mile, when you hit on the backside, the riders would pull out to make their move.

"I did not necessarily do that. I stayed on the rail because some of them were done. Then you might kick in for a 1/16, but (on the rail) I didn't have to get around other horses and that saved ground."

Jockey Calvin Borel, born in 1966, who won the Kentucky Derby in 2007, 2009 and 2010, frequently used the tactic of skimming the inside rail. His nickname: Calvin Bo-Rail. Long before it became fashionable, Servis rode the rail. "It was a style and you looked who was in front of you. I'd wait until later and wait to see if I could get through or have to go around."

In the sixth race at Charles Town on July 19, 1958, Servis won with a brown gelding named Sparkle Rock for trainer W. H. Edwards and owner Dorothy N. Lee. In the next race, the seventh, Servis was riding for Sylvia on Mr. R.C. in a 1 1/16 mile contest worth $1,500. They finished fifth, five lengths behind the winner.

For jockeys, a horse race is an addictive chess match at warp speed, with a possible big payday at the end. Sylvia's little black book reveals the jockeys of her era earned twenty dollars per ride and ten percent of the first place money. Today, the fee in Charles Town ranges from seventy-five to $100 per ride and ten percent of the purse. In turn, the jockey pays five percent of their take to a personal valet, who organizes the silks to be worn and carries their tack to the paddock.

Servis said he always asked each trainer what idiosyncrasies his mount might have: Did they "lug in," where the horse pulls toward the inside rail? Does the horse prefer to change his lead going into the far turn? At this point, the horses are leading with their right front leg at a gallop, then switch to the left leg to go smoothly and safely around the turn. When they come into the stretch, they go back to the right lead.

"And," Servis added, "don't hit the horse (with a whip) right-handed going into any turn. That was one of my beliefs on any turn."

Their own body weight is always on a jockey's mind. The assigned weight of the rider is dictated by the Jockey Club in New York in coordination with each track. A number of factors are taken into consideration: distance, age of the horse, purse amount and experience of each jockey. Servis started at 107 pounds as an apprentice known as a "bugboy" (because a bug-looking *asterisk is printed after his name in the program).

"As a veteran rider in the mid-1950s, I was doing 115," Servis said, adding that for the races in July 1958, he was at 122. "From the word go, I had to reduce, always."

Roger Hudson started riding races in 1973. Now retired from racing, he works part-time as a card dealer at the Charles Town casino at the track. He and his wife, Carole, live near Harpers Ferry. He remembers the "sweatbox" in the jockey's room and a square toilet (which still exists at some tracks) where the jockeys make themselves vomit, if necessary, to shed a pound or two. Lasix pills help lose water weight. The same drug, known as furosemide, is used on horses to alleviate blood clots that form in the lungs during racing.

In the constant battle on the scales, jockeys of Sylvia's era turned to a laxative called "Pluto Water." Servis recalled the bottle had a red devil on it, and there's even one displayed at the Smithsonian Museum in Washington, D.C. According to Servis, Pluto Water "would flush you out in one day. Clean you out by two or three pounds."

Some riders jogged in a rubber suit, then drove a car with the heat up full blast while still wearing the sweat-inducing get-up. They drove to a nearby fountain and put their head in the water to cool off, but never drank a drop. The results could be a four- to five-pound loss.

One top jockey had the ability to simply flex his stomach muscles to flip an entire meal. Some used capsules to keep their appetite at bay. Black beauties and "speed" were very popular.

Servis quit riding after he suffered a crushed heel in 1960, one of many riding injuries. One day, while taking a horse out to the track, it reared up and jumped. Servis was thrown into a protruding gutter as he came off the horse's "back end" and broke his arm. And, he added, "it seemed like my wife was pregnant every time I got hurt."

Joe Snyder was only twenty-six when he attempted to avoid a collision and fell and fractured his skull in the third race at Charles Town on Wednesday, June 11, 1958. After a two-hour surgery at Johns Hopkins in Baltimore, he died the next day.

Joe Servis, Sammy Palumbo and Patsy Grant-who had all ridden for Sylvia through the years-were among the pallbearers at Snyder's funeral at the Charles Town Presbyterian Church on Monday, June 16. Located in the middle of town on West Washington Street, it was founded by Charles Washington. Snyder's survivors included his wife, Jean, and two sons, five-year-old Steve and sixteen-month-old Bryan.

Hudson broke his pelvis in 1996 at age forty-seven while racing in Abu Dhabi. He had to take four different flights home, accompanied by nurses, and never rode again.

Jessie Davidson, a Hagerstown, Maryland native, had 319 victories in 1965 and was the winningest jock in the United States. He broke his leg in a starting gate accident in November 1958, and returned to ride five months later. He eventually went on to fulfill a lifetime goal to ride in New York, and had some success there.

Joe Servis served as a Charles Town steward for twenty-five years and later was a manager of the Jockeys' Guild. He retired in 1996 and was inducted into the Charles Town Hall of Fame in 2010. Palumbo and Servis maintained a lifetime friendship.

"By knowing horses and saving ground," Palumbo once said, "you can steal a lot of races around here." He was inducted into the track's jockey Hall of Fame in 2008.

"As a developer of saddle talent, Charles Town stands out," Walter Haight of the Washington Post wrote on July 21, 1963. At that time, admission to the grandstand was one dollar, and two dollars for the clubhouse. They also held "Appreciation Days," with multiple give-a-ways of radios and televisions and a grand prize of a Buick Skylark.

"Although usually put in a bracket with the half-milers," Haight wrote, "the six-furlong tracks have been a big league in the caliber of riders sent to the major ovals."

And, finally, consider one last jockey story from Charles Town.

In 1970, thirty-year-old James Thornton was aboard Native Bird in the ninth race, a seven-furlong contest on a rainy night at the track. Along the backstretch, he raised his whip and accidentally struck a nearby five-year-old chestnut mare named Kandi Arm on the nose. They bumped. Kandi

Arm's rider, Dan Gallegos, was tossed and landed in the slop uninjured. As Thornton came off Native Bird, he somehow found himself on Kandi Arm and scrambled into the saddle. They finished sixth.

"I thought I was going down in between them," Thornton, thirty, told Washington Post racing columnist Gerald Strine right after the race. "I just remember reaching out, grabbing a mane, and getting my arms around the other horse's neck. I didn't go under and come up the other side, like some say I did. I was able to pull myself right up on the other horse. I remember I got my feet back in the irons within a sixteenth of a mile."

If either Thornton or Kandi Arm had finished first that night, the win would have been disallowed. Changing horses mid-stream or mid-stretch is not permitted.

"There is a saying at the race track 'Bad Beginning, Worse Ending',"

J.J. Graci wrote.

THE MACHINE

Stewards and judges watch each race for a number of possible jockey infractions: careless riding, permitting the horse to drift in or out and thus impede the path of another horse and rider, interference, and more. No one is immune, evidenced by a June 1964 ruling against Sam Palumbo, then fifty-four, for rough riding. He was suspended for ten days.

In 1970, jockey Kenneth Baker was suspended "for possession of an electrical device." Known as a "machine," it's battery-operated, produces a shock, and has been around tracks nationwide for years. One jockey confessed that he frequently tied a machine into the knot of his reins and would use it well before the finish line.

CHAPTER 25

MILKSHAKES AND GUINNESS

CHARLES TOWN, W.Va, July 1—It is 7 a.m., an hour that comes brutally quick here. Charles Town is a night racing town and the race-track people are obliged daily to somehow transform magically into day people, to shake the dust from their eyes at the first sound of a crowing rooster, and to heck with the traditional eight hours of sack.

- William Gildea, *The Washington Post*, July 2, 1967

When Sylvia was a naive sixteen-year-old and getting her first taste of working at the racetrack, the astounding news in June 1936, was about a horse named Banana. He was found to have been "touched" with a stimulant by his trainer, H. W. Wagely. It might have gone unnoticed had the horse not failed his post-victory saliva test and paid twenty-four dollars for a win ticket. The trainer, along with two other horses under his care, was suspended.

Later that year, trainer Aaron Kayfetz was suspended for sixty days when his charge, Icy Wind, tested positive for a forbidden energizing medication.

The most shocking drug-related case took place in December. As the 1936 season was coming to a close, trainer Jim Hill had been suspended for doping a horse called Jim Moss at Charles Town. The headline in the *Washington Post* read "Colored Trainer Suspended on Doping Charge at Charles Town." A saliva test given to all winners revealed that Jim Moss had been given a dose of the stimulant strychnine. Each winner is taken to a holding area, then known as "the spit box," for a saliva test. Larry Togans, who later became a respected member of the extended racetrack family for his work on horse's teeth, started his career in the post-race testing process.

"He took the test (for Jim Moss) after the race for the saliva," his son, Larry Togans, Jr., recalled. "He sealed it off and it was sent to West Virginia University. He also administered the urine test in which the horses peed in a cup. I helped him pack the gauze in a cup for the test."

Staff writer Walter Haight reported the Jim Moss infraction in two paragraphs in his *Washington Post* report on Sunday, December 13, 1936. The guilty trainer, Jim Hill, was suspended on doping charges. "He was responsible for the horse Jim Moss, a winner here on December 8," Haight wrote. "Stewards recommended that the trainer and horse be suspended for sixty days."

Twenty years later, in June, 1958, trainer John Selby Morris was suspended for six months after his mare, Sun Delores, tested positive by saliva for caffeine.

Meanwhile, forty miles from Charles Town, *Washington Post* White House correspondent Chalmers M. Roberts reported that President Eisenhower and Soviet Premier Nikita S. Khrushchev were in "talks" at the Maryland mountain presidential retreat of Camp David near Catoctin Mountain Park. In the same paper, there was an ad for a "brief little pantie-girdle for figures that need just a bit of firming" for $3.95 from S. Kann Sons & Co.

Fats Domino's "I Want to Walk You Home" was the current hit on the radio as Sylvia greeted some of her horses: Irish Dash, Bill Pack,

Sugar Loch and her beloved Chalkee. They stuck their heads out of the stalls, eager for breakfast. Sylvia was always up as the morning sun rose to prepare for morning training and racing that night.

All Thoroughbreds get a light breakfast on the day of a race. An hour or so later, they are hand-walked around the barn for thirty minutes. Next might come a ninety-minute "ice bath" for the front legs (actually a muck tub filled with ice). Later on race day, all feed and hay is withheld for at least four hours before and after the race in order to reduce metabolic stress on the horse. Temperatures are checked and a bath usually follows. Sylvia feels all four legs for swelling and undue warmth.

Six hours before the published post time, some horses might receive a popular concoction known as a "milk shake." Believed to boost stamina, it's a mixture of sixteen ounces of sodium bicarbonate, water, sugar and electrolytes that is administered through a gastro-nasal tube that delivers the substance directly into the stomach. Sylvia said she added powdered orange-flavored Tang to the mix. Strictly banned since the late 1990s, some trainers nevertheless have tried to administer this formula. They argue that levels established by testing officials are unfair.

Trainers continue to add several tablespoons of sodium bicarbonate (also known as baking soda) into the horse's water or feed as a supplement tonic, despite warnings of it's ineffectiveness and that it can possibly cause cardiac or digestion problems. They also might deliver a "bullet" of bicarbonate, sugar, amino acids and electrolytes down the throat with a dosage gun about five hours prior to race. Many get caught during the testing phase and face suspension and/or a fine.

Zirin Laboratories, based out of Hialeah in Miami, in 1960, used the Australian trainer A. W. Beuzeville for an advertising endorsement of their product, Stamin-Atom. "Zirin products have helped me keep all

Marani Leg Paint

8 oz. phenol
8 oz. Camphor } Blocks Shredded
2 oz. Iodine Crystals
1 oz. Menthol Crystals

Rom 90% 95%
to dissolve

get a good brush that will hold paint plastic brushes will dissolve and never let it soak in paint leave it open to air :—

paint lightly little scrubbing first few days to get it to work then just paint on after that (everyday until a good scuff appears) Then paint as you see it you can miss some days but keep this going until you see good results. keep as much water off area as possible never bandage over this paint.

my horses fit," he said. They also manufactured Dymasol in 1964, for "veterinary external preparation for pain, soreness and inflammation."

All types of drugs are a part of the dark side of racing now. They include strychnine, used more than eighty years ago and now considered a banned Class 1 drug by the Association of Racing Commissioners International. There's the opioid Dermorphin, an extract from the South American tree frog that is forty times more powerful than morphine, and Ractopamine, a banned steroid-type food additive.

Today, trainers are suspended or fined for the use of d-methamphetamine and amphetamine on their horses. For years, there has been support from horse owners, trainers, fans, and even the U.S. Anti-Doping Agency for national legislation to regulate the sport with a horseracing integrity act. Congress has not yet acted.

There is also the issue of horses "bleeding" while racing. Known as EIPH—Exercise Induced Pulmonary Hemorrhaging—fresh red blood regurgitates through the trachea and in acute cases, comes out through the nostrils. Based on age-old remedies shared among trainers to control bleeding, Sylvia fed her horses all parts (leaves, root, flower) of a dandelion or created a dandelion tea as a diuretic, a precursor to the diuretic Lasix, the most popular drug on the racetrack.

In 1964, it was discovered that Northern Dancer, trained by Horatio Luro, won the 1964 Kentucky Derby after receiving a dose of Lasix from Dr. Alex Harthill. Ever since, there has been constant controversy surrounding the use of the drug. Lasix creates dehydration by diminishing stress on blood vessels. It took thirty-one years before the medication became legal, with New York the last state to approve its use.

"Its popularity has no peer among horsemen," according to the Daily Racing Form. In a 2014 piece for ProPublica about Northern Dancer's victory fifty years earlier, racing writer Ryan Goldberg estimated that "at least 95 percent of American racehorses have the drug in their system when they leave the starting gate."

In Sylvia's career, forty years after her many early victories, she saddled With Royalty at Charles Town in a seven-furlong $14,500 allowance race on November 19, 1999. The five-year-old grey mare, owned by her daughter, Laverne, won by two lengths and earned $8,700 under cloudy skies in a seven-furlong allowance race that went off at 9:29 that night. She had been treated with Lasix, just like all the others in the field.

In today's racing world, state-of-the-art post-race testing of blood and urine samples can identify more than 1,500 illegal substances and medications. Each state uses a different technique of testing. "In the meantime, it appears there are certain racing jurisdictions in which it may be easier to get away with cheating than others," Natalie Voss wrote in April 2014 on the Paulick Report.

This ugly underbelly of performance-enhancing drugs in American racing has existed from the time Sylvia started training horses until today. It's a never-ending battle between track workers trying to outsmart the technicians testing urine and blood samples.

Sylvia often used her own concoctions to get the best out of her horses. She fed them wheat germ oil to make their coats shine. In the spring, they were fed flax meal, which encouraged them to shed their long winter coats. Sylvia also spoiled her horses with plenty of peppermint candy, a treat that remains popular. She even sprinkled Jell-O into their feed to strengthen hooves, the same principle that gelatin improves fingernail strength. She ordered supplements, such as the New York-based U.S. Vitamin Corporation's Chevinal, advertised to "set the pace as a source of health-essential vitamins and minerals which are too often deficient in the horse's feed." It came in the form of a syrup or powder.

Helio horse concentrate boasted that it could "Bring out the best in your horse." Based in Detroit, the distributing Gordon Service touted, "Your potential winners need the extra stamina…Try only a half gallon and you will be convinced. Therefore, if your veterinarian, druggist or dealer cannot supply you, order direct. $10.00 per half gallon."

Once in a while, Sylvia also poured a bottle of Guinness in their feed. She thought it encouraged the horses to eat up and also stimulated some horses to sweat more.

Racing writer Natalie Voss gives her horse, Jitterbug, the same Guinness treat from time to time. "It's legal," she wrote in an email. "You'd have to give a 1,000-pound horse an insane amount of alcohol to make him actually drunk, and then it's not like he's going to run faster...…or at least, not in a straight line. So, it's not particularly an issue I've heard about in modern day racing as far as someone trying to influence the outcome of a race."

And yet, consider this April 15, 1950 item from the Associated Press, with a headline that read "Drunken Horse Turns Out as Just Another Masher." According to the story, police in Portsmouth, Virginia, got a call about a horse called Dobbin that had passed out "dead drunk" in a cornfield. His owner said the horse had come across a still and "helped himself to fermenting mash."

The owner declared he was going to shoot Dobbin and concluded, "Any horse that'll go off and get drunk and stay out all night ain't worth nothing anyway."

CHAPTER 26

A LONG SHOT

The gambling known as business looks with austere disfavor upon the business known as gambling.

- Ambrose Bierce (1842-1913)

Showers were expected to pass through Charles Town in the late afternoon of June 26, 1962, as Sylvia ducked under the web stall front to prep a vibrant five-year-old chestnut gelding named Bright Gem for the eighth race. She noticed he'd "cleaned up" his feed, finishing all his breakfast before dawn at 5:46 that morning.

His usual portion of six quarts of pure jockey oats was cut in half—to three quarts—on race day. The hay and water were also taken away, a practice that is no longer utilized because progress in horse nutrition has changed the way of thinking at the track. In the 1960s, trainers believed horses would run better on an empty stomach and be lighter on their feet. Now, research shows that a horse's stomach would produce excess acid, resulting in colic and stomach ulcers.

Sylvia ran her fine hands down his front legs, searching for heat or bumps that could indicate a potential injury. Both hind legs looked like a matching pair of white socks in a height known as "half cannon." She detected no heat, no bumps.

The horse stood still and Sylvia didn't need or want to pay a groom at this time during the pre-race rituals. She checked the horse's temperature using a rectal thermometer, then took him out of the stall for a fifteen-minute hand walk. This was followed by a soapy bath and concluded with a cold hose run over each leg for five minutes. Pre-race procedures might include a standing ice bath for front and/or hind legs or all four, but not today.

A lone orange cat sauntered past in search of a stray mouse or random scraps of food. Most barn cats wander from barn to barn un-named because they never stick around for long. Sylvia went into the tack room to change from her work clothes of blue jeans and sneakers into a smart short sleeve shirtwaist dress and slip-on flats.

At about the same time, car dealer Jack Dempsey Weaver was making his way seventy-plus miles north from Culpeper, Virginia, the better to arrive in Charles Town in plenty of time to wager on the twin double.

According to local historian and writer Donnie Johnston, "Culpeper County, named for Lord Culpeper, an English nobleman, was founded in 1749, with the town, then known as Fairfax, established in 1759. There were a few industries but it was mostly a rural, farming area. Until 1958, flat races had been held every Fourth of July for 80 years at the Culpeper Fairgrounds. There were many local horsemen, including names like breeder Newt Lindsay and trainer Fritz Clatterbuck, who also trained at Charles Town."

Jack D. Weaver usually made the trip to Charles Town five times week, often with his father, Dick C. Weaver, the founder and owner of the town's Buick dealership. They were both stockholders in the Charles Town track and shared not just a love of horses, but a serious (and some might even say dangerous) obsession with gambling.

"The Weaver farm," Johnston noted, "was on the Hazel River on the west side of the county, five or six miles north of Rt. 522 off what is now Old Stillhouse Road. He'd have driven through Sperryville, where there was a Civil War skirmish in 1863, then turned north on Rt. 211/522 to Massie's Corner, where Rt. 522 turns north. Here he'd be following the route General Lee took in June of 1863, over Chester Gap and out of Rappahannock County into Warren County and through Front Royal."

Then Dick Weaver turned onto Rt. 340 at what is still today referred to as "Double Tollgate."

As Weaver rolled along, a roulette wheel of numbers spun through his head. He knew he'd use ten and nine as his winning picks for races five and six. Locking in on his decision had nothing to do with the horses' past performances, nor their names of Side Town and Fair Kicker. Their post-positions dictated his choices. They were his lucky numbers from a previous jackpot he'd won. On this summer day, he planned to bet on the 10 and 9—ten times.

The pending wager required Weaver to arrive at the track in plenty of time to make the multi-faceted bet by picking the winners in races five, six, seven and eight. The top on Weaver's black Buick LeSabre convertible was up as he cruised through the rolling Virginia countryside known as the Piedmont and through the Shenandoah Valley. The predicted rain never came.

There were, and still remain, tattered split-rail snake fences. Alluring dry-stacked stonewalls formed rigid ribbons around cattle and horse fields. Meadows of almost knee-high corn waved in the gentle wind.

Weaver eased on through Boyce and Berryville. Approaching Charles Town, he turned west onto the very same Augustine Avenue where Sylvia would spend the last years of her life.

He walked straight to the betting windows at the track. He glanced down at his notes on the race program. He asked for the 10-9, ten times for the first half of the twin double for races five and six. He wheeled, or combined, all of these horses with the number 7—Weather Lady in the seventh race. Then he added number 5 to win in the eighth race.

10-9-7-5.

After three races, his bet of 10-9-7 was alive going into the eighth race. Weaver couldn't even think about buying a hot dog, though his stomach grumbled with hunger at just after 4 in the afternoon. He paced back and forth, then headed to the rail to watch the race.

Sylvia led the strapping horse named Bright Gem, under her training tutelage for the very first time, out to the paddock for the eighth race. He remained calm, though he had not raced since September 29, 1961, at Atlantic City. He'd been racing four years starting as a two-year-old in 1959, running sixty-five times under a different trainer.

She paused before going in the saddling area to smooth her dress. The track's horse identifier was waiting as she and her charge entered. He curled up the top of the chestnut's lip to check the tattoo number.

Eight horses warmed up for the four-and-a-half-furlong allowance race with a purse of $1,500 for four-year-olds and up. They paraded to the starting gate and were loaded. Sylvia was able to follow the French grey with cerise dots silks that jockey Sammy Palumbo was wearing for this race.

The starting buzzer went off and the gates banged open at 4:45. Valley One was leading at the quarter pole. Mardanherst was first at the top of the stretch and then bolted away from the inside rail suddenly. This created the textbook opening for Sylvia's big chestnut to make it to the finish line first. The newspaper race chart reported the horse had "rallied" to the wire.

And, yes, number five, Bright Gem, trained by Sylvia Bishop, won by half a length. (Mandanherst was disqualified and removed to last for taking second-place Sagitate wide.)

"The big monetary punch was supplied by Bright Gem, owned by

Virginian, M. Tyson Gilpin, which paid $57 in the regular mutuels," Washington Post turf writer Walter Haight reported in the sports section the next day.

Jack Dempsey Weaver, who'd been named for the legendary heavyweight boxing champion Jack Dempsey, knew his numbers. After all, just six months before, on January 24, he'd hit the twin double and took home $17,737.80 for his two dollar bet. On this June afternoon outing, he cashed the only winning ticket—10-9-7-5—on the twin double.

His payoff this time was $10,733.80.

On his way back to Culpeper, Weaver stopped at the Royal Diner just on the south side of the Shenandoah River for a midnight breakfast. It was an old mobile diner setup, and it was a standing tradition among gambling friends that whoever cashed the most winning tickets bought dinner.

Half a century later, Jack Mason Weaver recalled his father and grandfather's wagering roller coaster. When agents with the Internal Revenue Service showed up at their 1,300-acre cattle farm to begin an audit and collect taxes on his 1962 payouts of more than $28,000, the session concluded quickly.

"My father told them he'd bet more than he won to offset the taxes," Weaver recalled. "He went down to the basement and brought up two wooden apple packing boxes and two huge baskets full of losing tickets. And that was that."

This was not the first, nor the last victory Sylvia would produce with Bright Gem for the horse's distinguished and debonair owner, Tyson Gilpin. We'll get to him in a bit.

For his part, Weaver continued to interpret past performances and speak the complicated wagering lingo of win, place, show, daily double, exacta, and wheeling one with the field. He remained a regular at Charles Town's betting windows for years.

Jack Mason Weaver was eleven years old and still remembers that remarkable day when his daddy came home with that $10,000. "I told him I wanted a baseball glove," he said. "I still have it."

Photo by Jennifer Shapiro Fleming

CHAPTER 27

MR. GILPIN

I hope it doesn't make any clients of mine nervous,
but I'd rather lose money in the horse business
than make it by working 9 to 5 doing anything else.

- Tyson Gilpin,
The Washington Post, June 29, 1964

Jack Dempsey Weaver's big night at Charles Town also marked the first time Sylvia saddled and was listed as the trainer for Bright Gem. She beamed with bliss as she walked the horse back to the barn for a bath and long cooling out walk. It was just after six o'clock when she splashed alcohol on his legs and rubbed them with her fine hands. Her brother, Donald Rideoutt, held the horse as she bandaged his legs neat and snug. She made sure the stall was clean and the horse had hay and water.

She walked down the row of stalls, checking Filly Lou, Prime Devil, Bad Penny and Martha's Star. The stalls were filled with bright yellow straw purchased from nearby farms. At this time of year, farmers spent long days cutting hay and straw, which sold for fifty cents per bale.

Sylvia poked her head back in Bright Gem's stall. After a high of seventy-eight degrees, the air was beginning to freshen at sixty-eight. The horse was settled and tranquil. She planned to return later that evening, as the sun set at 8:30, to give him some oats.

Before heading home, Sylvia stopped to look in on Twice Shy, a bay filly also owned by Tyson Gilpin. She glanced up at the almost full moon as she walked through the now quietly peaceful stables.

McGhee Tyson Gilpin had aristocratic good looks, a distinguished demeanor, a profoundly innate knowledge of exceptional equine bloodlines, and an eye for a well-built horse. He was born on September 26, 1919, in a year when the *Washington Post* cost two cents and a twenty-four-ounce double size loaf of Dorsch's "Old Mammy" bread was fourteen cents.

To put the era in some context, Polk Miller's Liver Pills were ten cents and, according to its newspaper ad, had been uses for "50 years without a change," and was good for headache, constipation and malaria. Laundry soap was five cents, brooms fifty-nine cents and metal polish nineteen cents a can. Also, a hog cholera was spreading in Clarke County, Virginia, and nearby Jefferson County, just across the state line in West Virginia.

Tyson grew up near the village of Boyce in Clarke County, only nineteen miles from the Charles Town racetrack. He was only a year older than Sylvia, but was born into a social stratum far above the one she occupied. Eventually, they would meet and uncover a shared love of horse racing.

The county's rocky countryside was home for Tyson Gilpin's entire life. He cherished the wide-open spaces, which were conducive to raising horses. Like the many Thoroughbreds he sold, bred and raced, his own bloodlines were impressive.

His father, Kenneth Newcomer Gilpin (1890-1947), was a member of the Virginia state legislature representing Clarke and Warren counties. His bid for Speaker of the House of Delegates came just as Tyson was born, and a clear majority of the new members of the legislature supported him.

In a three-paragraph editorial, the weekly hometown paper, the Clarke County Courier, published an editorial on Thursday, September 18, 1919: "Mr. Gilpin possesses those qualifications necessary for a good presiding officer. A good presiding officer must be fair; Mr. Gilpin is fair."

Tyson's mother, Isabelle Tyson Gilpin (1894-1983), was frequently referred to as a socialite. She came from a grand family in Knoxville, Tennessee. Her parents were U.S. Senator and Brigadier General Lawrence Davis Tyson and Betty Humes McGhee Tyson. She was a descendant of Charles McGhee and Knoxville founder James White. Those names might ring a bell for anyone who has flown into Knoxville's McGhee Tyson airport.

Kenneth and Isabelle Gilpin lived at Scaleby, in a home designed by Baltimore architect Howard Sill. The cornerstone was laid in July 1909, by Tyson's paternal grandparents, Harriet "Hattie" Newcomer Gilpin, and Henry Brooke Gilpin. Hattie (1861-1942) was the daughter of Benjamin Newcomer, founder of the Atlantic Coastline Railroad.

The stately Scaleby remains as a splendid twenty-room, three-story home. It's finished with handmade bricks that are larger than standard size for

Scaleby, the Gilpin family home in Boyce, Virginia.
Photo Clarke County Historical Association archives.

the exterior facing eighteen-inch walls. The architectural elements include every possible style, from Palladian, French Rococo and Renaissance, with traces of Greek and Roman influence. Interior touches offer examples in the approach of the Adam brothers from Scotland. This estate was named for the Gilpin family British seat in Westmoreland, England. In 2019, it was listed for sale at $22 million, including just over 200 acres.

The estate includes sixteen additional structures, including a gardener's cottage, pump house, stables, garages, tenant house, farm manager's house and more barns. Tyson Gilpin grew up romping through halls with pediment cornices, eating and greeting in formal dining and drawing rooms with imported marble mantles, dentil molding and carved doorways, and dancing under vaulted ceilings. A painting by an ancestor Sawrey Gilpin of a White Horse in a Wooded Landscape hung on the wall and sold at Christie's in New York for $80,000 in May 1981.

After attending a local military school, Tyson went on to the boys boarding school St. Paul's in Concord, New Hampshire, and then to Princeton University in New Jersey. During World War II, he earned the title of Captain in the U.S. Army, Commanding Officer-Military Intelligence Interpreter Team #436, 6th Armored Division. He was wounded in Plouviens, France on August 6, 1944, and later honored with a Silver Star, Purple Heart and French Croix de Guerre.

He married Catharine Ginna Mellick on October 23, 1942, in New Jersey. They shortly returned to his beloved horse country of Virginia and originally lived at Lakeville, a nearby 500-acre farm. They had four children: M. Tyson, Jr. (1943-), Donald (1950-), Lawrence (1956-) and daughter Catharine Drew Gilpin Faust (1947-).

His first son, M. Tyson Gilpin, Jr., a 1965 Princeton graduate, went on to law school at the University of Virginia. He is now an attorney in Winchester, Virginia, not far from where he grew up, and is chairman of the Education Committee of the local chapter of the NAACP. He has a scrapbook filled with photos of his father's horses in the winner's circle, including many with Sylvia. Although he did not have a long-time interest in horses, upon reflection, he finds racing interesting, even intriguing. He also said his father "never saw color."

Daughter Drew became an expert on the Civil War and the American South. As a young girl, "Drewdie" attended the private Blue Ridge Country Day School on sixty-four acres in Boyce. Founded in 1948, it became known as Powhatan in 1957, about the time little Drew was in the nearly all- white primary school. Drew Gilpin Faust, who earned her doctorate at the University of Pennsylvania, went on to become the twenty-eighth president of Harvard University on July 1, 2007, until she stepped down on July 1, 2018. She was the first woman, the first southerner, and the first non-Harvard graduate to occupy that position.

"I was nine years old when news reports about 'massive resistance' and battles over segregation made me realize that it was no accident that my school was all-white," she wrote in the August 2019 issue of The Atlantic magazine. She visited her grandparents at Scaleby and saw that the rear wing was a service and utility expanse, real estate speak for servant area. And all those servants were black and always called by their first names.

In a 2003 interview with Harvard Magazine, Gilpin said when she was born, "a half century after the (seventy-fifth anniversary of the end of the Civil War), the South was still breathing the air of war and defeat. The Lee-Jackson Highway took me to school, ubiquitous Confederate gray historical markers memorialized battles like Cedar Creek, Belle Grove or Bethel and seven small marble slats noted the presence of unnamed Confederate dead just behind my grandfather's grave in the Old Chapel cemetery. I have always known I became a Southern historian because I grew up in that particular time and place."

Three years after the Supreme Court's Brown v. Topeka 1954, Drew Gilpin penned a letter to then-President Dwight Eisenhower. "I am nine years old and I am white," she wrote, "but I have many feelings about segregation." In the letter, she expressed disappointment with the way black Americans were treated and urged the president to make schools more open to minorities. Years later, she told Harvard Magazine in June 2003, that she "also wanted the president to know that even though I was very young, even if I was not among those feeling the force of discrimination, I felt strongly about segregation."

She described her own situation growing up in a "privileged" family in the rural Shenandoah Valley in Clarke County in the 1950s, with a black population of about seventeen percent among 7,000 county residents. She also noted in an August 2019 piece for The Atlantic titled "Carry Me Back," that in her hometown of Millwood, "most African Americans lived in dwellings that lacked running water. This was not the deep south, and I remember no signs designating water fountains or waiting rooms as Colored or White," she said. "But it was a community of rigid racial segregation nonetheless, with lines drawn by custom and common understanding.

"There were separate black and white schools. Such restaurants and other public facilities as existed in the largely rural county were restricted to whites. In our own house, the black cook and handyman had a separate bathroom. When I once used it, my mother reprimanded me for invading their privacy."

While her father served in World War II, her grandfather, Kenneth Gilpin, was elected first president of the Virginia Horsemen's Association in 1941. After five months, the organization went on a hiatus during the war.

After Tyson Gilpin returned home, he soon became a respected voice in the Virginia Thoroughbred business. He was strongly in favor of having big-name stallions as part of the state's equine inventory. This would give the horse industry the necessary status at the large auction venues held each year in Saratoga Springs, New York.

One such sales venue was the Fasig-Tipton Company, an auction agency for horses. Kenneth Gilpin owned the controlling interest, and it was revived by the mid-1940s. Following his father's death in 1947, Tyson took over as president at the tender age of twenty-eight. He then formed a group of Virginia breeders to control the board, and the company flourished. At a meeting held at the Fauquier Springs Club near Warrenton in 1954, Tyson Gilpin was named president of the Virginia Thoroughbred Association, which his father had once led.

Tyson founded the Stallion Station Service Bureau in 1952. It served as an international source for Thoroughbred services and sales. His employees included his British assistant, Tessa Dole, who knew every detail of his business, and later Susie O'Brien. Other expert participants included Peter Pegg, Glenn Petty, John Stuart and Patrick Lawley-Wakelin. And, with the exception of Peter Pegg, who has retired, all the others remain involved in the Thoroughbred industry.

Gilpin's horse, Bright Gem, was foaled in Virginia on April 23, 1957, and sired by a British Stakes winner, Beau Gem, who was brought to the United States to stand at stud. Distinguished equine ancestors included War Admiral, Man o' War, and Hyperion.

Sylvia initially teamed up with Bright Gem for the August 1962 meet at the track in Bel Air, Maryland. As spectators and punters approached the 100-acre track in the afternoon, young boys would be hawking the Baltimore News American or Sun paper on every corner for five cents. Both papers included the lineup for the day with the latest odds and scratches. At the entrance and inside the track, tipsters were selling tout sheets with their own "expert" picks. Priced from twenty-five to fifty cents with names such as the Little Green Card, which was actually a green paper, the favorite horses were listed.

Anywhere from 6,000 to 15,000 racing followers streamed to the half-mile track, which opened in 1870. There was a live trumpeter blowing the "Call to Post" unlike the recording now heard at Charles Town.

Bel Air often was referred to as a "poor man's Saratoga" in reference to the iconic upstate New York track. The grounds of Bel Air resembled Saratoga, with a number of similar white wooden structures. The barns were set on a slope in the woods. There was a steeplechase and turf course and an air of gaiety flooded the environs from the shed row-type barns to the grandstands.

The big difference was that Bel Air was a small track, and the caliber of horses running couldn't come close to the sleek athletes vying for far more money in big-time races like the Travers Stakes.

A D.C. transit bus from the terminal at 1125 Pennsylvania Ave. N.W. offered "modern motor coaches" direct to the track. Reserved seats on the bus were three dollars one way, plus tax, and four dollars roundtrip, plus tax. Buses loaded between 10 a.m. to 11:30 a.m. with a reminder in their advertising that "Post time 1:30 p.m., daily double closes at 1:20 p.m."

Bel Air closed in 1966. The old dirt track is now hidden under layers of cement and asphalt beneath the Harford Mall, which conjures up a memory of a popular 1970s folk song about just such an act.

Bright Gem came in third on July 25 in a six and half-furlong contest with jockey Sam Palumbo riding for the Gilpin-Bishop team. All eyes (and wagering money) at Bel Air were on jockey Larry Reynolds, the fourth leading rider in the country the previous year. He was only twenty-one and had recently purchased a farm in Charles Town.

Reynolds was aboard Miss Nannette in the five-furlong seventh race on August 4, a $2,500 allowance contest. The previous day, Reynolds had won six of the nine races. Miss Nannette was in post-position five and came out of the gate in seventh place.

Jockey Palumbo, aboard Bright Gem, was in post-position four and jumped out fourth. At the 3/16 pole they were in fifth place and remained there at the 3/8 pole and into the stretch. More than 9,000 fans were on hand to watch as Bright Gem passed Monono, then West End Miss and flew past Tea Day. They sailed across the finish line in 59 3/5 seconds, to win by three lengths. A two dollar win bet paid $7.20. Miss Nannette was dead last.

The Palumbo-Gilpin-Bishop team took winnings of $1,625, with ten percent to the trainer, ten percent to the jockey (who was also paid twenty-five dollars for the ride, win or lose) and the rest, $1,300, to the owner. The day's total betting pool of $613,644 was the third highest single day in the twenty-five year history of the track.

Five days later, on August 9, 1962, the same team gathered again as Bright Gem was entered in the eighth race at Bel Air, a $2,500 allowance, this time at a mile.

Spectators studying the odds listed in their newspaper charts likely were also reading about the recent death on August 4 of actress Marilyn Monroe. It had been less than three months since she sang "Happy Birthday, Mr. President" (on May 19, 1962) to President John F. Kennedy at a New York concert.

For the eighth race at Charles Town, five horses stepped into the gate at 4:38 p.m. Palumbo and Bright Gem jumped out of the fourth gate in the $2,500 one-mile race to second place. They led all the way and won by a length. Once again, it was off to the winner's circle and winnings of $1,625, with a new bridle also awarded to Sylvia by the race sponsor. A win ticket was worth $10.40.

During mid-August of 1962, Sylvia took her string of horses to race at Timonium, the next stop on the half-mile circuit. Bad Penny, Martha's Star and Odd Lot all finished out of the money in fifth, sixth, or eighth place during the meet. But Bright Gem finished a respectable third in the eighth race, a seven-furlong contest, on August 18. Palumbo, at 113 pounds, was listed as one pound over. It didn't matter. The total purse was $5,000, with Bright Gem earning $500 for third.

The next stop for the Palumbo-Gilpin-Bishop team was back in Charles Town at the Shenandoah Downs track for the Iron Horse Mile Handicap.

In February 2013, Drew Gilpin Faust spoke at the Library of Congress about her book, *This Republic of Suffering: Death and the American Civil War*, which was the basis for the documentary *Death and The Civil War*, shown on PBS and directed by Ric Burns (brother of fellow filmmaker Ken Burns).

CHAPTER 28

THE WINNER'S CIRCLE

A horse is the projection of peoples' dreams about themselves—
strong, powerful, beautiful—and it has the capability
of giving us escape from our mundane existence.

- Pam Brown, British author

Following Bright Gem's victory in Bel Air, he was entered to race at Timonium on August 18, 1962 and finished third with Sam Palumbo riding once again. It was then decided the horse would be entered in the Iron Horse Mile Handicap at Shenandoah Downs on the Tuesday after Labor Day, September 9.

The race was named in honor of a star horse of the 1950s named Alerted. A winner of 104 races and more than $440,000, his nickname was Iron Horse. Leading up to this big race, Sylvia let Bright Gem have a few days off to walk. On the third day, the big chestnut was taken out for work on the track with an exercise rider for an easy three furlongs. Henry Allen, a clocker for many years at Charles Town, said his time would have been about 37.2 or 37.3 seconds.

While every horse is different to train, there is an accepted routine—walk in the barn, gallop, a walk around the track. Every trainer uses these parts, but each has their own particular order. Sylvia trained her horses according to how they responded to her personal prescription of work sessions along with her observations of their mood. Did they sulk in the stall? Were they frisky and maybe even aggressive toward other horses? She let them speak to her. So, it often was two days of walk, a work, and then another two days off to walk.

This would likely be followed by taking the horse out the next two days with a pony rider, who would lead Bright Gem, with no rider, at an easy canter. For the next two days, Bright Gem went out as the sun came up with a rider to gallop two times around for a total of 1 ½ miles. This is a fairly easy pace of twenty-five to thirty miles per hour, far from the speed in a race of about forty-three miles per hour. Two days before the race, Sylvia instructed the exercise rider to take the horse out on the track and work him hard for 1/8 mile at racing speed.

The day before the race, Bright Gem was hand walked around the shed row of the barn. The bugs were bad at this time of year, and Sylvia had access to the A-M-R bomb for horses approved by the Department of Agriculture. It was hand-pumped through a long metal tube-type nozzle atomizer and sold by Jeter's Saddlery out of Richmond at two dollars per bomb or twenty-one dollars for a dozen.

As the entries closed, Sam Palumbo told Sylvia he would not be riding Bright Gem in the Iron Horse. Instead, he chose to ride Silver Song, a huge grey owned by Dorothy Turner. Trained by former star jockey Patsy Grant, Silver Song previously raced on August 11 and set a track record for 5½ furlongs, followed by another track record on August 19, going six furlongs in 1.10 4/5 seconds.

Disappointing for Sylvia and Mr. Gilpin? Maybe. But they now had the talented and clever rider Carl Gamardella up on five-year-old Bright Gem.

M.TYSON GILPIN-OWNER
SYLVIA A.BISHOP-TR.
1 MILE 1:43

"THE IRON HORSE MILE"
BRIGHT GEM
SHENANDOAH DOWNS SEPT.4,1962

CARL GAMBARDELLA -UP
SACUM   2ND
SILVER SONG   3RD

Photo courtesy of M. Tyson Gilpin, Jr.

Sylvia was awake two hours before sunrise at 6:42 a.m. on Tuesday, September 4, 1962. On a bedside table, a brown fan rocked back and forth, circulating the smell of cigarettes, bourbon and men's cologne from her husband's softly snoring body. He had slipped into bed only an hour earlier.

It had been a rough year for Sylvia and John Bishop, who stayed out late at night working at a nearby nightclub. Laverne, their four-year-old daughter, was tucked into her bed upstairs at 122 South West Street when Sylvia tip-toed down to the kitchen. She was late and needed to get to her Thoroughbred barn to prepare for an important day of racing.

With no time to brew coffee, she grabbed an orange soda from the fridge and slipped out the door, also forgoing her usual toast and poached egg. Wearing work clothes of jeans and sneakers, she carried a madras shirtwaist dress over her arm for a later change. She also grabbed a raincoat and boots, just to be safe.

Only a mile away in Barn E at Shenandoah Downs, Sylvia's half-dozen horses rustled in the straw as they stood up and poked their heads out of their stalls. The familiar barn fragrance of fresh-cut hay with touches of liniment and pine wafted in the air as Sylvia entered the shed row.

"Hey baby," Sylvia said, patting Bright Gem on the nose. She hugged him around the neck, and then, as always, checked his legs for bumps or bruises.

"Hey," said a voice coming from around the end of the shed row, "you were talking to me, weren't you?" one of her grooms asked.

Soon, the sound of mostly early morning silence was broken by the demanding whinnying of horses hungry for their oats. Sylvia headed to the feed room, where a barn cat emerged, stretched, and also begged for breakfast. Every stable has a cat and, hence, no mice.

The tiny feed room doubled as a tack room. Bridles, leather lead shanks and blinkers hung on a tack hook in one corner; several buckets were stacked up along the wall. On top of a desk, a calendar featured notes on the training schedule of the various horses—walk a half hour, gallop half mile, gallop three-quarters mile and walk twenty minutes. A bill from the Purina feed store was tacked above the desk. The previous balance was $53.58, plus two bales of hay for $10.00, three bags of oats at $15.75. In red pencil below the total of $99.36, there was a note from the feed store: MAIL CHECK PLEASE BEFORE FURTHER ORDERS ARE DELIVERED. It was underlined twice.

Alongside leg wraps and blankets, a lone burlap bag with large black print announced "Jockey Oats-Special Quality for Thoroughbreds." As she easily lifted the bag, Sylvia declared, "Oh dear," of the unusual lightness of what had started out as a fifty-pound bag. Looking inside, she calculated there would be just enough oats for the rest of the day and maybe tomorrow morning.

On the other side of the barn, Ray Charles' velvet baritone voice crooned "I can't stop loving you," the current soul hit, from a radio. Sylvia began filling each galvanized steel feeding tub with two quarts of oats. The daily customs and rituals in a racing barn have not changed much over many decades, even generations. A visitor can walk into a barn at Gulfstream Park, Aqueduct, or Keeneland, and it's still the same old routine. Once the horses are fed, the water buckets (two in each stall) are scrubbed clean using a strong pine disinfectant called Kreso (now known as Kreso-D), then rinsed several times and refilled. Sylvia carried two full fifty-pound buckets to each horse. A hose is rarely used to fill water buckets in the stalls at the track. There is far too much opportunity for a horse to get tangled up and injured as he walks past.

As the horses finish their oats, which horsemen everywhere refer to as "cleaning up," the stalls are mucked out. Brother Bobby started in the first stall, while Sylvia went to work in the second. A bulky section of burlap is laid on the ground in front of the stall as the manure and soiled straw is piled in the middle. It's hand-carried outside to a collection area, then hauled out by truck later in the day. Before the sun even came over the horizon, Sylvia's white Keds were soaked in wet brown glop.

Before cleaning out Bright Gem's stall, Sylvia removed the white bandages that had been on all four legs all night. Kneeling down and talking to the five-year-old, she gently unwound each outer flannel before removing the thick inner cotton padding.

"There, there now baby," she quietly whispered to the horse. He turned and looked, then put his head down to sniff the straw. Horses not only remember but respond to people who have treated them in a positive manner. According to Carol Sankey, an animal behavior expert at the University of Rennes in France, a horse's attachment with a trainer or caretaker very clearly depends on how they're treated.

"Horses can be very forgiving," Jill Starr, founder of Lifesavers Wilde Horse Rescue of Lancaster, California, told Discovery News, "but they never forget."

Still on her knees, Sylvia took her right hand and put her palm on each front knee of the chestnut gelding to check for any unusual heat, which might indicate inflammation. "Uh-huh," she declared when no problems were apparent.

"The people who train horses do it because they're born into it, or they just love it," said D.W. Fries, who knew Sylvia as he was growing up in Charles Town and is now an assistant trainer based in Kentucky and Florida. "Sylvia loved it. She had a way with horses, a very special, natural way with horses.

"I'm not big on the term 'horse whisperers'. But she could watch a horse walk in front of the vet and the vet wouldn't really know what was wrong with it. Sylvia would be sitting on a chair at the end of the shed row. She'd watch and then she'd tell the owner which way they should go with that horse," Fries said. "She knew more than the vet did. The vet would say they thought the horse might be a little off on the foot. Sylvia would say, 'If you want to fix that horse, you need to go higher up' (meaning the problem could be in the shoulder). You don't see that much anymore."

Sylvia closed her eyes as her slender fingers made their way down the back of each front leg, exploring the tendons for lesions and caressing the ankles for possible swelling. She repeated the process on the rear legs, stood up, and patted the horse on the rump.

Each horse was then given two "flakes" (a four-inch wedge) of hay, which in 1962, cost fifty cents a bale. The cheap price of hay in Charles Town was noted in a 1962 Time magazine piece. The track was "a haven for penny-wise trainers (hay costs only fifty cents a bale, vs. $2.40 in Florida)." Between the cost of oats at $5.25 for a fifty-pound sack, medications and other supplies, Sylvia had very little budget for extra help to clean stalls and prepare horses for the races. If her horse won some money, she could pay her brother. If not, he would wait until next time.

The weather forecast interrupted Ray Charles on the radio… temperatures hovering in the mid-seventies and no rain, always a good thing. A sloppy track is a nightmare for most horses, and Bright Gem was no exception. Sylvia lit an L&M cigarette; sometimes it was a Winston.

She set about the pre-race routine with little exchange of words. Bobby went to the back of the track kitchen to get some coffee. He also bought two hot dogs at $1.60 each for a late afternoon lunch for he and his sister. If they had time and wanted to sit down at the kitchen for a proper breakfast or lunch, it would have been in a segregated area. On this special day, there was no time to linger.

Bright Gem's front legs were placed inside a large tub which then was filled with the ice. For the next two hours, Bright Gem stood in the ice while Sylvia stroked his head and patted him on the neck.

"You don't have to be crazy to do this," she once said of her life as a horse trainer. "But it helps."

As race time approached, Bobby brushed and groomed the horse.

Hattie and Henry Gilpin were among those contributing $17,500 during early 1912 when the Norfolk & Western Railway announced that it would replace the thirty-three year-old wooden station in Boyce, Virginia, near their home.

Hattie Gilpin preferred the stylish stucco appearance. The renovated depot included platform access to the white men's room. Additional touches included central heating and electric lighting in the expansive waiting room for the whites, but not in the twelve by twenty-four foot colored waiting room.

The Gilpin family horses were shipped to and from Boyce, pegging it as a "fancy stock" origin and destination.

Then he bent down at the back legs and put on elasticized bandages that covered the legs from halfway down to just below the ankle. Known as "run downs," the wraps protect the horse's legs from cuts and scrapes during the race, especially on the rear ankle.

The barn pigeons cooed and flapped their wings from the barn rafters as Sylvia administered a tube of glycerin and peppermint oil down the horse's throat. "It soothes the throat and opens the airway," explained Billy Bush, a horse trainer who worked for Sylvia. "She bought the peppermint at the pharmacy and mixed it. I don't know how much she used, but it sure made sense."

Bobby opened a bottle of Tuttles Elexer and rubbed it over the horse's back to relax his muscles. Once Bobby had put the D-snaffle bit and bridle on the horse, he led him out of the stall. Sylvia stepped inside quickly and changed into a smart-looking shirtwaist dress and sensible loafers. She walked out looking more like Donna Reed, a popular actress portraying a housewife on a hit 1960s television series, than a rumpled horse trainer.

As they approached the racetrack, a sudden lashing thunderstorm erupted, and 3,200 fans sought shelter from the pelting rain. No bug bomb was needed on this day. Fortunately, just as the first race began at 7:21 p.m., the weather cleared. The track was officially declared sloppy and Bobby tied Bright Gem's tail into a neat knot called a "mud tail." Sylvia grabbed her raincoat and mud boots.

She had also saddled Bad Penny for owner Ed Stephenson in the seventh race and ironically, Sam Palumbo was the rider for the one-mile starter-allowance for three-year-olds and up. The purse was $2,000, but it didn't matter; Palumbo and Bad Penny finished fifth.

The Morning Telegraph trackman had Bright Gem picked for third place in the featured eighth race Iron Horse scheduled to go off at 10:14 p.m. Six horses were in the field, with Bright Gem in the sixth slot. He was quickly running fourth at the first call, with Silver Song in first place by a head. It didn't last very long. With a quick burst, Bright Gem shot up to first place, then stretched to a five-length lead over Silver Song in second. At the finish, Bright Gem won by a whopping eight lengths in a time of 1:43 for the mile. Silver Song was third.

Tyson Gilpin, in an immaculately pressed and spotless sports jacket, joined a mud-spattered Sylvia in her raincoat and boots covered with dirty sludge. Bright Gem was in the winner's circle. His sons, Tyson Jr. and Donald, along with other friends, were all smiles. Carl Gambardella was oblivious to the muck all around.

Sylvia beamed as she accepted the trophy from Hall of Fame jockey Eddie Arcaro for the biggest win of her career. A two dollar win ticket on Bright Gem paid twenty-one dollars, and the Twin Double was worth $737. It's not known whether Culpeper gambler Jack Dempsey Weaver had another winning ticket.

We do know this: a photo in the Spirit of Jefferson newspaper the following Thursday, September 6, had a photo of Silver Song, who finished third. The headline read: "Silver Song Found Distance Too Long in Iron Horse Mile at Shenandoah Downs." The thirteen-line caption mentioned Silver Song's owner and trainer and, only in passing, mentioned that Bright Gem had won. And so sadly, but clearly a sign of the times, there was no mention of Bright Gem's trainer. Nor was there a photo of Sylvia Bishop in the winner's circle, or anywhere else.

Bright Gem raced four times following that victory, finishing first at Pimlico at 1 1/16 in a $5,000 claiming race against twelve other horses on November 27, 1962. He paid thirty-four dollars for a two dollar win bet. A year later, he ran second in Charles Town in May, was second again in June, and finished a weak sixth that July. Bright Gem was shipped to Laurel in Maryland on August 19, 1963, where he won a 6½-furlong race with a $2,500 purse. There was just one hitch. It was a $5,000 claiming race, and when the races were over, Bright Gem had a new owner.

Tyson Gilpin's wife, Catharine, died on New Year's Eve in 1966 at age forty-eight.

On November 5, 1977, Tyson Gilpin married Hortencia "Tencha" Mesa Heard. They also lived at the 500-acre Lakeville Farm along the meandering Shenandoah River in Clarke County. He rode to hounds with the Blue Ridge Hunt and started a new business called the Stallion Service Bureau, advising clients in the Thoroughbred industry.

In 2000, he was elected president of the Virginia chapter of the Horsemen's Benevolent and Protective Association. In 1968, the Virginia legislature gave counties the option of pari-mutuel racing. A year later, five counties voted to permit such racing. The first track, Colonial Downs, was built in New Kent County and opened in September 1, 1997.

A reporter once asked Tyson his secret to longevity. "Cigars and whiskey," he answered, then added, "What else could it be?" On May 7, 2000, Tyson Gilpin, Sr. died. He was eighty.

On August 10, 2019, M. Tyson Gilpin, Jr. presented the trophy to a group from Eagle Point Farm, owners of What The Beep, winner of the $100,000 M. Tyson Gilpin Stakes at Colonial Downs. It seemed only fitting because the winning trainer was a woman, Karen Dennehy Godsey, as was the jockey, Forest Boyce. Tyson Gilpin, Jr., in a summer suit very much like his father often wore, had binoculars around his neck. He bears a strong resemblance to his father, who would have been very pleased to see his son in the winner's circle.

CHAPTER 29

MR. GILPIN'S OTHER HORSES

Marry me and I'll never look at another horse.
- Groucho Marx (1890-1977)

Sylvia and John Bishop separated in 1963. "We reached a point where we weren't getting along," John Bishop recalled. "She told me she wanted to separate and I left. I would go by and tuck Laverne in and lay down until she went to sleep. She would hold my thumb and she held on hard and she cried.

"The building on South West Street where we ran Payne's Tap Room was meant to be a black hotel. Sylvia had a fear that I might cause problems and I could have sued her for the business. I decided to be friendly because of the child. There was no more romance and I'm that type of person."

John Bishop rented a house trailer near the racetrack and stayed close to his old home. He began to travel to big fairs from New Jersey to Florida with his entertainment business. He eventually remarried, moved to Maryland and kept in touch with Laverne.

For her part, Sylvia continued to train for many owners, including some of the other horses owned by Tyson Gilpin, Sr.

Odd Lot, a chestnut horse, was bred by Tyson Gilpin. He foaled in May 22, 1958, by Double Eclipse out of Market Day. He ran 121 times between 1961 and 1969. He began racing with Sylvia and Gilpin and was claimed away in 1963. His career concluded with twenty-nine wins and a total of $35,626 in lifetime earnings.

His 121 starts are way above average by today's standards. According to Allan Carter, longtime historian at the National Museum of Racing in Saratoga Springs, N.Y., "If a horse runs forty times, it's a lot today and in the last twenty years."

Tea Tray, a chestnut bred by the Gilpin family at Kentmere Farm in Millwood, Virginia, foaled May 21, 1959 by Your Host out of Fussbutton. He began his career as a two-year-old with Sylvia and won his first race on December 29, 1961. Tea Tray brought home $780 in the 4½-furlong outing. The charts reported: "Tea Tray set the pace under strong pressure to the stretch while along the outside and drew off in the drive." He finished his first year with $960 in winnings. In 1962, he traveled north to Garden State and Monmouth Park and was claimed for $4,000 in a six furlong race on July 5, 1962, by C.E. Stable, with trainer P. Scalcione.

Photos courtesy of M. Tyson Gilpin, Jr.

Twice Shy was a bay mare bred by the Gilpin family at Kentmere Farm in Millwood, Virginia. She was foaled April 17, 1959, by Double Eclipse out of Damaged Goods. The mare first raced with another trainer at Belmont in New York and one description of the race on October 3, 1961, reported that "Twice Shy showed nothing." On October 17, 1961, at Aqueduct, Twice Shy ran last in a field of fourteen and "was unable to enter serious contention." She raced four times in 1961 with no winnings.

Just after the new year in 1962, Gilpin brought Twice Shy back home to run under Sylvia's tutelage. They won at Charles Town with Sam Palumbo riding on January 4, 1962. A two dollar win ticket paid $25.20, and it was noted in the Washington Post that, "A parade of long shots dominated the program, with the result there were no twin double tickets sold on M. Tyson Gilpin's Twice Shy." The bay filly, who loved to lean her head against Sylvia's shoulder in the stables, won again on Tuesday, January 16, 1962, with jockey Raymond Arduini. In the larger world, it also was the same day that it was announced in Rome that actress Elizabeth Taylor and her then husband, singer Eddie Fisher, had adopted a one-year-old orphan girl named Maria.

Twice Shy traveled to run in Bowie and Laurel in Maryland with respectable placings. In mid-October of 1962, she was claimed for $5,5000 at Garden State Park by Mr. and Mrs. H.M. Harris, using Arnold Winick as trainer. She had fifty-three lifetime starts, with seven victories and $19,825 in earnings.

Wounded Knee won a one mile at Shenandoah Downs on March 30, 1966, with C.C. Smith as the jockey. Tyson Gilpin, Jr. was in the winner's circle with Sylvia in hat and coat. On August 11, 1966, Wounded Knee won a 1 1/16 mile race at Shenandoah Downs. Carl Gambardella was the jockey. Don Gilpin, the second son of Mr. Gilpin, represented the family with Dr. Dan Madden, a veterinarian from Charles Town.

In Hock was a brown horse foaled on April 3, 1958, bred in Michigan by Mrs. William O. Bridge by Gold Note out of a mare called In. He had an astounding number of starts—103—and was initially owned and trained by E. J. Hillman throughout 1964. He won on April 20, 1964, at Gulfstream Park in Hallandale, Florida, where the temperature was a balmy seventy-eight degrees. He ran again at Hialeah Park with little success, and by 1965, he was owned by Tyson Gilpin. In 1966, Gilpin was still the owner and Sylvia was listed as the trainer. She won four straight races with In Hock at Charles Town, including June 11, a seven-furlong claiming for $1,600; Donald Gilpin and his school friend John Stuart were there to pose for a win photo. John Stuart went on in 1981 to become a co-owner of Bluegrass Thoroughbred Services as an agent and advisor in all aspects of breeding and racing. On June 22, In Hock won a six and a half furlong claiming for $2,250 and was described in the race chart as "easily the best"; on July 13, in a six and a half furlong contest at $2,500, he won with a "brisk drive," and Gilpin was pictured with sons Donald and Lawrence in the winner's circle. He won again on July 21 in a $1,250 allowance race at seven furlongs. The charts said In Hock "kept to pressure" for the victory, and his owner, Virginia gentleman Tyson Gilpin, was front and center for the victory presentation.

By 1967, In Hock, now age nine, was listed as owned by Sylvia. He had seventeen starts that year, won once and was second once with a total of $1,400 in winnings. His last race was on December 1, 1967, at Shenandoah Downs, when he finished seventh.

The bay horse Dancing Ghost, foaled in Kentucky on March 2, 1963, was by Gray Phantom by Prom Queen. He began running in early 1966, and was owned by Mrs. A. Lowenthal and trained by J. B. Bond. He became part of the Gilpin/Sylvia team in August of 1966. In a five and half furlong race at Shenandoah Downs on September 3, he won with jockey C.C. Smith and paid $31.20. Sylvia's nephew Skeets Holland, Jr. remembered it well: "It was a big payoff and I felt like I had paper money."

CIVIL RIGHTS TIMELINE

July 2, 1964: President Lyndon B. Johnson signs the Civil Rights Act of 1964 into law, preventing employment discrimination due to race, color, sex, religion or national origin. Title VII of the Act establishes the U.S. Equal Employment Opportunity Commission (EEOC) to help prevent workplace discrimination. And, on August 6, 1965: President Johnson signs the Voting Rights Act of 1965 to prevent the use of literacy tests as a voting requirement. It also allowed federal examiners to review voter qualifications and federal observers to monitor polling places.

CHAPTER 30

THEY SHOOT HORSES, DON'T THEY?

There was a short, sharp sound and the colt toppled onto his left side, his eyes staring, his legs straight out, the free legs quivering.

- W. C. Heinz, The New York Sun, July 29, 1949

With the high of the winner's circle also comes the distressing low of reality when a horse is injured and damaged beyond repair. "I had a horse break a leg at the 3/8 pole," Sylvia recalled. "And all my money went up in smoke."

Such was the case in Charles Town on the showery evening of February 29, 2012, for Sharp Beauty, a four-year-old bay mare ridden by Carlos Marrero.

Trained by Leslie J. Frost and owned by James Schlehr, the mare was bred by WinStar Farm in Lexington, Kentucky, by Sharp Humor out of Call Me Chief by Chief Seattle. She was purchased at auction as a two-year-old for $4,500.

This was the twelfth race of the mare's career, a $28,000 allowance for fillies and mares four-years-old and up which have never won a race other than maiden, claiming or starter, or which have never won two races.

Eight horses left the starting gate for the four and one half furlong contest at 10:33 p.m. The track was listed as sloppy.

As the field entered the far turn, Sharp Beauty broke down, triggering a horrific seven-horse pile up. One jockey was hospitalized overnight. The remaining six, including Marrero, "were able to walk away at some point" following the accident, according to reports.

Danny Wright, a former jockey and chief steward at the time, issued a statement: "Let me make it clear. This was not an issue of the track condition causing an accident. This was a horse breaking down during the race that unfortunately took the field with them."

Before it was all over, Sharp Beauty faced the agonizing situation referred to as "putting a horse down." In veterinarian speak, it's known as "euthanasia," an ancient word of Greek origin meaning "good (eu) death (thanatos)." The intention: end all suffering of the horse. "It's a process that combines compassion and scientific consideration while providing each animal with a death that is free of pain and stress," according to the Humane Society of the United States.

When Sylvia began training horses in the 1950s, euthanasia was accomplished with a bell-shaped gun placed between the horse's eyes on the forehead. At the moment of execution, one attendant rang a bell with a hammer as another pulled the trigger.

At the racetrack in Charles Town today, a team of West Virginia state veterinarians supervises all aspects of safety and welfare concerning every horse scheduled to race. They go to the stable area the morning of the race to observe them walking and jogging to make sure they are sound. They palpitate the horse's joints and discuss training and fitness to make sure the horses are prepared to race. About eighty percent of the horses entered are stabled at the track; the other twenty percent are shipped in from remote farms and training facilities and must be on the grounds four and a half hours before their race.

Artwork by Crowell Hadden

Dr. Jay Joyce, who is in private practice at Total Equine Veterinary Associates in Leesburg, Virginia, is one of several vets working under contract for the state several times a month. The races take place at night under the lights at Charles Town. As the horses are led into the saddling area, Joyce pays close attention. "Scratches can be from a horse flipping while saddled, spooking, sitting down, losing balance or bleeding in any way or some type of lameness," Joyce said.

As the horses step on to the track for the pre-race warm-up, Joyce again watches intently. A U.S. Naval Academy graduate, he served in the military for nine years and later went to the University of Maryland to complete prerequisites for vet school. He was accepted into eleven schools and graduated with honors from the University of California-Davis School of

Veterinary Medicine. In addition, he spent three months in South Africa conducting research on tuberculosis in buffalo, lions, kudos and zebras before settling down in Virginia.

As the horses approach the starting gate in Charles Town one chilly autumn evening, Joyce is nearby. At that point, he can immediately order a horse to be scratched if deemed unfit, unsound and not ready to race.

If a horse breaks down while racing and has no chance of a recovery, he's put down. Horse people never use the term "put to sleep," words parents are told to avoid with their young children because they create anxiety. Dr. Joyce has the necessary medications in his customized truck "if something bad happens." He also has a phone list handy to quickly consult with the owner or trainer.

In most cases, a screen is put up to offer privacy if the injured horse is on the track and cannot be moved by horse ambulance.

Administration of a strong sedative of xylazine is the first step. Within thirty seconds, the horse is heavily sedated and loses awareness. This is followed by a lethal dose of sodium phenobarbital and succinylcholine given intravenously. This combination stops the heart immediately, invades the brain, and halts all vital functions. The death is painless, swift and humane.

The attending veterinarian checks with his stethoscope to be sure there is no heartbeat. Final gasps and muscle twitches are reflexive, because the horse has already died. What seems like a last breath is not; the horse has expired.

In Charles Town, one former administrative employee recalled driving home during the 1970s late at night and passing a spot known as the "rake yard," where horse corpses from the track are piled each night. Some trainers say this practice still exists.

The final destination of the body could be a rendering plant or an approved facility for discarded remains. Burial is not possible due to restrictions regarding rural water tables. Reporter Demmie Stathoplos addressed the notion of putting a horse down at Charles Town in a March 13, 1978 Sports Illustrated article. At the crucial moment of decision, the piece suggested anyone involved with race horses "might consider the time it takes to travel the short distance to Front Royal, Virginia, thirty miles away-where one of the major industries is a glue factory."

Safety measures in horse racing grew exponentially in 2018 and 2019 as a result of a dramatic spike in injuries at Santa Anita in California, which resulted in dozens of deaths by euthanasia at the track. The possible cause was attributed to poor footing and a push by some trainers to maximize winnings. Add to this management decisions at many tracks nationwide to schedule more races with larger fields, the better to encourage more wagering and create higher profits. This, in turn, "puts intense pressure on trainers to race horses that may not have had enough rest (between races) or been in the proper condition," according to a story by New York Times reporters Joe Drape and Corina Knoll in June 2019. In the wake of the Santa Anita surge as well as an uptick in deaths at several other tracks, numerous oversight committees were formed and new regulations were put in place.

Obtaining statistics on horse injuries and deaths at racetracks around the country is not easy. It's up to each track to reveal those numbers, and very few participate. The Washington, D.C.-based NBC4 television station did an investigation during the period of 2014 through August 2016. Their report concluded that, "More than 160 thoroughbred racehorses have died from injuries suffered before, during or after race days at Charles Town." One reason for that high number is likely caused by the track's 220 days of racing a year, far more than other tracks. A 2018 report gave the number of deaths at Charles Town as sixty.

Although veterinary medicine has moved away from the bell-shaped gun, some horsemen still prefer it. "It's fast and simple," said Andi Gilman, a horsewoman from Virginia. She added, however, that she would never pull the trigger, but would give permission for someone else to do it. Ironically, her uncle, Dr. Manny Gilman, a veterinarian with the New York Racing Association, participated in a 1949 euthanasia at Aqueduct. The horse, Air Lift, was a two-year-old full brother to the 1946 Triple Crown winner Assault.

Obviously, the euthanizing process for these majestic Thoroughbreds is excruciating for owners, trainers and jockeys. Sadly, as the saying goes, in many cases, these horses either win or die trying.

SHARP BEAUTY'S LAST RACE

MISS FIFTY was a bit rank at the start, advanced inside to force the pace down the backstretch, checked sharply to avoid the spill entering the far turn and was the only horse to not lose her rider. IDEAL THOUGHTS stumbled badly at the start, trailed outside down the backstretch and lost her rider avoiding the spill entering the turn. LIL MISS JANE fell over a fallen rival near the quarter pole and walked off. SPUNKETTE fell over a fallen rival near the quarter pole and walked off. SHINE FOR ME fell over a fallen rival near the quarter pole and walked off. PAGE'S PROMISE fell over a fallen rival near the quarter pole and walked off with cuts in her left front leg and left stifle. SIMSATIONAL pressed the pace two wide, fell over a fallen rival near the quarter pole and walked off. SHARP BEAUTY set the pace off the rail and broke down near the quarter pole, causing a chain reaction that left just one horse with a rider still aboard. The Stewards posted the inquiry sign before declaring the race official.

-Equibase

CHAPTER 31

A WEAVER, A PUDDLE JUMPER, A CRIBBER AND OTHERS

Attorney General Robert Kennedy told a crowd gathered at the Justice Building that the current administration, led by his brother President John F. Kennedy had made great strides working for Civil Rights. But, he added, "there is still a long way to go."

- The *Washington Post*, June 15, 1963

In the summer of 1963, more than 3,000 protesters assembled in Washington for a civil rights demonstration. The Washington Post described it as "one of the most restrained and friendly protest marches in history." The mostly black group gathered across the street from the White House at Lafayette Square, then marched east on Pennsylvania Avenue to the Department of Justice building. Civil rights leaders Rev. E. Franklin Jackson, president of the D.C. branch of the National Association for the Advancement of Colored People, Rev. Walter E. Fauntroy and Rev. Smallwood E. Williams of the Southern Christian Leadership Conference, as well as Rep. Charles C. Diggs, Jr. (D-Michigan) and C. Summer Stone, editor of the Washington Afro-American newspaper, were in attendance. Attorney General Robert Kennedy spoke to the crowd at the Justice building on Friday, June 14.

Meanwhile, sixty miles away, it was a clear afternoon at the Charles

Town racetrack. Sylvia had her eyes fixed on the nine horses in the sixth race as they loaded into the starting gate at 3:41 p.m. The seven-furlong race for four-year-olds and up had a purse of $1,000. She was particularly interested in a horse named Theresher in post-position one. The six-year-old chestnut mare, owned and trained by Anthony T. Allen, was the frontrunner most of the way and won by three and a half lengths.

The horses and riders returned to the front of the grandstand to check in with officials at the scale house. As jockey C.C. Smith stepped on the scales to weigh in, he was four pounds over, but it didn't matter. William Bushong, one of Sylvia's best customers, had already paid $1,200 to claim the mare for Sylvia to train. They were off to a good start.

Maybe.

When Sylvia and Bushong were considering claiming the mare, they examined the racing charts and scrutinized the results. They watched other horses in the races against the chestnut mare and kept an eye out on her morning workouts.

But it's not always possible to learn all a horse's quirks and kinks before making a claim. It's all about their idiosyncrasies and how to deal with them. For Sylvia, all it took was a walk back to the barn following that successful claim to discover Theresher had equine obsessive compulsive behavior. The mare immediately started to weave back and forth in her new stall in a fit of fret. She was what's called "a weaver."

A weaver sways constantly from side to side, typically while at the stall door looking out. Some attribute this quirk to boredom, others point to a genetic predisposition. Through many generations, horse owners have tried various distractions, from introducing a companion such as a goat or chicken, putting a ball on a rope to play with, and even a plastic mirror. Not much works.

This disturbing trait did not influence Sylvia's results with Theresher. Whenever she passed the stall, she'd pat the mare on the neck and reassure her in her gentle voice. Although her weaving never ceased, Sylvia's patience paid off.

The mare ran again four days after being claimed and finished second, earning $320. On July 3, Theresher finished third and earned $120, then ran second on July 11 for $280. A week later, the mare was out of the money, only to come back on July 26 to show for third and $130.

By August 9, Theresher won by a neck in a one-mile starter allowance earning $975 and paying $28.20 for a two dollar win ticket. Ten days later, Theresher won again. This time, there was an objection to her victory, which was disallowed. First place money of $875 brought her earnings with Sylvia to $2,700 within nine weeks, more than double her claiming price of $1,200.

One newspaper noted: "On a track turned sloppy by the hardest rains of the season, William L. Bushong's Thresher scored a front-running half-length victory over Rose Alley's Storr while Red Kent's Whitehead finished third."

Sylvia's Spring was a bay mare foaled on February 23, 1959, in New York, and was sent to Sylvia's stable in Charles Town in May 1963.

In her second outing under Sylvia's training, the bay mare, now four-years-old, won "driving" on a clear afternoon on a fast track, paying $36.40 for a two dollar bet.

The key to success on this day was a "clear" and "fast track," because this mare had an aversion to puddles. That presents another tricky problem. Many trainers say it's simply because the horse can't see the bottom of the puddle, or fear its reflection. Re-training entails months of gradual, gentle urging to put one foot in the puddle, hoping the rest will follow. At least one trainer said that vision problems are likely the most overlooked flaw.

Whatever the case, this bay mare refused to walk in or even near a puddle and never won on a sloppy track. Toward the end of her career, the horse once owned by New York investment banker James S. Abrams, Jr., was listed as owned by Middleburg horseman Roger Dodson. And, when Sylvia's Spring came across the finish line first on April 24, 1964...it was a clear evening at Charles Town over a fast track, no puddles included.

Wounded Knee was bred and born in 1961 at Kentmere, the Virginia estate of Tyson Gilpin, Sylvia's long-time client. Sylvia began training the horse in early September 1964. It did not take long for her to recognize this horse was a "cribber," who relentlessly grabbed the edge of the stall door or fence and sucked in air. This is not the worst habit a horse can have but, like a weaver, it's annoying and distracts from a tranquil atmosphere for the horse in question and others in adjoining stalls. It does not affect a horse's ability to run, and win.

Old cribbing remedies have included boiling down red pepper pods and spreading the concentrate on the fences or stall doors. Some owners and trainers believed that filing spaces between the horse's teeth can prevent the habit. French horsemen developed a spiked throat strap that was effective, and in the U.S., a similar throat latch with tacks has been put to use.

Sylvia fed the horse from a bucket on the ground instead of a built-in wooden feed tub, because horses will not crib on anything lower than their knees. Over the two years Wounded Knee was under Sylvia's training, he had twenty-six starts and won three.

In Hock also was owned by Tyson Gilpin. In 1966, the handsome eight-year-old brown horse started the year slowly in ten races, finishing second or third or just out of the money until he won four straight races on June 11, June 22, July 13, and again on July 21.

Not many horses are capable of racing four times within five weeks, much less winning each time out. Horses now run about once every four or five weeks. But Sylvia found the key to the winner's circle with In Hock. His four straight victories qualified him as a racetrack "streaker."

Dancing Ghost was a bay horse foaled March 2, 1963. His sire, Gray Phantom, foaled in 1953, had an impressive career, with eighty-nine starts and respectable earnings of $130,830. He won several big Florida races, including the Coral Gables Handicap, Ponce de Leon Handicap and the Robert E. Lee Handicap at Tropical Park as a four-year-old. He was bred by Kentucky-based Wheatley Stables, which produced many storied champions (Bold Ruler, Man o' War, Seabiscuit, and Bold Ruler). It was founded in 1926 by Gladys Mills Phipps and her brother, Ogden Livingston Mills.

Dancing Ghost began racing as a two-year-old at Garden State Park in Cherry Hill, New Jersey. This put him against strong horses. He failed to win his two starts that year. As a three-year-old in 1966, Dancing Ghost ran twenty-one times, winning several times at Pimlico, Bowie and Delaware Park. However, halfway through the year, negative comments creeped into racing charts—"no threat," or "tired," or "trailed far back."

When Dancing Ghost arrived in West Virginia in August 1966, he was owned by Tyson Gilpin, who immediately put the horse in training with Sylvia. He ran five times in August and September and won twice, each time in a late-night race.

At 11 p.m. on September 3, 1966, Dancing Ghost won a five and a half furlong $2,500 allowance contest at Shenandoah Downs. The Daily Racing Form race review said the horse was "evenly placed for a half mile, came between horses and for his bid in the drive and was along in time." The time was recorded at 1:07.1.

Dancing Ghost finished victorious at the exact same time and distance when raced again at Shenandoah Downs on September 26. That race went off at 10:22 p.m.

This was a night owl, or better yet, how about a dark horse? As Sylvia once said, "You take the bad with the good."

SPLITTING THE DISHES

The long hours at the track along with late Saturday nights proved to be an intolerable situation for Mr. and Mrs. John Bishop. It got that way because of the intense pace of Sylvia's early morning grind at the track and her husband's midnight-hour lifestyle. "He went in the music business," Sylvia said decades later. "And we didn't see eye to eye." After separating in 1963, a bill of complaint was filed on January 12, 1967, and John Bishop, the defendant, was served. Sylvia's attorney, Henry W. Morrow, declared that "the defendant has neither appeared, pleaded, answered, or otherwise made any defense to this action." Judge Gray Silver, Jr. considered testimony in support of Sylvia's complaint and ordered the parties divorced on July 28, 1967. It was noted in the court papers that Sylvia was "a fit and proper person to have custody" of their nine-year-old daughter, Laverne.
John Bishop could visit his daughter at "reasonable and seasonable times" and was ordered to pay fifteen dollars in weekly support for her care. He also was ordered to pay $150 in attorney fees.

CHAPTER 32

THE OLD BOYS NETWORK

My years in the horse world have been among the happiest
of my life. The caliber of people I have met in racing,
whether grooms or track owners, trainers, jockeys or owners,
have always impressed me as inspired people. Inspired,
I am sure, by the greatest of all athletes, The Thoroughbred.

- Nelson Bunker Hunt, November 2, 1987

Nelson Bunker Hunt's address for Sylvia to mail her training service bills for a horse named Bold Rider was at 700 Mercantile Bank Building in Dallas, Texas. Hunt (February 22, 1926-October 21, 2014), known to many simply as Bunker, inherited $250 million from his father, Haroldson Lafayette Hunt, Jr., and launched a quest to make more. At one time, his estimated worth was $16 billion.

An ultra-conservative Republican and a member of the Council of the John Birch Society, Hunt focused on an anti-communist ideology and also served as chairman of the board of the Bible Society of Texas.

He had a strong love of breeding and racing Thoroughbreds. He began what ultimately became an impressive and thriving business in 1955. Hunt owned the 8,000-acre Bluegrass Farm in Lexington, Kentucky, and was awarded the prestigious Eclipse Award as Outstanding Breeder in 1976, 1985, and 1987. Lifetime totals for Hunt included twenty-five champions that he bred or owned and 158 stakes winners. He was also honored as the British flat racing Champion Owner in 1973 and 1974.

Along the way, Hunt invested enormous amounts in silver. Prices soared, then plummeted, and he (and his brothers) had billions of dollars in losses and legal fees, and declared bankruptcy.

The financial saga forced Nelson Bunker Hunt to sell oil fields, his house, an extraordinary coin collection, a cattle ranch in Australia, and his beloved string of successful Thoroughbred horses. At the 1988 Keeneland Sales in Kentucky, a special auction of 580 of his horses went for $46,911,800.

Eleven years later, he bounced back and bought fifty-one young Thoroughbreds for $2,075,000.

Edward L. Stephenson (February 13, 1926-September 12, 2019) and Nelson Bunker Hunt were members of "the Old Boy's Network," as roommates at the Hill School, the tony all-boys boarding school in Pottstown, Pennsylvania. In 1952, they went to a Kentucky yearling auction at Keeneland and together purchased six yearlings.

Although they did not meet with great success with their first group of racehorses, they continued occasional partnerships. They remained close friends, sharing a passion for racing. In 1975, they purchased a yearling filly for $90,000, later named Trillion, because at a huge 17.1 hands high, they felt she deserved a big name. Trillion became a French and American champion.

Stephenson, originally from Cincinnati, later owned Kilmaurs Stud in the Virginia horse country of Warrenton. He sent several horses to Sylvia to train. His farm was not far from Meadowville Farm, where Hunt's horse, Bold Rider, was bred and born. Stephenson's philanthropy in Warrenton extended to donating the Town Hall and a building that housed the public library. During his career, he commuted to New York and worked in finance. In later life, he lived in Palm Beach and invested in building condominiums.

Leonard David Fruchtman was eighty-six when he died on December 22, 2007. A steel mogul from Toledo, Ohio, he served as president of Donovan Wire and Iron and its subsidiary, Peters Stamping. His many horses ran in red, white and blue colors under the name of Edgehill Farm. He owned part of Miles Park racetrack in Kentucky and was a member of the board of directors at Santa Fe Downs, which closed in 1997.

One of Fruchtman's paramount racing accomplishments was a bay horse called Bally Ache, purchased for $2,500. After the horse placed second in the 1960 Kentucky Derby to Venetian Way, he sold a majority interest in his colt for $1.25 million just before the Preakness Stakes, which Bally Ache won.

Photo courtesy of Ed Stephenson

He also gave female jockey Julie Krone her first ride in a race at Tampa Bay Downs on January 30, 1981, on a horse named Tiny Star.

His son, Gary Fruchtman, recalled that his father loved to name his horses after family members: June's Crocodile (after his mother, June Fruchtman) and Gary's Star, Gary Dear, Our Gary, David's Sin (brother) and Our Michael (after his brother). Another was named for his aunt, Martha's Star. The horse was trained by Sylvia Bishop.

James S. Abrams, Jr. was a New York investment banker with multiple financial accomplishments. He was also a co-founder of the New Jersey Natural Gas Company.

Abrams and his wife, Marguerite DePoe Abrams, lived in the sixteen-story circa 1958 Cumberland House on the corner of 62nd Street and Madison Avenue in the fashionable Lenox Hill section of New York City. He loved to fox hunt and would travel to Middleburg, Virginia, to pursue his passion. He also invested in several large horse farms in the area, less than an hour from the track in Charles Town. At the time, he told one real estate executive he felt Middleburg real estate would always hold its value, which holds true more than fifty years later.

Abrams bought several well-known estates and hired Ray Bates, a Middleburg decorator and interior designer who operated out of a building at the southwest corner of Washington and Madison Streets in the still magical village. Bates, often referred to as "Master Bates" behind his back, later sold the building to real estate guru Phil Thomas. It's still the location of the Thomas and Talbot Real Estate firm, anchoring one corner of the town's only intersection with a traffic signal. President Kennedy and his equestrienne wife, Jackie, were often weekend residents. Pamela and industrialist Averell Harriman, the former governor of New York, owned a large estate just outside the town. Elizabeth Taylor, Dick Smothers, Tab Hunter and Robert Duval also were residents. Over the years, the area included a colorful collection of characters, with a few scandals to boot, all leading to what is known as "the Middleburg Mystique."

Abrams, who died in October 1991, age eighty-one, was forward-thinking in buying, restoring and selling large estates, always at a considerable profit, long before the term "flipping houses" became a real estate catchphrase.

Abrams had several Thoroughbreds racing in his gray and white silks trained by Sylvia. Pete's Pet was bred by Abrams and foaled in January 1957. The dark brown horse started forty-two times in his five-year career and only won three times, once with Sylvia when he was six-years-old. He ran hard, but mostly as an "also ran."

Marble Top, a dark bay mare foaled May 20, 1958, won twice in sixteen races. Her first win was on the evening of September 7, 1962, at Shenandoah Downs in a $1,000 six-furlong race. Then, on September 22, with the temperature reported at fifty-three degrees, there was a slight drizzle as the first race took off at 7:31 p.m. The mare led all the way in the $1,000 5½ furlong claiming race.

Abram Stevens Hewitt (1902-1987) also had a connection with Nelson

Bunker Hunt. As an expert in equine genetics and pedigrees, he often consulted with the Texas businessman.

Upon his death, Eslie Asbury wrote in the Thoroughbred Times that Hewitt "was the most accomplished intellectual who ever devoted his entire career to breeding, racing, and turf writing." His theories and research were published in his books: Sire Lines, published in 1977, and Great Breeders and Their Methods, 1982.

An Oxford graduate, Hewitt also had a law degree from Columbia. In 1947, with funds borrowed from the trust fund of his heiress wife, Griselda Higginson, he purchased the 1,200-acre Montana Hall Farm in White Post, Virginia, where he began breeding Thoroughbreds.

Located in the southern part of Clarke County, the property included several barns for horses. One such white wood-framed structure included a gable roof with an extended hay hood and ridge vent. This particular board and batten barn in the middle of a large open space had a cross aisle so that horses could be walked or ridden inside around the stalls. The farm, with a vast fertile canvas of growing corn and hay, offered a spectacular backdrop that included the Blue Ridge Mountains to the west. The farm still exists decades later.

The main 8,400 square-foot two-story brick colonial with a center hall was built in 1953. Outbuildings at Montana Hall included tenant cottages, an ice house, a white board and batten smokehouse with a cupola vent and steep roof, and a handsome green structure used for storage. It also included two ponds.

Wayne Chatfield-Taylor, who lives nearby at Morgan's Ford Farm, has been to Montana Hall many times. An architect by training and now a breeder of racehorses, he was also impressed by a covered, airy springhouse. "It's still functional and protecting the mansion's drinking water," he said. "There must be a really good spring inside and it's the reason for this plantation's location, surveyed by George Washington himself."

Hewitt's first successful homebred horse was the 1947 three-year-old champion Phalanx, who raced in partnership with C.V. Whitney, followed by Royal Governor, the champion sprinter of 1949. He later divorced Higginson and was forced to repay the loan for the farm to her trust.

Hewitt's lineage was as noble as some of his horses. He was named after his grandfather, Abram S. Hewitt, a mayor of New York who played a role in setting up the New York subway. His namesake later married wife Dorothy Furey, who had flown for the RAF during World War II. Hewitt had been with the Office of Strategic Services, the forerunner to the Central Intelligence Agency. In 1957, they purchased the circa 1811 property Long Branch in nearby Millwood, Virginia. They raised four boys on this sprawling farm.

The estate included a two-story Federal-style brick mansion built by

Robert Carter Burwell. Burwell sought architectural input via letters to Benjamin Latrobe, who designed the U.S. Capitol building, and suggested a servant's staircase should be included in the home.

The estate also came with stables. "Abe Hewitt was a true master of knowledge of the Thoroughbred horse," Chatfield-Taylor said.

In 1968, Long Branch became a Virginia Historic Landmark. In 1969, it was listed in the National Register of Historic Places. Now open for tours, weddings and meetings, it appropriately serves as a facility for retired racehorses.

Hewitt bred a bay horse called Man o' Mails (by Correspondent out of *Donavala by Donatello II). He had a three-race career in West Virginia, winning once at Waterford Park on June 1, 1963. Danger Zone, a half-brother to Man o' Mails (by Call Over out of *Donavala by Donatello II) ran fifteen times and won three races. Both were trained by Sylvia and owned by her longtime client, W.L. Bushong.

The engagement of Harvey Wallace Shaffer (1893-1970) and socialite Eva Cochrane Stewart was announced in the New York Times on January 18, 1920, under the headline "Junior League Member to Wed."

Born as Harvey Lyman Shaffer, his middle name was later changed. He went to Yale, and then served in the Overseas Air Service. She lived with her parents at 903 Park Avenue and also in Plainfield, New Jersey. Their wedding took place in March with a guest list of blue-blood attendants. A dance at The Plaza hotel followed a dinner party the night before. They divorced in 1933.

Eva married Baldwin D. Spilman, Jr. in 1934. They divorced in 1938. In 1940, she married Laurens Morgan Hamilton, the grandson of J. Pierpont Morgan. They were to live at her Byrnly estate in the heart of the Virginia fox hunting country of Middleburg. Clearly, her love of horses was just as strong as that of her first husband.

In January 1940, Mr. Shaffer purchased Sherwood Farm near the Shenandoah River in the Milldale section of Front Royal, Virginia, in Warren County.

Sherwood Farm was located next to Rock Hill Farm, owned by fellow horse aficionado and polo player Raymond Guest, America's ambassador to Ireland from 1965-1968.

Harvey Shaffer had a dairy in addition to his fine racehorses. His "dairy barn" was actually a disguised racehorse barn, as were others in the area: "In order to build after the war, the project had to be approved to qualify for materials for livestock of sheep and cows, not horses, because of post war shortages," one neighbor recalled years later.

Sylvia trained a number of Shaffer's horses. She recalled that he kept "racing forms to the ceiling, all tied up with bailing twine." Dante's Hope, a dark brown mare by Dante's Faith out of Prickly Pear, was foaled May 5, 1963. She won her first start at Shenandoah Downs on September 29, 1965, then had dismal results and was sold in late October 1966. Shaffer bred three other horses out of Prickly Pear. Her offspring—Red Ash, Sickle Pear, Black Bart and Rope Walker (a full sister to Dante's Hope)—were all winners.

Lady Lucifer was also sired by Dante's Faith, as was Dante's Hope. This shimmering chestnut mare ran with Sylvia as trainer thirty-six times between 1964 and 1966. She won nine times and earned $14,370.

Alfred Alexander Biddle (1885-1967), often referred to as "A.A.," was a member of an old Philadelphia family. A 1909 graduate of Yale, he also studied at Balliol College in Oxford and was an artillery captain in World War I.

A stockbroker for fifty years, he was a partner in the Philadelphia investment group of Biddle, Whelen & Co. on Walnut Street. He married Gertrude Heckscher in 1922, and they lived on a 100-acre farm across from the Aronimink Golf Club along Route 252, known to the locals as Newtown Street Road near Newtown Square.

According to local historians, "He married into his farm—his wife's mother apparently owned Boxmead Farm first." They had four children: Constance, Anne, Julian, and Edith.

Biddle raised American Hampshire Sheep and rode to hounds with the Rose Tree Fox Hunting Club and the circa 1883 Radnor Hunt. His hunting journals, in which he recorded the weather, scent, hounds, horses, kills and more from 1912 to 1920, are in the Special Collections at the University of Virginia Library in Charlottesville. He also bred, raised and raced Thoroughbreds. Neighbors in the area of Newtown Square included other gentleman farmers such as William du Pont Jr., who had a training track on his farm and likely allowed Biddle to exercise his horses there.

Sylvia trained some of them. He bred a bay horse named Mr. Fizz born on February 26, 1962. He was owned and raced by Harvey Shaffer and sired by *Acramitis, the stallion owned by W.L. Bushong. This was clearly what has come to be known as "the Old Boys Network." It's not necessarily connected to where a boy went to school, but to who that boy knows.

Biddle also bred Lady Scattercash, foaled May 7, 1960, Major Tinhead, foaled June 21,1961, and Lord Lionel, foaled March 12, 1963. All three were sired by *Advocate II and all three were trained by Sylvia.

And what does all this prove?

As someone once wrote, "A racehorse is an animal that can take several thousand people for a ride at the same time."

William Lee Bushong and his wife, Maxine, were longtime supporters of Sylvia Bishop. She trained many of their racehorses, and they coordinated a breeding program. Bushong also served as her attorney.

He died age seventy-seven in 1992, and Maxine survived him. They had no children, and she remained in their home at Antram Farm in Hedgesville, West Virginia twenty-five miles from Charles Town. She recalled Sylvia as a hard-working and fascinating woman. She also shared recipes for Sylvia's home remedies her husband collected over the years.

Though Maxine Bushong was slow to get around, her longtime caretaker was never far away as she reminisced about outings to watch their horses race.

Mrs. Bushong died of a heart attack on January 4, 2010. In Article III-C of her will, she left her caretaker jewelry, and "all the trophies, portraits and scrapbooks relating to my racehorse 'My Sailor'."

The caretaker, who was never particularly enamored with Maxine over her thirty-year tenure, felt she'd been short-changed and claimed she'd been promised several hundred thousand dollars. Not long after Maxine's death, a small shop along Washington Street in Charles Town had some of these items for sale. The shop owners confirmed the caretaker had brought them to be sold for cold hard cash.

So much for sentimental value.

CHAPTER 33

DOUBLEDAY AND BAKED APPLES

Love doesn't grow on trees like apples in Eden—it's something you have to make. And you must use your imagination too.

- Joyce Cary

As a single mother, financial reality eventually forced Sylvia to take on extra work in 1974 in the shipping department of a Doubleday publishing factory in nearby Berryville, Virginia. In November, Sylvia welcomed a new granddaughter, LaToya Jones, and on January 1, 1975, she lost her mother, seventy-six-year-old Bertha Rideoutt.

A viewing took place on Friday evening, January 10, at the Melvin T. Strider Colonial Funeral Home, the very same establishment that handled the funeral of abolitionist John Brown on December 2, 1859. Reverend J.R. Thacker of St. Philip's Episcopal conducted the funeral service on Saturday, January 11, at 2 p.m. Those mourning the strong and hard-working matriarch laid her to rest at Fairview Cemetery.

In her will, written in 1972 and probated in 1975, Bertha Rideoutt left her estate to her son, Robert Lee Rideoutt, and lists Sylvia R. Wells as executor. At that time, Sylvia was still married to her second husband, Theodore L. Wells. They were divorced on July 14, 1976, and there was one interesting caveat in the two-page divorce document: "And it appearing to the Court that the plaintiff desires to have her former name of Sylvia R. Bishop restored to her and that this is a proper case for the granting of such relief, it is accordingly adjudged, ordered, and decreed that the former name of the plaintiff, Sylvia R. Bishop, be, and the same hereby is, restored to her."

The astonishing circle of life and death continued in 1976, as Sylvia's brother, Magruder, passed away in May. Then came a second beaming granddaughter, Michelle Nicole born on December 29.

By then, the Shenandoah Downs track had closed down and Charles Town remained open for business. There are no records of any of her horses racing at the track, although she did have several offspring to look after from her first mare, Chalkee.

Irvin Kovens, Ruby Stofbert, and Irving T. "Tubby" Schwartz from Baltimore, who owned the track in Charles Town since 1968, entered into a legal understanding with the owners of Shenandoah Downs. The tracks shared the racing dates and pooled all financial responsibilities. Both tracks were then sold to the Rapid American Corporation.

The U.S. government had imposed a twenty percent withholding tax on pari-mutuel betting throughout the country. The track was teetering on going out of business unless taxes were lowered and Sunday racing was re-instated. The state legislature agreed, and by 1979, racing resumed at the original facility.

Meanwhile, Sylvia settled into her work in Berryville, a twenty-minute, thirteen-mile drive past rocky fields and farms. Along the way, she also passed the Orchard Inn, once owned by her first husband, John Bishop, and renamed as the Rainbow Inn. She always tried to put him out of her mind, but couldn't help ruminating about their marriage and divorce.

The geology of this area is complex. Outcroppings of limestone are everywhere, and there are numerous horse and cattle farms. Founded in 1734 in Clarke County, the population in 1970 was 1,569, growing to 4,342 by 2018. The Battletown Inn at the main intersection was so named, according to urban legend, because early in its existence, so many fights broke out inside.

Sylvia was well acquainted with Berryville, named in 1798, when Benjamin Berry divided the town into lots. The four main blocks included a pharmacy, school, several pubs and a pharmacy. The Berryville Farm Supply in a weathered frame building was just over the railroad tracks on the east side of town. It still looks like something out of a Hollywood movie set after a recent renovation. This was where Sylvia bought oats, feed, hay and straw for her horses.

The farm supply depot was owned by Charlie Stuart and Milton Ritzenburg during the 1960s and '70s. Richard Loughborough managed the store for thirty-five years, unless he was off down the road at the Clarke County Fairgrounds training his racehorses. His wife, Ruth Loughborough, ran the front counter and sold the oats and sweet feed for the horses. For sixty-two years, she kept the accounts meticulously in a ledger. She owned the building and sold it for $375,000 in 2019.

The 2,400 square foot structure, built in 1902, had no heat or air conditioning, but did have a large parking lot and ample space and ramps for oversized delivery trucks. Its proximity to the railroad tracks once provided the opportunity for delivery by train. It was here that farmers and horsemen gathered to talk about the weather, their cows and horses, and maybe a bit of local gossip.

Meanwhile, Sylvia continued to occupy her home at 122 S. West Street in Charles Town. "It was a two-story house at the end of the block," recalled D.W. Fries, a white horse trainer who grew up in Charles Town and was a frequent visitor to Sylvia's house as a child and adult. "The left side was level with the porch," he added while drawing a floor plan of the 1937 structure. "You had to walk down outside to the basement, and from the basement, you'd walk out to the backyard. That's where she had that little pub. The stairs when you walked in the front door went straight up to the second floor."

Fries and his wife, Melony, tried to pick Sylvia's brain any time they visited her. "She was a celebrity to my wife," he said. "Miss Sylvia would always tell her how hard it was for a woman at the track. But she never complained. Back then, when she was training, a woman on the track was kind of a joke. Sylvia was definitely a pioneer. Because of where she was working, nobody really knew about her at the bigger tracks."

Even as she worked at the publishing plant, Sylvia fastidiously read the racing charts from the track. She was always telling friends and relatives about horses to bet on, or not.

She was a frequent smoker and occasionally liked a sip of Southern Comfort. She had bottles hidden everywhere, all over the big drafty house. And while she kept working in Berryville, she always intended to get back to the racetrack she loved.

In the local primary elections in June 1979, Democratic voters designated incumbents President Jimmy Carter and West Virginia Governor Jay Rockefeller to return. Republicans voted for Ronald Reagan over George Bush to run for president, and Arch A. Moore, Jr. ran unopposed for governor.

Sylvia was a devoted Democrat, and the final general election results in November were somewhat disappointing to her. Republican Ronald Reagan was elected to replace Carter, but Rockefeller was re-elected.

At the racetrack, horsemen boycotted in 1981 until a state law was put into place for additional funding from tax revenue to track management and horsemen. Receipts at the track went up and, in turn, there were larger purses. That year, a record crowd of 21,480 packed Charles Town to watch the Sugar Ray Leonard-Thomas Hearns boxing match on closed circuit television.

Two years later, the West Virginia Breeders' Association began an incentive program. It was also around this time that the track once again changed hands. Kenton Corp./Rapid American sold the facility to fifteen investors, including eleven locals operating as Charles Town Racing, Ltd.

As a blizzard inched its way toward Charles Town in mid-December of '81, schools were closed and roads were impassable. Sylvia did not miss the track on days like this. With Christmas around the corner, she began a list of gifts for friends and family and made a note that the Santa Clause Express train from Harpers Ferry to Winchester would stop in Charles Town near Shenandoah Downs race track on Flowing Springs Road. She was forever making small notes on scrap paper scattered everywhere. She cherished Christmas and took time to wrap each little gift with holiday paper, tagged with names and a cheerful ribbon. No stick on bows for this lady.

The Spirit of Jefferson Farmers Advocate newspaper reported that the Board of Directors of the Charles Town Civic Center and Library gathered on the northeast corner of East Washington and South Samuel Streets on Sunday, October 2, 1983, to celebrate the opening of a two-story brick museum.

"Did you know that Sylvia Rideoutt Bishop, a native of Charles Town, was the first licensed female African American thoroughbred trainer in the United States?" read a 2020 museum Facebook post, illustrating how times had changed. "Find out more about these women in our new exhibit. The museum is hosting a FREE opening reception Saturday, March 14, from 1 to 4 p.m. Come to see the new exhibits and enjoy refreshments from Alfredo's Mediterranean Grille."

Little could Sylvia have imagined while reading the 1983 newspaper account of that new museum opening that her family and friends would gather fifteen years after she died in the very same building for the opening of "Six Notable Jefferson County Women."

As for Doubleday & Company of New York City, the well-known book publishing house opened a massive printing plant in Berryville in December 1956. It was three-tenths of a mile away and just around the corner from the farm supply store. When Sylvia began working at Doubleday in 1974, there were 500 employees.

Sylvia was still at the plant when it was sold in 1986 to the German-based Bertelsmann, a private mega multinational media conglomerate. According to Social Security reports, this was Sylvia's last year as an employee at the now high-tech plant, capable of turning out 110 books a minute.

She was about to return to the horses and the racetrack she adored.

Berryville and Charles Town are located in the northern Shenandoah Valley. The region is well-known for producing apples: think of festive apple harvests, apple cider, apple sauce and apple butter. It seems only fitting to include this recipe from *A Christmas Sampler of Feasts* published in 1981 by Doubleday while Sylvia worked at their printing plant.

BAKED APPLES
Serves 4

4 large baking apples
$3/4$ cup sugar
$2/3$ cup sugar
$2/3$ cup water
1 tablespoon butter or margarine
Pinch cinnamon and/or nutmeg
2-3 drops red food coloring

Photo by Leonard Shapiro

Preheat oven to 350 degrees. Core apples, then peel about $1/3$ of the way down from the stem end, or, if you prefer, peel entirely. Arrange in an ungreased shallow baking pan. Boil remaining ingredients about 5 minutes to form a clear syrup, pour over apples, and bake uncovered $3/4$-1 hour, basting often with syrup, until crisp-tender. Serve hot or cold, topped if you like with custard sauce or whipped cream.

From: The Doubleday Cookbook by Jean Anderson and Elaine Hanna, 1975.

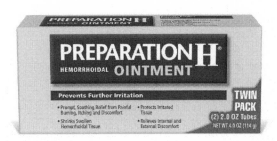

CHAPTER 34

BE PREPARED WITH PREPARATION H

Shrinks hemorrhoids a new way without surgery.
The secret is a new healing substance (Bio-Dyne)—*
discovery of a world-famous research institute.

- Preparation H newspaper ad, circa 1963

Since 1973, when she started working at the nearby Doubleday plant, Sylvia had not been training at the racetrack. She was sixty-seven when she retired from the book publishing firm and made a comeback to racing on October 12, 1987.

"I still remember when she came out of retirement and bought a horse called Half Quacked," her nephew, Devin Walker, recalled in an online post in February 2011. "Aunt Sylvia would yell for me to cool the horse out for her. I would say 'Aunt Sylvia, when are you gonna run this horse. She is ready.' Aunt Sylvia would say 'Be patient. When she runs, she will win because she will be a racehorse.' Guess what? She was right. She won the first time she ran her! That was the type of person and horsewoman she was."

It was the only time the bay mare Half Quacked won in her sixteen lifetime starts. They earned $1,396 for the effort, and Sylvia once again was back in the winner's circle.

Top Mac was a chestnut horse Sylvia also owned and trained. She was back in the game, caring for several horses and often making purchases at the Three Acres Tack Box over in Shepherdstown. Top Mac was five-years-old when they finished first on July 24, 1988. Jockey Laurie E. Strickland was up wearing Sylvia's blue and yellow silks. The horse was seven when they won again on January 6, 1990. Jack Kent Cooke, who owned the Washington Redskins and a number of racehorses and lived at his 180-acre Kent Farms in Middleburg, was not far away that day, in a Warrenton, Virginia courthouse. He was arguing with his ex-wife, Suzanne Martin Cooke, who was asking for $140,000 a year in child support for their soon-to-be two-year-old daughter Jacqueline. "Preposterous," he said. The back and forth between them continued for years. And, by the way, a two dollar win ticket on Top Mac paid $64.50 that day.

Six weeks later, in February 1990, Sylvia won with Barbi Aunt Connie in a 4½-furlong $2,100 race that paid thirty dollars for a two dollar win ticket.

As often happens at the racetrack, everyone knows what everyone else is doing and when they're doing it. Sylvia met Jack Ferguson, who owned a 147-acre farm in rural Maryland. She eventually learned how he indulged his passion for racehorses with a methodical and regimented training schedule on his farm. He kept charts and made meticulous notes on index cards. He had a typed list called "Going to the Track" so as not to forget silks, blinkers, bridles, hose, sponge and scraper, brushes, screw eyes, snaps, cotton, cold water wraps, Ice-O-Gel, the Racing Form, a fan and a chair.

Not on that list was a tube of Preparation H, which he always kept on hand. Preparation H has nothing to do with a horse's rear end. Rather, its function is to reduce swelling and sooth the stressed tendons of the horse's legs.

Ferguson preferred to train his horses at home and took them to Sylvia at the track closer to the day of the race. It was known as "racing off the farm," or working as "program trainer."

Essentially, the program trainer is listed as the trainer of record for a horse and may not have daily contact with that horse. "Usually this is a situation where someone either can't get a license (because of legal issues) or doesn't want to get a license," trainer Diana McClure said in 2020. "Or they can't afford the workman's comp required, which was not required during Sylvia's earlier era. Basically, the real person training the horse is not the one listed in the program."

Whatever Ferguson's motive was in hiring Sylvia didn't much matter. She constantly consulted with him, handling Wolf Call, King's Bay, Wink's Surprise, John's Rollick and Kathy Ann Alden.

And now, she was back at the track she loved so much in Charles Town, among friends and family. "She treated the horses as they wanted to be treated," Ferguson said. "They're just like kids; all are different. Most trainers treat all the horses the same, but they're all different."

On October 16, 1991, Sylvia saddled Terminally Gray in the first race at Charles Town for a win. It was partly cloudy and in the mid-sixties that afternoon, but news in Washington was red hot as the senate confirmed Clarence Thomas, a black conservative judge, to serve on the Supreme Court.

Ferguson's horses were winners, and their photos were displayed all over his farmhouse. Nevertheless, one photo of a gray mare called Betyerbrass was not on his wall.

That's because Betyerbrass, once owned and trained by Ferguson off his Hargett Farm, never won while he was in charge. He eventually gave the horse to Sylvia, and she did not waste the opportunity. Betyerbrass' only victory came while she was under the full care and training of Sylvia Bishop on September 12, 1990.

Photo courtesy of Hollywood Casino at Charles Town Races

CHAPTER 35

THE CLUBHOUSE TURN

A horse gallops with his lungs, perseveres with his heart, and wins with his character.

- Federico Tesio, Italian Thoroughbred breeder (1869-1954)

In 1987, the West Virginia Breeders' Classics races based at Charles Town were established by West Virginia native and National Football League Hall of Famer Sam Huff and his partner, Carol Holden. It grew into a spectacular annual weekend event, featuring a Friday night dinner dance, a golf tournament, and a popular breakfast lecture featuring speakers like former teammate and Hall of Fame quarterback Sonny Jurgensen and Hall of Fame coach Joe Gibbs. In thirty plus years, the Classics have offered more than $28 million in purses.

In early May 1988, Sylvia lost an older sister, Irma Rideoutt Berry. Born June 4, 1925, the ninth member of the family, Irma, sixty-two, was married to John Berry, also a horse trainer at Charles Town. She retired in 1987 after twenty-two years as a machinist with Badger-Powhatan in Ranson. They had four children—Alisha, John III, Linda and Timothy. Family and friends gathered for the funeral on Monday, May 9, with Rev. David Bicking and Rev. Joseph Washington officiating. She, like many other family members, was buried at Pleasant View Memory Gardens.

The news out of Washington in the early 1990s brought the latest in the soap opera saga of disgraced former Washington Mayor Marion Barry, whose legal team filed a $5.5 million damage suit against the Virginia Bureau of Prisons. Prison officials, who had accused Barry of alleged sexual misconduct in the form of oral sex from a visitor, were now under the microscope for violating his rights by making public comments on his alleged transgressions.

An 800,000-page archive on the assassination of President Kennedy was set to be released for research. Washington Post sportswriter Leonard Shapiro gathered stories from the tennis world in Wimbledon, England, and the sensational murder trial of O.J. Simpson went on in a Los Angeles courtroom.

Sylvia's brother, Robert Lee Rideoutt, sixty-seven, died on Friday May 25, 1990, and she and five sisters and one brother, many nieces and nephews and friends again gathered at the funeral home in Ransom.

Jesse Jackson's National Rainbow Coalition sponsored and convened a Washington conference to discuss the escalating growth of violence in the African-American community. Publisher Malcolm Forbes died in 1990, age seventy. A $50,000 certificate of deposit could earn 8.10 percent at Perpetual Bank, and boneless N.Y. strip steaks were $4.98 per pound at Shoppers Food Warehouse.

Just before 8 p.m. on Friday, January 17, 1992, Sylvia walked Wink's Surprise from the barn area at Charles Town toward the paddock for the second race. It was cloudy as she guided the four-year-old bay mare owned by Jack Ferguson (of Preparation H infamy) in the darkness. She greeted all her friends, grooms, hot walkers and fellow competitors and along the route with a simple nod or modest "Hey." In a familiar routine of a lifetime, she paused at the gate to the paddock while the identifier checked the lip tattoo on her charge.

Prior to this race, Ferguson had taken on training his horses with mixed and often poor results. Put simply, the mare's record reveals no wins and a meager $420 in earnings with Ferguson, and $5,243 with Sylvia. This included the only lifetime victory for Wink's Surprise on this dreary night.

During 1993, Sylvia lost two more sisters. Clara Howard Rideoutt

Holland died in January, age seventy-four, and Madge Virginia Rideoutt Thorne, fifty-five, died on February 26. That year, she saddled and trained more winners, including Mishavere for William E. Montgomery and John's Rollick for Jack Ferguson. Leon L. Taulton, Jr.'s Munden's Michele won twice, including the seventh race on Sunday afternoon, August 22. Track denizens that day also were focusing on television monitors inside the clubhouse to watch as Kentucky Derby winner Sea Hero captured the Travers Stakes in Saratoga Springs.

"I couldn't be more delighted," eighty-five-year-old Sea Hero owner Paul Mellon of Upperville, Virginia, told the Associated Press. It's very likely Sylvia felt the same way about her own victory in Charles Town.

For owner Franklin Rice, Sylvia took his West Virginia homebred Hunting Tower to the winner's circle in 1993. This bay gelding had twenty-six lifetime starts, which included three wins, two with Sylvia. And Sylvia's Blushing Andrea also won for owner Sandor Horvath.

The races in Charles Town were canceled on Friday January 7, 1994, because the roads were expected to be hazardous. The next day, Blushing Andrea won the seventh race and returned for another win in early February during Black History month.

For owner Dale Rice, Sylvia trained Classical Herb to a photo finish victory that spring. She was also listed as trainer for Rice's Lean n Loose for the only victory of the gray gelding's four-race career. Maurice Pendleton III's Alitango won a maiden claiming race that spring, and Blushing Andrea won for the third time in three months. By the end of April, Classical Herb recorded two more victories.

Gini Go Go broke her maiden for owner Michael B. Ott with Carol Bradshaw riding in October 1994. Yet, by the next year, Charles Town once again seemed in danger of closing when the track was put up for sale.

In 1995, the track was in decline, with very little money set aside by the legislature to support the races. This was, most likely, the reason Sylvia had few horses to run in 1995 and none in 1996.

The track's future was in question until 1996, when West Virginia voters approved video lottery terminals at the track. Some have speculated that the track would have gone under without Penn National Gaming Inc.'s purchase of the facility a year later.

Daily racing purses increased nearly ten-fold in the years after Penn National took over operations at the track, pulling some old-time horsemen (and horsewomen) back and bringing in many newcomers. The casino gaming center, filled with scads of computerized slot machines, opened to elaborate fanfare. Four hundred video lottery terminals were installed for the "Silver Screen Gaming Center," followed by a multi-million-dollar, simulcast center called "Longshots." TV monitors showing races from tracks around the country also allowed Charles Town racing gamblers to wager elsewhere. It eventually led to sports betting of all kinds. It was reported that Penn National Gaming spent $175 million for track improvements, which included new and renovated stables.

Sylvia had thirteen starts and one win with Really a Devil in '97. For a bit of extra income, she rented rooms in Payne's Hotel, the twenty-room, two-story frame house she had inherited at 122 South West Street. Payne's Tap Room was still running on the bottom floor at street level. It was a busy section of town and always popular with the African-American community. Years later, Alan Williams of Middleburg, Virginia, recalled renting a room at Payne's: "I was a jockey at the time and it was nice to be with her and talk about horses."

Back in the day, there were other popular establishments catering to the black population, including Fisherman's Hall, the Grand United Order of the Galilean Fishermen built in 1885 for "the empowerment of slaves" by the Charles Town Industrial Association at the northeast corner of South West and Academy Streets. Jefferson County had more slaves than any county in the state.

Sylvia also recalled other black-owned businesses: Frank Bradford's Billiards, James and Mamie Bradford's Barber Shop and Restaurant, Rideout's 1st Dry Cleaners, along with John Smith's Dance Hall, and Amanda Galloway's Gold Kettle.

In early 1998, Sylvia found herself struggling with bills from her doctor, Allegheny Power, Citizens Communications Phone, Charles Town Water Department, Mastercard, West Virginia Cable Television, Cigna Health Insurance, and a bill for $19,325 from the U.S. Department of the Treasury for unpaid income tax.

In February, she borrowed $33,789.30 as a mortgage note against her home. It was to mature in full one year later. At 8.5% interest, she would owe $36,661.38. Her optimism did not wane, bolstered by an occasional investment in a Powerball ticket.

She kept in contact with her friends and neighbors from long ago: Russell Roper's Taxi Service, Ella Hughes' Candy Store, George Harris' Barber Shop, Mable Smith's restaurant, and T.I.A.B.L.E. (an acronym for "This is a Black Local Enterprise") that sold wigs and ethnic attire in the 200 block of South West Street.

She reminisced about her parents and brothers and sisters and all the good times they had with big gatherings and many laughs. She remembered stories of Samuel Galloway's Livestock Yard and Lou Rutherford's Stables. Just walking around a certain corner or past a place where she'd been with one of them brought memories bubbling up, not all of them perfect.

She harked back to when she was nine-years-old and her Uncle Edgar Snowden went to jail for "stealing cement in sacks from the negro school being built on Harewood Avenue in the western part of town."

Then there was her Uncle Edgar Rideoutt. He was sentenced to six months' labor on the country roads and fined fifty dollars after being caught carrying a straight razor, a portent of a lifetime of mostly petty law breaking. But this was nothing when compared to the 1967 conviction of her brother Govenear Paige Rideoutt, then thirty-four, who murdered their brother Donald, age thirty-six. As a sweet adolescent boy, Govenear held horses and worked for Sylvia. He had used a butcher knife to stab Donald, who had also worked for her, in the kitchen of their mother's home on Davenport Street.

Court documents reveal there was an altercation between the brothers, and alcohol likely was involved. More than one butcher knife may have been involved, and somehow, Govenear killed Donald and wrapped the knives in newspapers.

He was arrested and initially held without bail before being granted a $5,000 bail. He hired Henry Morrow as his attorney and initially pleaded not guilty. Morrow filed a discovery order requesting, among other things, the blood alcohol and autopsy report of the deceased. A jury was impaneled and witnesses subpoenaed. At trial, the jury was escorted to the scene of the alleged crime on Potato Hill.

At some point shortly thereafter, Govenear changed his plea to nolo contendre, which is no contest but still considered a plea of guilt. The judge then sentenced him to a year in jail, with all but sixty days suspended, and a period of ten years' probation with numerous conditions.

Not long after the trial, their mother, Bertha Rideoutt, requested the court to return the butcher knives, which she said would be used for household purposes.

It remained a hideous family episode.

The People's Supply and Feed in Charles Town extended credit to Sylvia and she was prompt to pay and keep this account current. Her purchases included: oats ($12.59 per fifty-pound bag), a liquid iron and vitamin supplement called Red Cell for twelve dollars per gallon in 1989 (twenty-seven dollars in 2020), wheat germ oil for a shiny coat ($ 22.32), and lime to neutralize the smell of ammonia and soak up urine in the stalls ($3.75 per fifty-pound bag).

Her shopping list also included one pound of diuretic leaves-UvaUrsi (which translates to "bear's grape" because bears love the stuff that grows on a shrub). It's used to reduce fluid as an organic alternative to the use of the drug Lasix. She also frequently bought flaxseed meal, high in omega-3 fatty acids to protect joints and soft tissues as well as equalize the immune system, and rat and mouse bait called "Just One Bite." This also was much needed, and all of the above was delivered to Sylvia at Barn D on the backside of the track.

During Sylvia's return to the track, the Independent Fire Company acquired and put into service a 1999 Pierce Dash Fire engine to replace a 1978 version that had been in service for twenty-one years.

The Spirit of Jefferson newspaper reported two cases of rabies in the fall of 1999, from raccoons to pets. The Jefferson County Chamber of Commerce honored new teachers and the board of education concluded an agreement with the Smithsonian's Naturalist Center in nearby Leesburg, Virginia, for sharing science and biology techniques.

Racing fans once again gathered around the television monitors inside the track's clubhouse to watch Charismatic with jockey Chris Antley win the 125th Kentucky Derby on the first Saturday in May. Two weeks later, Charismatic won on a day when a man ran onto the Pimlico racetrack in Baltimore during the Preakness. He later pleaded guilty to reckless endangerment. In the Belmont Stakes on June 5, Charismatic, the 3-2 favorite, finished third but was pulled up as he broke the sesamoid and cannon bones in his left front leg, ending the chance of winning the Triple Crown. He survived the injury and went on to stand at stud. Longshot Lemon Drop Kid won the race.

Back in Charles Town, it was all in the family in 1999 as With Royalty, owned by Sylvia's daughter, now using her maiden name, Laverne Bishop, won an allowance race. Betweenopportunity and Regard The Dream, owned by her granddaughter, Michelle N. Bishop, also won. And, Dixie Danny, owned by her daughter and granddaughter, won on a cloudy fall evening over a fast track. Virginia River, a four-year-old dark bay mare owned and trained by Sylvia, finished off the year with a win.

A small cellular antenna was installed against the water tower in Charles Town, a co-agreement between a larger antenna that would have disturbed "the visual and historic landscape of the area." Julia & Jacques Cooking at Home by Julia Child and Jacques Pepin became available at the library. The Fruit and Veggie Wagon advertised the "best prices in town" for their annual pumpkin sale along with plenty of apple types, from Red Rome varieties to Matsu. D&D Meats offered boneless chicken breasts, $1.99 per pound, baby back ribs for $2.99 per pound, and NY Strips at $4.99 per pound.

A pickup truck collided with another vehicle in November of '99, resulting in the death of a ten-year-old girl, whose name was withheld. And, Page Jackson Elementary School launched a grant-funded program to promote one-on-one learning for reading, listening, and writing skills.

As Sylvia's favorite time of year, the holidays, approached in December 1999, the Spirit of Jefferson newspaper was filled with advertisements from local farms for Christmas trees. The Jefferson Memorial Hospital Auxiliary/Volunteers raised $1,700 at a book sale to fund patient needs. And a there was a note: "Cheers to Midnite Blizzard, It's Only Money, and Clever Champ among others at the Charles Town Races in the past weekend."

In this final year of her career in 2000, Sylvia's horses raced thirty-one times with her only win with Lone Wolf, owned by her great-granddaughter, Mildred L. Twyman.

On April 15, she saddled previous winner Lust for Gold, owned by Reminda Morris, on yet another overcast night. Post time was 10:11 p.m. for this seven-furlong contest. As the field of ten thundered to the final "clubhouse turn," the announcer boomed "and down the stretch they come."

The dark brown gelding finished in ninth place. The report was "showed little." It was Sylvia's final race.

During her comeback, between 1987 and 2000, she raced 349 times with forty-four victories. The horses she trained gathered $166,663 in earnings.

CHAPTER 36

RECOGNITION

D.W. Fries and his wife Melony returned to West Virginia in 1998 to celebrate Sylvia's October birthday at the Cliffside Inn in Harpers Ferry.

"At the party, Miss Sylvia asked us to take her home," Fries recalled. "Her nephews and nieces were fighting over who would take her back home. We did. Miss Sylvia always called us her childrens. Not children. Childrens. She told everyone: 'No, my childrens will take me home,' and that was that. She told us they were all acting like a bunch of idiots. She was a tough nut. She didn't take any shit."

He recalled her large home at 122 S. West Street as "drafty as all get out. Her family was trying to talk her into moving to the Charles Towers. Her daughter Laverne told us that we should talk to her to see if we could get her to go there. We just talked to Miss Sylvia, didn't try to convince her or tell her what to do.

"She asked us, 'Do you think it's the best thing I should do?' We told her she knew some of the people over there and she'd like it. Then she just said, 'Okay then, that's what I'll do.' She agreed to it and she moved in. We told her that any time we came home from Kentucky we'd come visit her there, and we always did."

On January 14, 1999, Sylvia sold the property she'd inherited from the Paynes at 122 South West Street. The sale price was $65,000. After paying off a mortgage of $36,543 and an income tax lien of $15,184, there wasn't much left. She received a monthly Social Security check thanks to her years at Doubleday.

Sylvia's career and life on the track were winding down and she retired. She moved into apartment 5-P at Charles Towers, the low-income housing building on Augustine Avenue. Every day in the comfort of her dark Naugahyde vinyl lounge, she read the Daily Racing Form and studied the entries. A steady stream of visitors, including friends Grady Sellars and "Mr. Butler," came by and called at all hours of the day and night. A fellow resident a few floors below ran bets for her to the track and brought back cigarettes, too.

Six minutes and one and a half miles away at the racetrack, there were 2,000 slot machines in the casino by 2000, along with an indoor parking garage. Penn National Gaming had now spent close to $61 million on casino improvements and expansion. Quickly, these numbers evolved to 3500 slots and $175 million worth of renovations. The complex now boasted three million visitors annually. Outside, new stables were built and others were renovated. Inside, a new simulcast center was unveiled.

In 2003, the West Virginia Legislature honored Sylvia as "the first licensed black female thoroughbred horse trainer in the United States and West Virginia." The plaque she received read: "She overcame racial prejudice, innuendoes of all types,

Courtesy of Sylvia Rideoutt Bishop

and limitations of public education offered to blacks, but never gave up on her ambitions and her love of horses..."

"Sylvia was a steady worker," her longtime friend Tony Bencivenga recalled. "When spectators would harass her as a 'nigger bitch', she knew they were ignorant."

"Horses respect you more than most people," Sylvia said.

Ann Hilton, whose husband, Robert Hilton, was a top trainer in Charles Town for forty-five years, committed her time and talent as a writer to preserving memories at the track. A former president of the Charles Town's Horsemen's Benevolent & Protective Association, she created the "Wall of Fame," which displays photographs and memorabilia. She also unveiled the track's Hall of Fame, and her husband Robert Hilton and Sylvia Bishop were among the inductees in 2008.

"There's just so much history here," said Hilton, who was inducted in 2011. "It's worth preserving."

Home Going Celebration
In Loving Memory Of
Sylvia Augustua Bishop
October 5, 1920 -December 27,2004

January 1, 2005
Saturday, 2:00 p.m.

Melvin T. Strider Colonial Funeral Home
3rd Avenue, Fairfax Blvd.
Ranson, WV 25438
Elder Richard Rideoutt, Officiating

CHAPTER 37

HONEY BAKED HAM II

Don't grieve for me, for now I'm free;
I'm following the path God laid for me.

- Anne Lindgren Davison

A sensible-sized dining table in Sylvia's one bedroom apartment in the Charles Towers was heaped high with intriguing personalized notes and pretty paper for Christmas Day, 2004.

Sylvia woke up and was violently ill. Her blood pressure soared, and she was whisked by ambulance to nearby Jefferson Memorial Hospital. Her best friend, Nellie Lawson, had the flu and was broken-hearted that she couldn't visit Sylvia. Instead, she sent her own daughter, Sylvia's goddaughter, Johnetta.

Sylvia's daughter Laverne was there as her mother lingered another day and died at 5:37 the morning of December 27.

On a magnificent sixty-degree afternoon of January 1, 2005, 200-plus mourners gathered at the all-too-familiar Melvin T. Strider Colonial Funeral Home, minutes away from Charles Town across the railroad tracks at Third Ave. and Fairfax Blvd. in Ranson. The imposing building has glossy white columns and an expansive porch covered in bright green artificial turf, like the kind used at a miniature golf course. Sylvia had been there many times for the funerals of friends and family.

The service began with the opening hymn of "What a Friend We Have in Jesus," What a friend we have in Jesus, All our sins and griefs to bear, written by Irish immigrant Canadian Joseph Medlicott Scriven in 1855. There were eight pallbearers and four honorary pallbearers. In addition, there were funeral attendants, heavy-set ladies in white nurse's uniforms, wearing white gloves. They were ready to catch the swooners, of which there were several. One of Sylvia's granddaughters sang "Wind Beneath My Wings" and "Eye on the Sparrow."

Elder Richard Rideoutt gave the eulogy and spoke about going to visit his Aunt Sylvia at Potato Hill and how she'd take him to the Tastee Freeze and buy him ice cream. She always lent him money. Her award from the West Virginia legislature was mentioned, but not much more about her life with her beloved horses or the racetrack.

A spread of food was laid out at the Lion Center. Among the provisions on the table was a honey-baked ham brought to Sylvia by a young admirer shortly before she died.

She was buried at Pleasant View Memory Gardens in nearby Martinsburg, West Virginia.

CHAPTER 38

THE (HOOF) BEATS GOES ON

It is 11 a.m. and suddenly the place is still.
Western music swings out of a transistor radio
and, periodically, a horse whinnies under the shed,
but there are no other sounds.

- William Gildea, *The Washington Post*, July 2, 1967

Trainer Michael Jones is grazing a bay mare named Wagered near barn twenty-one in the stable area of the track in Charles Town. It's July 2018, just past ten in the morning, and the sun is strong. The temperature will top out at ninety intense degrees by 8:26 p.m., the conclusion of a sweltering and scorching fourteen hour and sixteen minute day.

"I always was around horses and always had horses," said the forty-something Jones as the five-year-old horse yanked bits of grass. "Everything I know, I learned from my grandma."

That would be Sylvia Bishop.

"I called her grandma, but around the track, everyone called her 'Moms'. I was walking hots when I was six years old."

In his twenties, Michael had several brushes with the law, but said his decision to return to the racetrack to care for horses was the best path he could have imagined. With lessons learned from his late and beloved grandmother still stored in his memory bank, he said there was a renewed purpose in his life.

"I'm out here every day at 5 a.m." he said. "We live right across the

Michael Jones is carrying on the traditions of his grandmother Sylvia Rideoutt Bishop
Photo by Vicky Moon

street."

Jones is tall and lanky, with a scraggily beard and a warm smile. He seemed hesitant at first to chat, but loosened up after a few minutes and we later followed up several times on the phone. He speaks softly, and is far more interested in watching his horse munch on grass. Asked if he rides, he said, "No, I don't ride 'em. I'm way too big to ride now."

The rules at Charles Town have changed since Jones' grandmother was a trainer six plus decades ago. Some trainers "ship in" to race their horses. They must be inside the fenced stable area by 1 p.m. for a race with a purse of $300,000 or more, or at least three hours before post time for their race.

In addition to a trainer's license, there are numerous permits involved these days: a registered stable name, hot walker, jockey or jockey agent, owner, exercise rider, pony rider, veterinarian, groom, chaplain and, of course, various "gaming" dealers—mutuel clerks and poker dealers. The fees range from twenty dollars and up.

Trainers who want stable space on the property for the long-term must apply for a revocable stall license agreement. Of the sixteen terms listed, several are of note. For example, the track "may refuse admittance to or eject anyone whom it considers undesirable in accordance with applicable law." Or, "Applicant shall purchase and maintain workers compensation insurance." Stalls are allotted "with the understanding that their horses are ready to run" and any horses that are no longer eligible "must be immediately removed from the grounds."

Unlike other tracks around the country, there are no dormitories for the grooms or other track workers at Charles Town. The price of fifty pounds of Legends racehorse formula is $16.49. The high fat of eight percent and twelve percent protein are intended to provide extra calories that translate into "optimal fuel for maximum performance," according to Southern States.

Brome grass hay is $7.50 per bale. Straw used for bedding is $5.79 per bale at Southern States in Charles Town. Some horse people use wood shavings as bedding in the stall, but it's rarely allowed at the track. The feed store delivers twice a week, no extra charge.

Inside the barn, swallows chirp and dart in the air among the eighty stalls. There are fans on the horses, whirling and stirring the still and stale air. The country and western music is coming from a box tuned to WUSQ-FM 102.5 out of Winchester, Virginia. Their current favorite is "Heaven" by Kane Brown.

The Hollywood Casino at Charles Town Races Horse Racing Guide of January 2018 dictates that "Goats and or other hooved animals used to assist a horse in the stall must provide a health certificate when entering the barn area and are not allowed to roam freely in the shed row or stable area. Goats or other hooved animals leaving and subsequently returning to the barn area, must resend a new Health Certificate."

There's more. Part seven of the stable memo orders that "all fans must be UL approved with 3-prong grounded cord, no extension cords, no box fans, all fans must have a cage or screen cover over the blades, all fans must be securely mounted and out of the reach of all horses."

It also should be noted that Michael Jones is hardly the only one in the stable area to go astray of the law, or the track rules. On this hot summer day, there's a fan on the floor, with a few bits of possibly flammable hay nearby.

"Right now, we have eight horses in barn 21 and three across the street," Jones said. "I go to Laurel and Delaware Park (racetracks) and I've got eleven horses in training right now." Some are stabled at Media Farm, a large 100-plus acre facility on Flowing Springs Road, outside of town.

Trainers and owners rent stalls and pastures where the horses can get outside to stretch their bodies and sniff fresh air. At the farm, there are forty-plus stalls and seventeen pastures and two smaller turnout areas.

"The stalls are beautifully built and quite nice," said Elizabeth Rogers, a horse gal who also works at the track.

There is an automated exercise machine (think fancy equine treadmill) called a EuroXciser that trainers can use, and a solid panel round pen, 190 feet x 190 riding arena, and a large field where trainers gallop horses.

Jones races several horses under the name of Imaginary Stable, owned by John Guarnere, Jr., who has horses in training with two other trainers around the country. Jones trains several of them in Charles Town.

Guarnere, Jr. is the general manager of Hylton Paper Company, Inc., based in Bellmawr, New Jersey. It began in 1984 with his father, John Guarnere, Sr., the CEO and president of the company. B.G. Graphic Services is also part of the company, which does die-cutting, embossing, shrink wrapping and finishing work for all types of products, from Benadryl to door hanger advertising, shipping and packing boxes.

One of Guarnere's racehorses trained by Jones is Pekin, a three-year-old bay gelding. He ran second the night before we met.

Perkin began racing as a two-year-old and had yet to win, with four second-place finishes as of this writing. (Sound familiar? Sylvia certainly experienced the same situation.) There were total winnings after fourteen starts of $15,290, a respectable statistic, but a sum that may or may not cover the training costs.

The 2021 fees for keeping a horse with a trainer based at Charles Town range from thirty five dollars to $150 per day. This includes care, feeding and exercising. Veterinarian bills and blacksmith fees are extra. Sylvia charged owners between eight to ten dollars per horse per day.

There's also a long-standing track tradition going back to Sylvia's era, of "ten percent for 1-2-3." This translates to: the trainer gets ten percent of all purse money for first, second or third place.

Guarnere spends half the year in South Florida and describes himself as what is known as a "snowbird." It's mid-August, and he has commuted from his home in Ft. Lauderdale to the air-conditioned comfort at Gulfstream Park on a Sunday. He's also there to watch the simulcast from other tracks as some of his fifty-plus horses run. Four of them were, at the time, with Michael Jones.

"Michael has done well," he said. "He's wonderful to deal with and having the horses up north, they don't get beat up in the heat of Florida. He and Brandy (Michael's wife) are down to earth."

Love Your Humor, a seven-year-old dark bay also owned by Imaginary Stables, was credited with a second place earning of $1,980 on the evening of July 13, 2018. In this claiming race, the gelding crossed the finish line in third place, but ended as second when Triple Black Jack was disqualified for bearing in on another horse in the late mid-stretch.

Love Your Humor's earnings halfway through 2018 were $7,090 in ten starts, with no victories yet; he was second once and third four times. His lifetime earnings after fifty-six starts were $103,563. One can only speculate, but at age seven, he might find a second career as an "off the track" show horse or pleasure horse. Some racehorses even go on to become police horses. And later, in fact, they did find a new home for the horse.

Some of Jones' horses race under the name of his wife, Brandy Dawn Jones. She is far more loquacious and outgoing, has a strong work ethic and truly loves to talk. She appears to enjoy her life around horses and the man who got her into it.

Brandy married Michael in 2014 and never met Sylvia. Still, she said, "She would've loved that Michael was doing this, working with the horses. It's what he does best. He always talks about her, all the things she used to say, how she did stuff with the horses. And we always say, those horses eat better than we do. He got that from his grandmother, too. His heart is right here at this track. He loved his grandmother and it sounds like he's very much like her."

Jones is wearing a t-shirt that reads: "I Can't Keep Calm, I'm a Jones."

Five days after we met at barn 21, Wagered won a claiming race for fillies and mares going six and half furlongs on the dirt. Of the $10,000 purse, with Brandy listed as owner and Michael as trainer, they took home $5,940 for first place. At the time, Wagered's lifetime earnings were $59,479 after twenty-six starts and four wins.

The Equibase report said: "WAGERED broke in and bumped Anyladysinthehouse at the start, then rushed up to rate a clear pace inside, was met at even terms past the three-eighths pole and dueled from there through the turn on the rail, then drew clear past the eighth pole, drove down the lane under steady handling, and just lasted first."

It all sounded very familiar.

Clearly, Jones adored his grandmother, credited her with everything he knows about horses and seemed to enjoy speaking about her. Not long after we spoke, the Sylvia Bishop Memorial $50,000 for West Virginia-bred three-year-old fillies at seven furlongs was coming up. Jones did not have a filly that qualified for the race. Maybe he will someday.

"My grandmother always said, 'Take care of the animals first. Feed the horses before you feed yourself. And what you take out of them on the track, you better always put it back in.' She was a woman, but she was a horseman in every way, and there aren't a lot of them out here now. Just seems like everyone is out to make a buck."

Jones entered each stall and ran his hands along the horse's back and down every leg. His grandmother taught him how to make up different braces and wraps, and he added, "little tricks she'd use to put in the food to make them eat.

"I couldn't see myself doing anything but horses. I just love it."

And neither could Sylvia Bishop.

Eighteen days before she died, she said, "I accomplished it, thanks to God and willpower. I knew I was black and I turned my cheek and I said: 'I will and I did.'"

EPILOGUE

THEY (ALSO) HAVE A WAY WITH HORSES

Diana McClure is a white female racehorse trainer. At fifty-something-years-old, she wasn't even born when Sylvia raced in Charles Town in the 1950s and '60s. "I don't know how she did it," she said. "She broke down barriers that were concrete."

For McClure, there's no tension within the racing industry. Instead, it's more a matter of "client relations," especially with men: "The male clients cannot stand taking orders, direction or advice from a woman, even if it involves their horse. They take it personally."

She added that she's even had wives call and offer advice on how to handle their horse-owning husbands. "Nine out of ten times, the man will take his horse elsewhere, most likely to a male trainer," she said.

While working on this book, which actually took fifteen years, my husband and I traveled to the annual September tradition of the Timonium State Fair. We drove the same route Sylvia traveled. I wanted to get a feel of the place in the best possible manner seven decades after she had driven there with her husband. (See the chapter on The Holy Land.)

The stomach-churning rides, the funky food trucks, the barns bulging with flowers, produce, pigs and cows and so much more are still there. We didn't bother to see if that elusive Baltimore reptile from 1954 might even be inside the much bally-hoed 'Killer Snake' sideshow.

Just beyond the bingo tent at the far end of the fairgrounds, we arrived in time to see nine horses loading into the gate for the fifth race. There was one black jockey in the lineup, a rare sight in this era and a far cry from the late 1800s and early 1900s, when black jockeys were the norm, not the exception.

As I leaned over the rail at the tiny walking ring before the sixth race, I spotted Donald Rideoutt, large and lumbering as he led number 1A, Spring Dragon, around and around. Spring Dragon was part of a double entry (when two horses have the same owner). It was a maiden claiming race for fillies and mares three-years-old and up. The claiming price was $5,000, with a purse of equal value.

The five-year-old gray mare he was leading has had a mediocre career with eight lifetime starts, never better than fifth place, and total earnings of $780. Rideoutt smiled when he recognized me from a recent family reunion I attended.

Donald Eugene Rideoutt was born September 12, 1952, at Charles Town General Hospital, the second child and only son of Sylvia's fourth younger sister, Shirley Devonne Rideoutt, and an unnamed father with whom he eventually united. He later learned his father was William Awkard, a highly accomplished molecular biologist in Baltimore, who trained his own racehorses as a pastime.

Fondly called Donnie, he was named for his uncle, Don Rideoutt (who was murdered by his brother Govenear in 1967). The younger Donnie followed the horses all his life, as did his namesake. He started out walking hots for his Aunt Sylvia during the 1960s, before he was a teenager.

As a kid, Donnie made fifty cents per horse, frequently leading two horses at a time for extra money. (Today, this hot walking service goes for about $8.50 per horse.) Recently, he worked at the Thoroughbred auction sales, pushing a broom "to clean the piles up" as the horses were walked

© Daily Racing Form, LLC

195

around the pavilion for prospective buyers.

"I'm idle right now," he said. "Money is short."

He's come to the races with his cousin James "Skeets" Holland because "helping out, that's family." Another one of Sylvia's horse-loving nephews, Skeets is the son of Sylvia's older sister, Clara, who married an accomplished jockey from Maryland named Raymond "Skeets" Holland. While working on this book, I came to adore Skeets, Jr., a fine horseman, and his wife, Carlyne Tapscott, a trainer.

Number one, Dippity, a chestnut mare with twenty-one lifetime starts and total earnings of $15,455, was being saddled by Skeets and trained by Carlyne. She is a stakes-winning trainer and her horses have won close to a half million dollars.

Of the seventy-something trainers listed on this glorious September afternoon in 2011, seven are women and Carlyne is the sole black woman, a modern day Sylvia.

"The rules for a black and a black woman have never been the same. All eyes are always on you," Carlyne said. "In racing, the drawback is not being able to get quality horses of championship caliber. Those owners of these horses go to Rodney Jenkins [a former show jumper turned racing trainer in Maryland] or Nick Zito [a nationally-known Hall of Fame conditioner]. It's a different ball game for a woman. They can turn down horses, but a woman has to prove what she can do with a good horse."

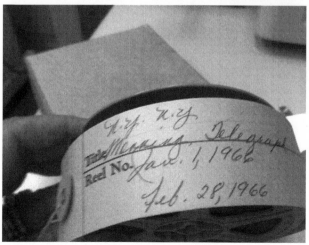

ACKNOWLEDGEMENTS

Thank YOU ALL past and present: Henry Allen, Don Bell, Keith Berkeley, Alicia Berry, Bill Berry, Johnnycakes Berry, Lucille Berry, Tony Biencivenga, John Bishop, Sylvia Rideoutt Bishop, John Blackburn, Coley Blind, Lambert Boyce, Bonnie O'Rourke Brannon, Billy Bush, Maxine Bushong, Allan Carter, Wayne Chatfield-Taylor, John Coles, Wilson Dillon, Cary Embury, Valerie Embrey, D.W. Fries, Jack Ferguson, Gary Frichtman, Michael Fruchtman, M. Tyson Gilpin, Jr., Butch Gore, Melissa Phipps Gray, Carol Hackney, Lenny Hale, Bill Higgins, Roger Hudson, Carol Holden, James "Skeets" Holland, Shannon Hull, Doug Humes, Sarah Huston, Angela Marzani Ingenito, Virginia Jenkins, Donnie Johnson, Jay Joyce, Gordie Keys, Robin Keys, Donna Kercheval, Nellie Lawson, Dale Leatherman, Frank Lee, Punkin Lee, Marion Maggiolo, William McCormick, Diana McClure, Dickie Moore, Mary Mullett, Mark Munden, Ross Peddicord, Doug Perks, Elizabeth Rogers, Phyllis Rogers, Russell Roper, Vinnie Perrone, Laverne Purnell, Anne Reilly, Donald Rideoutt, Kevin Rideoutt, Rachel Rideoutt, Steve Roman, Russell Roper, Randy Rouse, George C. Rutherford, Cathy Schenck, Joe Servis, John Servis, Steve Sfarnas, Vicki Shannon, Deborah Sharp, Laurie Shifflett, Michelle Spero, Bill Steinkraus, John Stuart, Carlyne Tapscott, James L. Taylor, Larry Togans, Jim Tolbert, Sr., Michael Veitch, Laurie Volk, Natalie Voss, Helen Wiley, Don Yovanovich, Erich Zimmy.

Amazing Researchers:

Carmen Creamer, Alexandra Heidler, Ann Hilton, Kathleen Short, Deetzie Bayliss Sigl, Hunter Sigl, Gracie Sigl, Genie Ragan, Clancey Yovanovich.

Selected Online Sources:

Afterthefinishline.org, Equibase.com, Equineline.com, History.
com, Jockeysguild.com, Paulickreport.com, Pedigreequery.com,
Thoroughbredracing.com

Selected Publications:

*A Collection of Black History Events in Jefferson County, Lexington News Leader,
Morning Telegraph: 1839-1972, Sports Illustrated, The Blood Horse, Daily Racing
Form: 1972- , The Farmer's Advocate, The Mail in Adelaide, The Martinsburg
Journal, The Maryland Horse, The New York Times, The Spirit of Jefferson, The
Washington Post, Thoroughbred Times*

Selected Books:

Bushong, Millard Kessler. *A History of Jefferson County, West Virginia.*
Charles Town, West Virginia: Jefferson Publishing Company, 1941.

Bushong, Millard Kessler. *Historic Jefferson County.* Boyce, Virginia: Carr
Publishing Company, Inc., 1972.

Farland, Mary Gray and Greenhalgh, Beverly Byrd. *In the Shadow of the
Blue Ridge.* Richmond, Virginia: William Byrd Press, 1978.

Greer, Margaret R. *Prose and Poetry Journeys.* Chicago: The L.W. Singer
Company, 1935.

Hadden, Will A. III. *Horseman's Veterinary Encyclopedia.* Guilford,
Connecticut: The Lyons Press/Equine Research, 2005.

Magner, R. Magner's Standard Horse and Stock Book. New York: The
Saalfield Publishing Co., 1901.

Mooney, Katherine C. Race *Horse Men: How Slavery and Freedom Were Made
at The Racetrack.* London, England: Harvard University Press, 2014.

Nasby, Dolly. *Images of America: Charles Town.* Charleston, S.C.: Arcadia
Publishing, 2004.

Jefferson County Black History Preservation Society, Inc. *Images of
America: African Americans of Jefferson County.* Charleston, S.C.: Arcadia
Publishing, 2009.

A NOTE ABOUT THE TYPE AND DESIGN

This book was set in Garamond, a typeface characterized by its smaller-than-average apertures that are closed off early on the stem, low line contrast, slightly cupped bases on the serifs, downward-sloping upper serifs, calligraphic terminals, serifs that are both heavily bracketed and rounded on the edges, pronounced diagonal stress, higher x-height and large difference between cap and ascender. Garamond is considered one of the most legible and readable fonts in print, and also one of the most eco-friendly major fonts due to it's lower ink usage.

Garamond is a group of many serif typefaces, named for sixteenth-century Parisian engraver Claude Garamond, generally spelled as Garamont in his lifetime. Garamond-style typefaces are popular and particularly often used for book printing and body text.

Designer Pam Owens of PamOwensDesign.com has designed three of Vicky Moon's books.

PRINTED AND BOUND BY
BERRYVILLE GRAPHICS, BERRYVILLE, VIRGINIA

DESIGNED BY PAM OWENS OF
PAM OWENS DESIGN, DELAPLANE, VIRGINIA

ABOUT THE AUTHOR

Vicky Moon is a writer, editor and photographer. She has chronicled the lives of the famous, and the not-so-famous and covered major murders and prominent lives for People Magazine and The Washington Post. She writes a monthly life-in-the-Virginia-countryside column "Over the Moon" for Washington Life magazine. She's reported on hunt balls, steeplechase races, and parties from Palm Beach to Saratoga Springs for Town and Country and Millionaire. She's written about homes and gardens for Veranda and Southern Accents and served as a contributing editor for House and Garden. She appeared on the A&E network's "City Confidential" and served as a producer for Dominick Dunne's "Power, Privilege and Justice." She is currently the co-publisher and a writer for Country ZEST magazine and middleburgmystique.com. She is the author of nine previous books, many involving horses and racing. Ms. Moon lives in Fort Lauderdale and Middleburg, Virginia and is married to sportswriter Leonard Shapiro. She can be reached at www.vickymoon.com

WWW.VICKYMOON.COM

Made in United States
Orlando, FL
09 February 2023